The Cambridge Introduction to
Modern Irish Poetry, 1800–2000

Over the last two centuries, Ireland has produced some of the world's
most outstanding and best-loved poets, from Thomas Moore to W. B.
Yeats to Seamus Heaney. This introduction not only provides an
essential overview of the history and development of poetry in Ireland,
but also offers new approaches to aspects of the field. Justin Quinn
argues that the language issues of Irish poetry have been misconceived
and re-examines the divide between Gaelic and Anglophone poetry.
Quinn suggests an alternative to both nationalist and revisionist
interpretations and fundamentally challenges existing ideas of Irish
poetry. This lucid book offers a rich contextual background against
which to read the individual works, and pays close attention to the
major poems and poets. Readers and students of Irish poetry will learn
much from Quinn's sharp and critically acute account.

Justin Quinn is Associate Professor of English and American Studies at
the Charles University, Prague.

Cambridge Introductions to Literature

This series is designed to introduce students to key topics and authors. Accessible and lively, these introductions will also appeal to readers who want to broaden their understanding of the books and authors they enjoy.

- Ideal for students, teachers, and lecturers
- Concise, yet packed with essential information
- Key suggestions for further reading

Titles in this series:

Christopher Balme *The Cambridge Introduction to Theatre Studies*

Eric Bulson *The Cambridge Introduction to James Joyce*

Warren Chernaik *The Cambridge Introduction to Shakespeare's History Plays*

John Xiros Cooper *The Cambridge Introduction to T. S. Eliot*

Patrick Corcoran *The Cambridge Introduction to Francophone Literature*

Gregg Crane *The Cambridge Introduction to the Nineteenth-Century American Novel*

Kirk Curnutt *The Cambridge Introduction to F. Scott Fitzgerald*

Janette Dillon *The Cambridge Introduction to Early English Theatre*

Janette Dillon *The Cambridge Introduction to Shakespeare's Tragedies*

Jane Goldman *The Cambridge Introduction to Virginia Woolf*

Kevin J. Hayes *The Cambridge Introduction to Herman Melville*

Nancy Henry *The Cambridge Introduction to George Eliot*

Leslie Hill *The Cambridge Introduction to Jacques Derrida*

David Holdeman *The Cambridge Introduction to W. B. Yeats*

Adrian Hunter *The Cambridge Introduction to the Short Story in English*

C. L. Innes *The Cambridge Introduction to Postcolonial Literatures*

M. Jimmie Killingsworth *The Cambridge Introduction to Walt Whitman*

Pericles Lewis *The Cambridge Introduction to Modernism*

Roman McDonald *The Cambridge Introduction to Samuel Beckett*

Wendy Martin *The Cambridge Introduction to Emily Dickinson*

Peter Messent *The Cambridge Introduction to Mark Twain*

David Morley *The Cambridge Introduction to Creative Writing*

Ira Nadel *The Cambridge Introduction to Ezra Pound*

Leland S. Person *The Cambridge Introduction to Nathaniel Hawthorne*

John Peters *The Cambridge Introduction to Joseph Conrad*

Justin Quinn *The Cambridge Introduction to Modern Irish Poetry*

Sarah Robbins *The Cambridge Introduction to Harriet Beecher Stowe*

Martin Scofield *The Cambridge Introduction to the American Short Story*

Emma Smith *The Cambridge Introduction to Shakespeare*

Peter Thomson *The Cambridge Introduction to English Theatre, 1660–1900*

Janet Todd *The Cambridge Introduction to Jane Austen*

Theresa M. Towner *The Cambridge Introduction to William Faulkner*

Jennifer Wallace *The Cambridge Introduction to Tragedy*

The Cambridge Introduction to
Modern Irish Poetry, 1800–2000

JUSTIN QUINN

CAMBRIDGE
UNIVERSITY PRESS

CAMBRIDGE UNIVERSITY PRESS
Cambridge, New York, Melbourne, Madrid, Cape Town, Singapore, São Paulo

Cambridge University Press
The Edinburgh Building, Cambridge CB2 8RU, UK

Published in the United States of America by Cambridge University Press, New York

www.cambridge.org
Information on this title: www.cambridge.org/9780521609258

© Justin Quinn 2008

First published 2008

Printed in the United Kingdom at the University Press, Cambridge

A catalogue record for this publication is available from the British Library

ISBN 978-0-521-84673-8 hardback
ISBN 978-0-521-60925-8 paperback

That there is an Ireland where
Trees suddenly fly away
And leave their pigeons standing
Baffled in the air.

Michael Hartnett

Contents

12 The disappearance of Ireland

Acknowledgements

Many individuals helped in many ways during the writing of this book and it is a pleasure to acknowledge them here: Michael Allen, Fran Brearton, Garrick Davis, Andrew Fitzsimons, Tomáš Fürstenzeller, Sylva Fischerová, Daniela Furthnerová, Robert Greacen, Aleš Klégr, Tereza Límanová, James McCabe, Peter McDonald, Síle Ní Bhroin, Štěpán Nosek, Luán ó Braonáin, Dennis O'Driscoll, Colm Quinn, Jack Quinn, Christopher Ricks, Ray Ryan (who came with the idea), Pavlína Šaldová, Moynagh Sullivan, Bill Tinley and Tereza Vohryzková. And thanks go to Audrey Cotterell for her copy-editing.

Especial thanks go to the following, who commented in detail on one or more chapters: Louis de Paor, Selina Guinness, Maria Johnston and Jill Siddall. Matthew Campbell supported the project from the beginning and read the manuscript in the final stages. I am extremely indebted to him for his valuable criticism and encouragement. Also, David Wheatley was a constant support, source of information and valuable objection throughout the writing of this book. Much of my understanding of Irish poetry developed out of our conversations and correspondence since the early 1990s.

I also wish to thank the Princess Grace Irish Library, Monaco, as well as the Ireland Fund of Monaco, for providing a month-long haven in 2005, which enabled me to get about a third of this book written.

The final draft of the book was prepared while I was teaching for a semester at the Department of English at Villanova University, Pennsylvania, and I would also like to acknowledge their support here.

Research funds were provided by a Research Grant from the Czech Ministry of Education awarded to an interdisciplinary collective at the Faculty of Arts, Charles University, Prague ('Foundations of the Modern World as Reflected in Literature and Philosophy', MSM0021620824).

The excerpt from 'For my God-daughter, B. A. H.' and 'Water Baby' by Michael Hartnett is reproduced by kind permission of the Estate of Michael Hartnett and The Gallery Press, from Collected Poems (2001). 'Love Poem' by Maurice Craig is reproduced by kind permission of the author.

The book is dedicated to my parents Anna and Jack Quinn.

Introduction

What is 'Irish poetry'? Is it written in Irish or can it be written in English too? Must it be about the history, mythology and contemporary life of Ireland, or can it range wider, through Europe, the world, the cosmos? Does it include the work of poets from Northern Ireland, a territory that belongs to the British Crown, or is it restricted to poets from the Republic of Ireland? What are we to do with a poet who was born a subject of that Crown, receiving a Civil List pension from that same Crown, who could neither speak nor read Irish yet claimed he was in touch with the spirit of the nation? Does it include poets who lived and published for most of their lives in England? Does it include second-generation emigrants? What about a poet whose family lived for centuries in the country and were Protestants who believed in the Union with Britain? What if that same Protestant poet is one of the century's best translators and interpreters of ancient Irish poetry? Is he somehow less Irish than a Catholic peasant poet who wrote in Irish? There are many more such questions, but they do not proliferate as thickly as their answers; which is to say, there is no consensus about what Irish literature is, let alone Irish poetry.

For the purposes of this brief book, I have had to answer provisionally many of these questions, and here I wish to state these answers along with the contradictions and difficulties they involve. First of all, the question of period. The overarching theme of the book is indicated by the titles of the first and last chapters. In the year 1800, the Act of Union was passed, thus joining Ireland's political fate with Britain over the next hundred years. In the following decades, nationalism became the motive force in poetry written in Ireland, and although poets would react in different ways to this æsthetic ideology, their work was deeply marked by it. This is what I mean by 'The appearance of Ireland', the title of the opening chapter. The last chapter is entitled 'The Disappearance of Ireland' and it points to the gradual abandonment of the nation as a framework for Irish poetry – on the level of theme, technique, forebears, etc. – what one commentator has called the post-national moment.

Nationalist ideology informs much of Ireland's finest art and literature in this period, as well as many of the most intense cultural debates. That ideology

1

both imagines an origin back in the vague ancient past and fantasises a glorious utopian future for the nation. It is fundamentally *un*nationalist then to say that the effects of the ideology are restricted to one particular period. While researching this book, I found myself constantly in disagreement with neo-nationalists as various as Thomas Kinsella, Eavan Boland, Seamus Deane and Declan Kiberd: these writers, with force and imagination, modernise the idea of Ireland in interesting ways, but the fundamental concept of the Irish nation itself remains unquestioned. That concept is only about 200 years old but to read these writers one would think it goes back to the Big Bang. Even a critic as sophisticated as Colin Graham in his *Deconstructing Ireland* (2001) still requires the Irish nation – in however vestigial a form – as raw material for his deconstruction, and he provides us with no glimpse of the theoretical and imaginative work to be done after the concept has been dismantled.

Why then write a book like this? Because although nationalism is on the wane, it was nevertheless the most important cultural force in much of the best literature of Europe, and perhaps the world, over the last two centuries. However much one might disagree with the tenets of nationalist literature, that the literature exists and is sometimes excellent cannot be denied, any more than the importance of *Paradise Lost* can be denied by an atheist. Furthermore, I attend to work which falls outside this debate – for instance, the poetry of James Henry in the nineteenth century, and the poets at the end of the twentieth century – and I show the way that nationalism is being overtaken by other concerns. I also examine elements of other poets' *œuvres* that are unconcerned with issues of Ireland. The approach is valedictory and as such must characterise what is being left behind and outline what is to come. It is probable that books of this kind will not be required in twenty years.

The second important issue is that of language. It is reported that Joseph Brodsky was once asked at a reading what the poet's political responsibility was, and he answered 'To the language.'[1] In the Irish context, I see the following implication: Yeats, Kavanagh, Clarke, MacNeice, Heaney, Carson, to name a few, are above all poets of the English language, and that they are Irish is only of secondary importance. They have more in common with the poets of England than they do with the Gaelic bards. In the chapter on Seamus Heaney, I quote the following passage from an interview when he was asked what makes him distinctly an Irish poet and not a British poet, and he responded thus:

> Well, the issue probably wouldn't arise at all were there not the political situation in the North. All of those remarks about Irish versus British are actually intended as irritants rather than definitions. The adjectives have

nothing essential to do with the noun. They have to do with the aggravation of the political and current situation. They're a form of game-playing.[2]

I do not wish to say that Anglophone Irish poets have not been deeply and variously influenced by Gaelic literature – most of this book traces that variety – but rather to say that the influences of, for instance, Shelley, Blake, Wordsworth and Tennyson have been more profound. While Tennyson boomed and gloomed at Ireland for all he was worth, the language he shared with Irish poets was infinitely more important than differing opinions about British imperialism. Yeats is not often thought of as a Tennysonian poet, in large part because of those differing opinions, but the *poetic* influence is there and is at least as significant as his engagement with Shelley, if not perhaps Blake.

What of poetry written in Irish? This is only mentioned insofar as it impinges on Irish Anglophone poetry – a separate book would be required to trace its development in the period. However, I have throughout tried to attend to the *border* between the two languages, especially to the occasions when writers pretend it doesn't exist. For instance, it does not seem strange to monoglot Irish audiences that J. M. Synge's *Playboy of the Western World* and Brian Friel's *Translations* are performed in English.[3] The situation is similar to the film *The Piano Teacher* (2001): because it was a French-Austrian co-production it bizarrely depicted the population of Vienna talking French. This is a type of linguistic imperialism that presumes that all of the Gaelic world is accessible through English.

The book was written mainly in the Czech Republic, where I have lived for many years. In my personal life, English is a minority language, constantly eroded by Czech syntax, vocabulary and idioms. The experience has shown me how much is left outside English, how much cannot be brought over the linguistic border. It ranges from a way of breathing when one speaks to moral and philosophical concepts. I have also learned how difficult it is to explain those excluded elements, as monoglots often listen to such explanations as they would to fairy-tales. One cannot explain what is like to live in another language. At the same time, I have also learned that much can be brought over, but that conveyance is strongly conditioned by social, cultural and historical forces which often erase themselves in the end result.

I have not lived in Irish in the same way I live in Czech, as I only have reading knowledge of the language. It is still considered acceptable for a scholar of Anglophone Irish literature to have no knowledge of Irish. Some critics might defend this by saying that since the material they work with is in English, they have no need of Irish. But that very material frequently claims to express the spirit of Gaelic literature; critics without, at the very least, reading knowledge cannot assess that claim and thus can be fairly accused of professional incompetence. Only those critics with a knowledge of both languages are in a position to assess those deceptive social, cultural and historical forces I mention above. I do not claim such a purview for this book; rather I merely bring attention to this border at key junctures.

Perhaps the most important of those junctures is the poetry of W. B. Yeats, the poet with the Civil List pension that I mentioned in the first paragraph. He established modern Irish literature and yet had no knowledge of the Irish language. Yeats scholarship is voluminous and while his ignorance of the language is noted, little more is said of the matter, few critics have addressed the matter fully. His poetry, drama, criticism and autobiography can be read for the ways he compensated for that ignorance, presenting other nationalist credentials in lieu of knowledge of Gaelic. He rather uncharitably described Keats thus:

> I see a schoolboy when I think of him,
> With face and nose pressed to a sweet-shop window,
> For certainly he sank into his grave
> His senses and his heart unsatisfied,
> And made – being poor, ailing and ignorant,
> Shut out from all the luxury of the world,
> The coarse-bred son of a livery-stable keeper –
> Luxuriant song.[4]

The description fits Yeats's relationship with Gaelic culture surprisingly well – if we substitute his Anglo-Irish Protestant details in the penultimate line.

Seamus Heaney asked whether Yeats was an example for Irish poets or not. Modern Irish poetry would be impossible without him for many reasons, foremost of which is that he enabled it to be monoglot. He could depend on nationalist ideology to compensate for that lack, but at the end of the twentieth century, with the withdrawal of that ideology, poets have been left floundering ever so slightly. In an interview in 1997 the poet Vona Groarke was pressed on the issue of whether she saw her poetry as distinctively Irish. She responded as follows:

> That's a difficult question, you know, for myself to answer. I mean, it's easy to say what *has* been an Irish poem, but now that glass has been shattered and there are so many different parts of it. It used to be a rural poem, but it's not anymore. Now it's equally likely to be urban as it is to be rural, it's equally likely to be about a woman as it is about a man. I find it quite difficult to define what an Irish poem is now, and I think that's a healthy thing. It's not as easy to immediately pigeonhole it as it

would have been, say, thirty years ago. I'm sure, I'm sure, I'm sure I must read like an Irish poet. I wouldn't attempt to deny or to contradict my background in the poems that I write, I mean I write out of what has been my life to date and I'm sure there are hints of that in what I do. So I think it would be fatuous for me to say that I wouldn't read as an Irish poet, but . . . That kind of elusiveness in being able to define what an Irish poem is widens the scope an awful lot . . .[5]

Clearly, 'my life to date' does not guarantee a poem's Irishness. Groarke hardly seems convinced herself, yet she has nothing better to offer. I quote the passage at length because the confusion and uncertainty that Groarke expresses are not merely her own. This brings us back to the flurry of questions at the beginning. But it is also of note that the passage follows an exchange where the interviewers ask Groarke if she would be interested in translating Gaelic poems, and she jokes in response that it's sort of ruled out as she doesn't know Irish.

The third issue which is important for my reading of Irish poetry is the British Empire. Many postcolonial critics try to align the Irish with the wretched of the earth; however, I repeatedly found poets – from Thomas Moore to Seamus Heaney – who express their indebtedness to and complicity with the Empire. My approach has been influenced by a general change in attitude towards the British Empire. Niall Ferguson remarks:

what is very striking about the history of the Empire is that whenever the British were behaving despotically, there was almost always a liberal critique of that behaviour from within British society. Indeed, so powerful and consistent was this tendency to judge Britain's imperial conduct by the yardstick of liberty that it gave the British Empire something of a self-liquidating character.[6]

Thomas Moore, as English Whig, participated in exactly such a tendency; Seamus Heaney has been lionised by a British audience eager for accounts of Irish imaginative resistance to the Empire. It is then a distortion to read Irish poetry as continually opposed to the British Empire, because the attitude of both the colonising society and the colonised is more nuanced.

Only two of the twelve chapters are devoted to the nineteenth century because of the relative weakness of the poetry of that period. There is a cluster of three chapters on the Revival, with Yeats at the centre. In chapter 6, I deal with the legacy of Modernism in Irish poetry, and how it has been adapted to Irish materials by two successive generations. Chapter 7 groups Derek Mahon, Michael Longley and Richard Murphy together and considers them in relation to the theme of Empire. The more usual grouping would substitute Heaney for Murphy in order to provide a detailed discussion of the Northern Irish Renaissance at the end of the 1960s (Heaney is dealt with in chapter 8). It is not the point of a book like this to be original, but there are so many treatments of that phenomenon elsewhere that I considered it superfluous. Nevertheless, readers unfamiliar with the Northern Ireland Renaissance still receive an account of it, although cross-hatched by another narrative. Chapter 9 deals with poetry translation from Irish, French and Latin, and might be described as the nerve-centre of the book. Chapter 10 deals with the explosion of women's issues in Irish poetry in the 1980s and early 1990s; chapter 11 with Paul Muldoon and the theme of emigration in Irish poetry. In the last chapter – with the wave of a wand – Ireland vanishes into other concerns, such as city-writing, cosmopolitanism and the sea. I do not have a better answer than Vona Groarke to the question of what now is a distinctively Irish poem; I merely attempt to describe some of the most exciting, though disparate, elements in contemporary Irish poetry. My bet is people will soon no longer think in categories such as the interviewers' 'distinctively Irish'.

Chapter 1

The appearance of Ireland

Thomas Moore, J. J. Callanan, James Clarence Mangan

In 1801, the Act of Union came into force, stripping Ireland of its own parliament and bringing the country under direct control of Westminster; thus it was dissolved into perhaps the greatest European empire after that of Rome. Over the following century it would shed its native language and adopt English. Even after achieving independence 121 years later, it would keep English as its first language de facto (though Irish would be designated the first official language in 1937); it would also keep the principles of English law at the centre of its jurisprudence. Of course, English had been a native language in Ireland for almost a millennium, but only in parts of the Pale on the east coast. Now, within a century, it spread westwards across the whole country, leaving only small pockets of Gaelic speakers on the Atlantic shores. After a slow start in the nineteenth century, when there was little of great literary worth, Irish writers were at last completely at home in English, and produced some of that language's greatest works in the twentieth century. The claim was occasionally made that the national spirit had been brought over from Gaelic into English. However, Irish speakers themselves rarely confirmed such a smooth conveyance of the national spirit. As the novelist Tomás Ó Duinnshléibhe made one of his characters remark:

> Tig le náisiún an tsaoirse a chailleadh agus a ghnóthú, agus a chailleadh agus a ghnóthú arís agus arís eile, ach dá gcailltí an teanga ní bheadh fáil ar ais againn uirthi. Ní thig le tír ar bith a teanga a chailleadh gan a hanam a chailleadh agus nuair a bhíonn an t-anam caillte tá deireadh léi mar náisiún.[1]

It is ironic that many writers who claimed that the spirit of Gaelic literature and culture was transferred to the Anglophone literature of Ireland had scant idea of the real contours of Irish literature and would not be able to understand the passage quoted here. It is perhaps just as well for them, as they would find cold comfort in its message.

These facts suggest that this chapter should not be titled 'The appearance of Ireland' but 'The disappearance of Ireland'. But the disappearance I have outlined above set a counter-motion going. As Robert Welch remarks: 'In the nineteenth century the strategy was to invent as many Irelands as possible. Because there *was* no Ireland, because there was no language, no system for it, then it was as well to try out as many possibilities as the brain could invent.'[2] The ideology of nationalism, which was spreading through Europe at this time, took hold in Ireland also, and writers and politicians endeavoured to preserve and develop the essence of Irishness often in the face of British hostility, and – what was often more difficult to manage – British interest. Prompted by the curiosity about James MacPherson's Ossian (1760–3), a work in which a Scottish writer claimed to have discovered the texts of Scottish legends (they were in fact Irish), as well as by the growth of French and German scholarship in the area of Celtic culture, there was a surge in antiquarian activity in Ireland during the nineteenth century, as scholars attempted to get a clearer idea of the outlines of the Irish past. Translation of Irish texts became increasingly refined and accurate. The fruits of this labour were pounced upon by Irish propagandists of every hue. This interest in things Irish led to the phenomenon of the Gaelic Revival at the end of the nineteenth century, and to the revolution in 1916 that precipitated the end of British rule in the greater part of Ireland. The revolution came from within the British Empire at a time when it was fighting an enemy without, and the shock was very deep for the imperialists, as it was for their subject peoples throughout the world. Three decades later the Empire would lose its greatest possession of all, India, and that country's statesmen would point out how instructive the Irish example was for them. Now, a mere century after the time of its finest flowering, the British Empire is but a memory: in comparison with the decline of that of Rome, the British Empire collapsed like a house of cards, leaving in its wake many countries around the world attempting to achieve national definition.

In the eighteenth century, Irish poets writing in English did not have as their goal the expression of national spirit, but viewed their work as an integral part of the British tradition, and wrote for a British audience. Matthew Campbell remarks that, in the nineteenth century, 'while many writers published for the large literary market in Britain and the new, English-speaking audiences of Irish origin in the United States, the poetry was often more concerned with its responsibility in preserving the authenticity of the cultural achievements of Ireland's past'.[3] The audience of that literature and the Irish 'nation' were not identical. The intriguing fact about Irish culture at this time, and in some respects well into the twentieth century, was that English opinion often counted for more. Critics of several generations have tried to obscure this fact in order to preserve some pure Gaelic quality, but it no longer seems either desirable or possible to do so. For once we admit such a complication, we acknowledge a richer idea of Irish culture than we were previously accustomed to. The edges of Ireland become blurred and we see that Irish culture was not formed out some unsullied source in the misty Celtic past, but out of centuries of negotiation and conversation with Rome and early Christian Europe, and then most importantly with England in its earlier embodiments, and later as imperial centre. Like most other European cultures, Irish culture is hybrid, and becomes interesting as soon as the liens of ownership and lines of influence are most tangled and messy.

By admitting the existence of this complex situation, we immediately have a better chance of understanding Irish poetry at the beginning of the nineteenth century, both its failings and achievements. We must also recognise, as Welch again points out, that the work of Irish poets in this period was not underwritten by an Irish tradition in English – there was no secure frame of cultural reference for their work;[4] and this made it clichéd and fissiparous, occasionally within individual poems, and more generally across the century. In what follows, I will look at the work of three poets often said to express the essence of the Irish national spirit. They often try to do that, and they often do other things, and I will follow their work as they move in and out of the nationalist frame of reference.

The works of Thomas Moore were often published in the nineteenth and twentieth centuries in large green tomes gilded with designs incorporating shamrocks, harps and other Irish symbols. The cover of one edition has, among these insignia, a short text: 'The hearts and the voices of Erin prolong for the answering future thy name and thy song'; and this is curved around a solid-looking female in gold-tooling who bears a harp.[5] The front papers more or less repeat this arrangement, but now the woman is pointing with a wand to a vignette of Moore. This is Moore canonised as Irish saint with all the regalia of nationalist iconography, whose reputation lies on his *Irish Melodies*, lyrics he wrote to old Irish airs. The edition was published in London, and there were many others like it, in Britain, Ireland and the USA. After the application of a little astringent, however, a different design emerges that incorporates the cross of St George and, if not a John Bull figure pointing approvingly to Moore, then certainly a Prime Minister such as Lord John Russell, who was in power during the Irish Famine in the late 1840s, and was a close friend of Moore's. These British and Irish symbolisms are complementary not contradictory.

Moore was born in 1779 in Dublin (in a building which is now famed for its jazz sessions), the son of a grocer and spirit dealer. Both his parents were Roman Catholic. He entered Trinity College, Dublin, a year after it was opened to Catholics. There he became friendly with a law student named Robert

Emmet who would later lead an unsuccessful rebellion against the British in 1803, and be executed as a result; this had an important bearing on Moore's poetry. He went to England in 1799 and his first book, *The Odes of Anacreon* (1800), translations from the Greek, was dedicated to the Prince of Wales. The dedicatee had to agree to the dedication, and the approval of *The Odes* is a indication that Moore had ensconced himself in the highest echelons of English society with astonishing speed. As George Saintsbury remarked: 'He had, indeed a catlike disposition to curl himself up near something or somebody comfortable.' However, he was never a sycophant. Saintsbury continues: 'But it does not appear that Moore was any more inclined to put up with insulting treatment than the cat itself is.'[6] In 1803 he was appointed Registrar to the Admiralty Prize Court in Bermuda, which dealt with the apportionment of booty among the officers and men of the Royal Navy. He, in his turn, appointed a deputy to look after these affairs. In 1818, Moore's appointee fled Bermuda, leaving him answerable for a large debt; because of financial embarrassment, Moore had to leave England temporarily, despite the great critical and financial success of his poetry at the time.

In 1807 he engaged to write the *Irish Melodies*: Moore provided the lyrics and Sir John Stevenson adapted the melodies that had been recorded and published by Edward Bunting in his *General Collection of the Ancient Music of Ireland* (1796). The first two instalments appeared in 1808 and eight more followed till 1834. These songs had original lyrics, but Moore could not read Irish, and indeed had scant respect for the language, writing his lyrics with little reference to them.[7] But there is a more general sense in which it is possible to understand Moore's work on the melodies as translation. Stevenson smoothed away the rougher edges of the original melodies and Moore provided words that would be palatable to the drawing-rooms of England; they did this in order to bring what they considered the 'national spirit' to a wide audience. Moore's description of this spirit is noteworthy:

> It has often been remarked, and oftener felt, that our music is the truest of all comments upon our history. The tone of defiance, succeeded by the languor of despondency – a burst of turbulence dying away into softness – the sorrows of one moment lost in the levity of the next – and all that romantic mixture of mirth and sadness, which is naturally produced by the efforts of a lively temperament to shake off or forget the wrongs which lie upon it. Such are the features of our history and character, which we find strongly and faithfully reflected in our music; and there are many airs which, I think, it is difficult to listen to without recalling some period or event to which their expression seems peculiarly applicable.[8]

The political implications of this 'national spirit' are of interest. Moore was careful to imply that the 'defiance' of the melodies would never grade into revolutionary violence. Faced with the regiments of imperial soldiery, Moore refused outright battle in favour of a more oblique contest for the hearts of the mothers, sisters, daughters, wives and betrothed of those soldiers. (The same pattern appears within his works also, as we shall see in *Lalla Rookh*.) Most critics view this as the substitution of revolutionary passion for something as devalued as sentiment. The earlier instalments of the lyrics were particularly rich in references to Emmet's recent revolution; but there were other immediate political contexts that would have been obvious to his first audiences and which are lost to us now. These references have exactly the pitch that Moore describes above: they are a fine exercise in keeping the pot warm, and never bringing it to the boil. This is perhaps best exemplified by 'Oh! Breathe Not His Name':

> Oh! breathe not his name, let it sleep in the shade,
> Where cold and unhonour'd his relics are laid;
> Sad, silent, and dark be the tears that we shed,
> As the night-dew that falls on the grass o'er his head.
>
> But the night-dew that falls, though in silence it weeps,
> Shall brighten with verdure the grave where he sleeps;
> And the tear that we shed, though in secret it rolls,
> Shall long keep his memory green in our souls.[9]

This requires little exegesis, apart from the remark that the man is often taken to be Robert Emmet. If one is on the revolutionary wavelength, one will easily understand the tenor of the poem. His memory will stay locked away in the souls of true Irishmen, and the greenness implies not only Irishness, but also that his legacy will bud again. However, consider the text again from a forensic point of view, and there is nothing to connect it with the theme of Irish revolutionaries: it is simply a lament for a loved friend. Moore is a master of this kind of ambivalence.

The texts of the *Melodies* also meditate on their own strange relation to the music, as well as to the Gaelic lyrics that they replace. It is a kind of temporising: by considering things from a philosophical point of view, Moore once again can avoid addressing political issues directly; once again, he 'breathes not his name'. Such meditations are Moore's attempt to empty out the meaning of his own language (with the result that most of the texts of the *Melodies* are, to modern taste, vapid and listless). But they also display an acute self-awareness, which if it does not ultimately save the poems, it does at least provide an excuse for their blandness.

> Music! oh, how faint, how weak,
>   Language fades before thy spell!
> Why should Feeling ever speak,
>   When thou canst breathe her soul so well?
> Friendship's balmy words may feign,
>   Love's are even more false than they;
> Oh! 'tis only Music's strain
>   Can sweetly soothe, and not betray![10]

Terence Brown remarks that 'the messages of the *Melodies* were the poignancy of loss, the charm of ruination, of buildings, of people's youth, and the poetic appeal of the buried life. The *Melodies* treat of Irish history as if its true significance was to provide a drawing-room audience with metaphors of its own indulgent sense of personal mutability.'[11] This is too harsh. It would be fairer to Moore's aims and achievement to say that he opened a conduit between Irish history and English hearts, and he did so by being deliberately vague and refusing to name names. To speak with intention, to treat language as meaningful and not just as a succession of sweet sounds, is to become involved in history and politics – in short, in the messy business of the world. To write a language without meaning, a language with only the vaguest of implications, is Moore's aim. The danger is the 'betrayal' of language, and that word is particularly poignant in the wake of two failed revolutions in Ireland, in which traitors played important roles.

Moore himself was aware that his lyrics depended heavily on the melodies, and referred to the music as the better half of the work.[12] One does Moore a disservice, then, by considering them purely as literary texts: they deserve to be experienced in performance rather than on the page, and indeed remain justly popular as songs, and justly ignored as poems.

Moore's opinions in the first decades of the nineteenth century do not accord with his high status in nationalist hagiography. In 1815 he visited Ireland and excoriated nationalist agitators, suggesting that they be put to the sword. He was disgusted by the crude methods that Daniel O'Connell employed in his campaign for Catholic emancipation.[13] Although Moore's ideas of Ireland changed in the subsequent decades as he acquainted himself with the history of his country, it is worthwhile dwelling on them for a moment. They provide an index of how deeply Moore had become a part of the Whig grouping in English politics. The Whigs could hardly be called a political party in the modern sense, but, generally speaking, they espoused religious freedom as well as wide-ranging political and philanthropic reforms. In principle, the Whigs supported the drive for Catholic Emancipation; Moore's reservation about O'Connell and his methods was on a point of taste: nothing could mark his distance from the Irish scene more than this.

As a satirist, Moore mordantly pilloried anti-Catholic prejudice. An excellent example of this is to be found in the *Twopenny Post-Bag* (1814), published under the pseudonym of Thomas Brown, the Younger. We are told 'a Popish young lady' plotted deviously against the status quo:

> (For though you've bright eyes and twelve thousand a year,
> It is still but too true you're a Papist, my dear)
> Had insidiously sent, by a tall Irish groom,
> Two priest-ridden Ponies, just landed from Rome,
> And so full, little rogues, of pontifical tricks,
> That the dome of St Paul's was scarce safe from their kicks.[14]

What is particularly to be relished here is the pun on 'priest-ridden'. But to read his satirical poems of this period is to know Moore as an English insider. The main aim of his satire was to heap scorn on the Prince Regent, in true Whig style. His insider status is demonstrated best by the tone and the presumption of knowledge shared by a coterie. The following few lines from 'Parody of a Celebrated Letter' (1812) illustrate precisely these qualities. The speaker is the Prince Regent himself:

> Neither feel I resentments, nor wish there should come ill
> To mortal – except (now I think on't) Beau Br – mm – l,
> Who threaten'd last year, in a superfine passion,
> To cut *me*, and bring the old K – ng into fashion.[15]

This needs a few footnotes, not just because it is taken out of context, but because it is coded for English readers in precisely the same way that 'Oh! Breathe Not His Name' was coded for Irish readers. In the last nine years of his reign, George III was insane, and his son, the future George IV, acted as regent. The Regent threw his favours on Beau Brummell, who, with this patronage and the inheritance of a tidy fortune, became the arbiter of London fashion and taste. He was also something of a wit, and this was the reason for his eventual break with the Regent in 1812, who did not like to be the subject of it. Moore depicts the Regent as a simpering fool who is afraid of Brummell, and has a go at the King himself, wickedly scouting the idea of his ever coming back into fashion. The same type of insider humour is apparent in *The Fudge Family in Paris* (1818). Mr Philip Fudge and his family visit France to write a book displaying the perniciousness of the new regime there in order to please his friend 'Lord C – stl – r – gh' (in the 1790s, Fudge used to write revolutionary tracts, but then betrayed the cause and became an establishment lackey). I provide this detailed explanation to demonstrate that these poems were emphatically for an English audience.

Moore made a splash in 1817 when he received a large advance for a long poem about the Orient. It was entitled *Lalla Rookh*, and it would richly reward the publishers' investment as it became one of the most popular poems in Europe. Much as in the present day when the financial transactions behind a book or film can become part of its marketing, so did the wealth that Moore gained from literature become the stuff of puffs.[16] The poem's lack of connection with Irish subject matter, heavily influenced as it is by Byron's *The Giaour* (1813), worried subsequent editors and critics. Just as Moore's satires are omitted from the patriotic edition of his poems that I described above, there is no mention of *Lalla Rookh* in a recent history of Irish poetry.[17] (Both editor and critic overlooked Byron's comment to Moore in the introduction to *The Corsair* about the strong parallels between Moore's story of the Orient and his own country's troubled state.) In both cases, there must have been a concern that these works would somehow discredit Moore's credentials as a poet of the Irish nation. Certainly, it confirms Moore as a poet of the British Empire, but there is no reason why that should make him any less of an Irish poet for that.

The poem is set in seventeenth-century India, during the reign of the last Mughal emperor, Aurangzeb. His daughter, Lalla Rookh, is betrothed to a prince in the Northern provinces and makes her way with her retinue to Kashmir, where the nuptials are to be celebrated. Along the way, a young Kashmiri bard joins their party and entertains the emperor's daughter with four long tales in verse. The princess gradually becomes fonder of the bard, and more apprehensive of meeting her betrothed, Prince Feramorz. All ends happily when it turns out that the bard is indeed Feramorz, who adopted the disguise in order to discover the true character of his bride-to-be. Feramorz's tales constitute the body of *Lalla Rookh* itself, and they immediately take us out of India to Persia, and back nine centuries in time. The first is a complex story of lovers caught on opposite sides of a violent revolt against Muslim rule; and this pattern of a love-relationship cross-hatching a military and religious divide repeats itself in the third and most gripping of Feramorz's stories, 'The Fire-Worshippers'.

This story takes us back a further century in Persian history, as the Pan-Arab invasion finally deposes the dynasty of the Sasanids. These latter are Guebres, or Zoroastrians (the fire-worshippers of the title), and the Arabs are Muslim. Al Hassan is an Arab Emir, or prince, leading the suppression of the Sasanids, and through a convoluted set of events, his daughter, Hinda, falls in love with the Sasanid leader, Hafed. Just as Moore's *Irish Melodies* wished to conquer the hearts of British ladies, after all military resistance in Ireland was conquered by the Empire soldiers, so does Hafed conquer the heart of the Emir's daughter, and thus receive the opportunity to talk eloquently of the Zoroastrian culture that was in the process of being destroyed. Military victory is achieved, only to be closely followed by cultural defeat. Hafed also indicates that resistance will merely go underground for a while:

> Is Iran's pride then gone for ever,
>   Quench'd with the flame in Mithra's caves? –
> No – she has sons that never – never –
>   Will stoop to be the Moslem's slaves,
>   While heav'n has light or earth has graves.
> Spirits of fire, that brood not long,
> But flash resentment back for wrong;
> And hearts where, slow but deep, the seeds
> Of vengeance ripen into deeds,
> Till, in some treachr'ous hour of calm,
> They burst, like Zeilan's giant palm,
> Whose buds fly open with a sound
> That shakes the pigmy forests round!
>
> Yes, Emir! he who scaled that tower,
>   And, had he reach'd thy slumb'ring breast,
> Had taught thee, in a Gheber's power
>   How safe even tyrant heads may rest –
> Is one of many, brave as he,
> Who loathe thy haughty race and thee;
> Who, though they know the strife is vain,
> Who, though they know the riven chain
> Snaps but to enter in the heart
> Of him who rends its links apart,
> Yet dare the issue, – blest to be
> Even for one bleeding moment free,
> And die in pangs of liberty![18]

'Tyrants' and 'liberty': this was true Whig talk, and Terence Brown, discussing the reception of *Lalla Rookh*, mordantly refers to 'some predictable captiousness in the Tory journals, who knew Moore for a Whig, even when bedecked in a turban'.[19] Of course, it is possible to read a passage like this as an allegory for Ireland, but it is important to recall, as I remarked above, that Moore, at the period of writing, disapproved of Irish extremism.

The poem is accompanied by copious notes which situate the personæ and places of the poem in Indian and Persian history. Stephen Gwynn remarked that 'whereas Scott's and Byron's descriptions savour of actual experience, Moore's reek of the lamp',[20] but later readers have perhaps lost something of the original effect of Moore's scholarly exactitude. In the era of *Lalla Rookh*, the British Empire was undergoing an unprecedented expansion in many of the areas the poem refers to. India, for instance, was becoming less exotic to the British. For many decades they had been involved intensely in the country, first, as the East India Company established itself, and, second, as it became part of the British Empire in 1818. (Also, the East India Company set up an office in Basra in Iraq in 1763, and British interests were consolidated in the country in the subsequent century.) The place-names, and to an extent the historical personages that the poem refers to, would have been familiar to British readers. It is not hard to imagine all the family members who went back and forth to the country throughout the eighteenth and early nineteenth centuries, not to mention the extensive investigation of Warren Hastings's activities in India at the end of the eighteenth century. A contemporary analogy might be an American novelist setting a historical novel in Iran and Iraq. Such a book would be intensely examined for modern parallels.

Terence Brown has referred to the 'strange mesmeric absurdity' of Moore's descriptions of Oriental luxury, for instance where Moore talks of Eastern spices and sandal burning.[21] At these junctures, Moore slows down the plot significantly (which elsewhere fairly races along), allowing his verse to luxuriate in these coulisses. Again it is worth recalling that these spices and smells were becoming widely available in Britain as a result of the Empire's consolidation in the Orient. The passages are the equivalent of what is to be found today in the supplements of Sunday newspapers. Certainly, this does not build a strong defence of the poem, rather it demonstrates the depth of Moore's imaginative investment in the British Empire. I do not wish to characterise him as an imperialist like Kipling; Kipling's was only one of the many forms that imperialist thinking took. Moore's ideal empire was an enlightened power that could profitably do business with various countries of the world, without suppressing those countries' cultures. He was not an apologist of the actual Empire.

Such arguments, however, cannot save the poem from Stephen Gwynn's judgement that it 'retains its place in literature mainly as an example of an extinct taste'.[22] The recent surge of interest in the history of the British Empire, as distinct from postcolonial history, provides a useful historicist context for the poem's revaluation, and *Lalla Rookh* holds its own among other Romantic long poems. And it holds our attention in the context of Irish poetry in the nineteenth century, not because it can be read as nationalist allegory, but for the way that it exceeds Ireland.

Some of the same complexity can be seen in the brief career of J. J. Callanan (1795–1829), a Cork poet who, weakened by tuberculosis, died at a young age in Lisbon, just a month or two before the publication of his only book of poems, *The Recluse of Inchidony and Other Poems* (1829), in London.[23] It was a début of considerable achievement, but its literary impact was negligible. In the same way that Moore was censored for a nationalist readership, so too was Callanan, even as late as 2005 in an edition of his poems which purported to select only the Irish material, as that was deemed superior.[24] Omitted and unmentioned was Callanan's fulsome poem of praise at the coronation of George IV (the same Prince Regent so despised by Moore), in which the Cork poet declares: 'God save great George our king / Honor and glory and length to his reign.'[25] (This praise is given in the hope that the new King will help Ireland; nevertheless, that George IV is referred to as 'our king' lingers in memory.) The effort at censorship is all the more acute as Callanan, unlike Moore, read Irish and many critic consider that his versions caught a great deal of the originals. How then could such a poet wish to inveigle himself into British affections? But how could he not, given that Irish poetry is not the expression of some 'otherness of Ireland's Gaelic culture',[26] as this editor has it, but a much more hybrid affair. Callanan's only book of poems is an achievement in precisely this way: it mixes works in the Romantic mode of Byron and Shelley, along with excellent versions, or amalgamations, of Irish originals.

The title poem is an expansive meditation in which a man finds consolation away from the crowds of mankind, in classic Romantic fashion, and this leaves him confronting the wild landscape of Callanan's native Cork. It is a strongly autobiographical poem, as Callanan also had a strong solitary streak. Moreover, the recluse of the title encounters a figure like himself who has taken ship to leave Ireland, as Callanan himself would in 1827, when he sailed for Lisbon. So far we are in the familiar territory mapped out by Shelley in *Alastor; or The Spirit of Solitude* (1816), but the poem then picks up some of the ghostly resonances of the defeat of the Earl of Desmond in the sixteenth century. Whereas Shelley's landscape is emptied of historical meaning, Callanan makes the egotistic sublime contiguous to Irish history. It is a unique moment in Irish poetry before Yeats. The Irish struggle is then compared with the struggle for Greek independence, which naturally leads to a eulogy for Byron, until the poem then concludes with a resounding meditation on Ireland's desire for freedom, and the recluse's own situation in relation to it. The verse-form is borrowed from Spenser's *Faerie Queene* (1590–1609), which had been used by Byron for *Childe Harold's Pilgrimage* (1812–1818) and by Shelley for *Adonais* (1821):

> Is this the Atlantic that before me rolls
> In its eternal freedom round thy shore?
> Hath its grand march no moral yet for souls?
> Is there no sound of glory in its roar?
> Must man alone be abject evermore?
> Slave! hast thou ever gaz'd upon that sea?
> When the strong wind its wrathful billows bore
> 'Gainst earth, did not their mission seem to be
> To lash thee into life, and teach thee to be free?
>   . . .
> The night is spent, our task is ended now,
> See yonder steals the green and yellow light,
> The lady of the morning lifts her brow
> Gleaming thro' dews of Heaven, all pure and bright,
> The calm waves heave with tremulous delight,
> The far Seven-Heads thro' mists of purple smile,
> The lark ascends from Inchidony's height,
> 'Tis morning – sweet one of my native Isle,
> Wild voice of Desmond, hush – go rest thee for awhile.[27]

As Callanan's note tells us, the Seven Heads refer to the headlands beyond Inchadoney (the modern spelling), on all of which 'the Irish formerly had duns, or castles': this is a slow-fade with martial resonance.[28] The difficult Spenserian stanza is handled with skill (although elsewhere in the poem it must be admitted that it becomes convoluted in order to get its rhyme), and the irony that Spenser came to Ireland as an important official in Elizabeth's administration just a year after Desmond died would not have been lost on Callanan. It is an irony of this kind that generated much of the best Irish poetry in the twentieth century.

Callanan has been celebrated less for his own work than for his versions of Irish poems. I say 'versions' as he did not translate particular poems, as Welch remarks, 'rather, his poems or versions seem to adapt certain kinds of Gaelic poetry to Anglo-Irish verse'. Thus while individual lines of Callanan's texts will correspond to lines in Gaelic originals, there is no case where a whole poem does. Welch continues: 'In his nine translations he extended and deepened the work of Moore. Through more immediate contact with Gaelic poetry he widened and deepened the range of expressive possibility for Irish poets writing in English.'[29] This is the beginning of tradition, as a younger poet picks up the tones and themes of an older poet and develops them. One of the more well known of these versions is 'The Outlaw of Lock Lene':

> O many a day have I made good ale in the glen,
> That came not of stream, or malt; – like the brewing of men.
> My bed was the ground; my roof, the greenwood above,
> And the wealth that I sought one far kind glance from my love.
>
> . . .
>
> 'Tis down by the lake where the wild tree fringes its sides,
> The maid of my heart, my fair one of Heaven resides; –
> I think as at eve she wanders its mazes along,
> The birds go to sleep by the sweet wild twist of her song.[30]

Critics have identified similar elements in the Irish poem, 'Muna b'é an t-ól'. Callanan reduces some of the sexual implications of the original ('Agus rún searc mo chléibh 's géaga tharm anall', translated by Welch as 'And the secret love of my breast with her limbs spread over me', is in Callanan's poem dispersed into its elements, i.e., there is a tree near where his lover resides[31]), but still expresses the same aching loss with a directness and lyricism that is very near the original. This represented a novel approach to translation. In the previous century, translators did not hesitate to change the technique and idiom in order to suit contemporary tastes; thus Alexander Pope's famed translation of the *Iliad* is in heroic couplets, where there is no rhyme and a very different prosody in the original. He also introduced many elements of periphrasis, again to suit contemporary tastes. Exactly the same approach was employed by Charlotte Brooke in her *Reliques of Irish Poetry* (1789). As L. G. Kelly remarks: 'One loses count of the number of times eighteenth-century translators tried to produce "a French Vergil", "an English Homer". In contrast the Romantics aimed to reproduce Vergil and Homer in their own languages, to show the foreign poet as he was, or rather, as he related to the basic energy of the "pure speech".'[32] Some critics have misunderstood this general shift in English translation and have criticised Brooke's as bad translations because they are not close enough to the originals;[33] the misunderstanding is given political ramifications by Seamus Deane: 'The translation of Gaelic into English was an action that had profound political implications. When read as the translation of something wild and savage into something regulated and polished, it becomes a metaphor of the translation of catholic [*sic*] into protestant [*sic*], of native and antique authenticity into modern and equally native civility.'[34] It has been suggested that Callanan's versions have a technical roughness which imitates certain rhythmic features of the original (usually this is merely the inclusion of more anapæsts in iambic lines), and this is a violence done upon the English poetic tradition. Such critics assume that this is a kind of compensation for military defeat. Again there is a critical confusion here: compensation for a military defeat is provided by subsequent military victory, not by prosodic innovation. Over a millennium, the English poetic tradition has proved welcoming of those elements that would extend its registers, and that is why Callanan's poem, 'The Outlaw of Loch Lene', is a fine poem in the English tradition, which makes it no less of an Irish poem.

Callanan received scant attention in his time and just a fraction more afterwards; Moore, during his life, received the adulation of Europe, but is remembered for only a small part of his work; however, James Clarence Mangan has perhaps received more critical attention than any other nineteenth-century Irish poet with the exception of Yeats. For his patriotic poems he has received the same hagiographic treatment as Moore;[35] for the incoherence of his work, he has been characterised offering resistance to both nationalist and imperialist literary forces;[36] for his generally louche lifestyle and grotesqueries, he has been figured as a *poète maudit*;[37] for one young poet he becomes a kind of Virgil figure who reveals a hidden Dublin;[38] a penny dreadful entitled *The Mangan Inheritance* has one of his descendants indulging in sex with a girl-child and another in incest;[39] one theory suggests that he is the model for the eponymous hero of Herman Melville's 'Bartleby the Scrivener'.[40] He wrote a fragment of an autobiography which was more fiction than fact, and in 2001 it was claimed that a further fragment was discovered; in true Mangan style, this turned out to be a hoax, not Mangan's own this time but one of his critic's.[41] One of his editors remarks:

> But there are other Mangans too, whose identities are as varied as the poet's many *noms-de-plume*: Mr James Mangan; M.; J. M.; J. C. M.; C.; C. M.; B. A. M.; Z.; Clarence; Drechsler; Selber; Terræ Filius; Hi-Hum; Whang-Hum; Mark Anthony; Vacuus; The Man in the Cloak; The Out-and Outer; Peter Puff Secundus; Monos; A Yankee; Lageniensis; A Mourne-r; Herr Hoppandgoön Baugtrauter; Herr Popandgoön Tutchemupp; Solomon Dryasdust; Dr Berri Abel Hummer.[42]

Mangan, in one poem-translation, described himself as 'Neither One Thing Nor T'Other', and the accuracy of the description has perhaps provoked critics to throw their various theories at him.

After so much uncertainty, some facts will be welcome. Mangan was born in Dublin in 1803, the son of a grocer. He received some formal education, including a grounding in Romance languages, but at the age of fifteen had to interrupt this to begin work as a scrivener; that year he also began publishing literary work in almanacs. A decade later he was appearing in the *Dublin Penny Journal* and the *Comet*; the former ran for two years and was co-edited by George Petrie. This proved a fateful connection for Mangan as Petrie was also engaged in important Irish antiquarian activities at the Royal Irish Academy and the Ordnance Survey Office. This last did not deal directly in bombs and artillery, but had the job, beginning in 1824, of establishing an accurate map of Ireland. Other antiquarians were drawn to the project, including Samuel Ferguson, and soon the Ordnance Survey became the means of gathering more information about local place-names and features of the landscape than could possibly be needed for the purpose of a military map, or any other type of map. Mangan was employed on the project from 1838 and it brought him into close contact for the first time with the Gaelic poetic tradition. Colleagues were able to provide him with literal English versions of the Irish originals – Mangan could not read Irish with ease – and from these Mangan would produce his poems, or versions. When the Survey's funds were reduced in 1841, Mangan took up a job at Trinity College Library. In 1842, when the *Nation* newspaper was set up by the Young Ireland agitators, Mangan began contributing. His link with the journal strengthened throughout the 1840s. A prominent Young Irelander, John Mitchel, would set the hagiographic tone in a memoir written after Mangan died in Dublin in 1849. Mangan had just recovered from a dose of cholera, and his constitution would have been considerably weakened by this, as well as by chronic alcoholism and by his possible abuse of other substances.

The writings of the last decade of his life fuel the nationalist account. Above all, there is his loose version of 'Róisín Dubh', a political Irish poem which in its turn is a version of an older love poem. The middle element – the political poem in Irish – figures Ireland as a woman. I give the first and final two quatrains, followed by a close translation:

> A Róisín ná bíodh brón ort fár éirigh duit –
> tá na bráithre ag dul ar sáile is iad ag triall ar muir,
> tiocfaidh do phardún ón bPápa is ón Róimh anoir
> is ní spáráilfear fíon Spáinneach ar mo Róisín Dubh.
>
> . . .
>
> Dá mbeadh seisreach agam threabhfainn in aghaidh na gcnoc
> is dhféanfainn soiscéal i lár an aifrinn de mo Róisín Dubh;
> bhéarfainn póg don chailín óg a bhéarfadh a hóighe dom
> is dhéanfainn cleas ar chúl an leasa le mo Róisín Dubh.

Beidh an Éirne 'na tuilte tréana is réabfar cnoic,
beidh an fharraige 'na tonnta dearga is an spéir 'na fuil,
beidh gach gleann sléibhe ar fud Éireann is móinte ar crith,
lá éigin sul a n-éagfaidh mo Róisín Dubh.

Róisín, have no sorrow for all that has happened to you:
the Friars are out on the brine, they are travelling the sea,
your pardon from the Pope will come, from Rome in the East,
and we won't spare the Spanish wine for my Róisín Dubh.

. . .

If I had six horses I would plough against the hill –
I'd make Róisín Dubh my Gospel in the middle of Mass –
I'd kiss the young girl who would grant me her maidenhead
and do deeds behind the lios with my Róisín Dubh!

The Erne will be strong in flood, the hills be torn,
the ocean be all red waves, the sky all blood,
every mountain valley and bog in Ireland will shake
one day, before she shall perish, my Róisín Dubh.[43]

(trans. Thomas Kinsella)

('Lios' can be a garth, a ring-fort or a fairy-mound.) The poem is loosely associated with the *aisling* tradition, in which Ireland is personified as a woman (*aisling* means 'dream') and the poet's love for her becomes the vehicle for an expression of his love of Ireland. Another important element is Catholicism, as *aisling* poems promise the return of the Stuart king. 'Róisín Dubh' ends in an apocalyptic scene (possibly the climax of their congress in the preceding stanza), which makes no reference to the English occupiers and does not need to in order for the import to be clear. Mangan's version follows:

I
O, my Dark Rosaleen,
   Do not sigh, do not weep!
The priests are on the ocean green,
   They march along the Deep.
There's wine . . . from the royal Pope,
   Upon the ocean green;
And Spanish ale shall give you hope,
   My Dark Rosaleen!
   My own Rosaleen!
Shall glad your heart, shall give you hope,
Shall give you health, and help, and hope,
   My Dark Rosaleen!

. . .

VI
I could scale the blue air,
  I could plough the high hills,
Oh, I could kneel all night in prayer,
  To heal your many ills!
And one . . . beamy smile from you
  Would float like light between
My toils and me, my own, my true,
  My Dark Rosaleen!
  My fond Rosaleen!
Would give me life and soul anew,
A second life, a soul anew,
  My Dark Rosaleen!

VII
O! the Erne shall run red
  With redundance of blood,
The earth shall rock beneath our tread,
  And flames wrap hill and wood,
And gun-peal, and slogan cry,
  Wake many a glen serene,
Ere you shall fade, ere you shall die,
  My Dark Rosaleen!
  My own Rosaleen!
The Judgment Hour must first be nigh,
Ere you can fade, ere you can die,
  My Dark Rosaleen![44]

This is a translation, or version, in the eighteenth-century sense: Mangan makes no effort to replicate the formal characteristics of the original, and if not exactly periphrastic, he adds a lot of expletive material. He also loses the goings-on behind the *lios*, but he compensates for this by the addition of some impressive effects, such as the priests marching along the Deep, the speaker scaling the blue air and the flames wrapping hill and wood. (Another persuasive reading of the poem is that it is voiced by a priest to his forbidden love.) The poem became the most important single text of nationalist literature in the nineteenth century. It moves Irish readers to protect their nation with the same passion as they would protect their lovers, were they threatened; it inures its readers to the idea of necessary bloodshed, and yet, as in 'Oh! Breathe Not His Name', it is innocent from a forensic point of view, as it never quite comes to the point. Among Mangan's other well-known versions of Irish poems are 'An Elegy on the Tironian and Tirconnellian Princes Buried at Rome', 'O'Hussey's Ode to the Maguire', 'The Woman of Three Cows' and 'Lament over the Ruins of the Abbey of Teach Molaga'.

Mangan also translated from German throughout his life (he was a private tutor of German for a while), and he introduced Irish readers to many important figures in contemporary German poetry such as Friedrich von Schiller, Johann Wolfgang von Goethe, Friedrich Rückert and Ludwig Tieck. Because German philological scholarship was unparalleled in Europe in the nineteenth century, the language also became a gateway for Mangan to poetry from further afield – especially Turkish and Arabic – as Mangan used the German translations as the basis for his own into English; he even produced some work 'from the Coptic', confusing Goethe's original poems for translations from the dead language.

To know more than one language is to be more than one person: moving between languages one changes one's breathing, facial gestures, posture and sometimes even one's disposition. Mangan was particularly aware of these possibilities in his work as a translator and began fabricating translations that had no original, and fabricating poets to go with them, such as the above-mentioned Selber and Drechsler. In magazine publications he would often attach mock-academic notes to his translations referring to non-existent scholars. His playfulness is also exhibited in the many travesties, parodies and comic verses that he produced, often with outrageously funny mosaic rhymes (one example from the 'Song for Coffee-Drinkers': 'sick, quits/poli-tic wits/liquids/quick wits'[45]). Reading Mangan is often like watching a manic comic actor let loose in a costume rental shop, and one often doubts his high pathos, as the memory of his burlesque performances still lingers. (Sometimes in the poems which seek to express violent nationalist passion, he employs mosaic rhyme, a device which belongs rather in comic verse.) David Lloyd expresses one implication of all this play:

> The difference between Moore's notes [in *Lalla Rookh*] and Mangan's lies in their opposed functions. Moore's provide a set of sources that substantiate the authenticity of the oriental scenario. To read among them is, almost literally, to be enriched and reassured of containing and possessing the Orient. In Mangan's case, the notes perform quite the opposite role, actually undermining one's sense of mastery of a certain field; while accumulating a vast capital of ostensibly authenticating sources, they turn the reader's investment of labor into a depletion of his resources. Both the poems and the articles absorb their readers in a quest for origins which, since those origins are perpetually falsified, becomes unendingly protracted.[46]

The point that Lloyd makes in his *Nationalism and Minor Literature: James Clarence Mangan and the Emergence of Irish Cultural Nationalism* (1987) is that Mangan's pseudo-translations call into question the Irish nationalist project of transferring the national spirit from Gaelic literature to English in order to build an Anglophone Irish nation.

It would be interesting if these comic subversions lost their strength as the 1840s progressed, with the decline in Mangan's health and Ireland's endurance of the worst era of its history. The terse strength of a poem like 'Siberia' encourages such a view. He writes that 'Lost Siberia doth reveal / Only blight and death'; the last verse reads:

> And such doom each drees,
>   Till, hunger-gnawn,
> And cold-slain, he at length sinks there,
> Yet scarce more a corpse than ere
>   His last breath was drawn.[47]

It would be difficult to get a more concise picture of Ireland in the late 1840s than is provided by this stanza. And yet, in the same issue of the *Nation*, we encounter a 'Persian' poem entitled 'To the Ingleezee Khafir, Calling Himself Djaun Bool Djenkinzun':

> *Thus writeth Meer Djafrit* (1) –
> I hate thee, Djaun Bool,
> Worse than Márid or Afrit (2),
>   Or corpse-eating Ghool . . .
>   . . .
> That thou thus shouldst disturb an
> Old Moslim like me,
>   With my Khizzilbash (4) turban!
> Old fogy like me,
>   With my Khizzilbash turban![48]

Many Irish nationalists did indeed hate John Bull, but the joke here is on them, even as Mangan deplored the ravages of British rule in 'Siberia'. He pops Khizzilbash turbans on the heads of John Mitchel, Thomas Davis and Charles Gavan Duffy, the leaders of Young Ireland, and does a merry dance about them. It is easy to see why James Joyce thought so highly of Mangan: here was a writer who engaged deeply with the issue of Ireland, confronting its travails with a mixture of solemnity and self-mockery, while flying by the nets of nationality and language, just as he would do himself.

Chapter 2

Tennyson's Ireland

James Henry, Samuel Ferguson, William Allingham

1849, the year of the death of James Clarence Mangan, marked a watershed in Irish history and culture. The Young Ireland organisation had become frustrated with Daniel O'Connell's movement for the repeal of the Union after he backed down from a confrontation with British forces in 1843, and this led to their failed uprising in 1848. This, like the other failed rebellion of 1867, was a minor event of no great military significance. British rule would not be seriously threatened until 1916. The movement's leaders were scattered abroad and the repeal movement guttered. This had an effect on poetry also, as those leaders were also prominent cultural figures who had built institutional contacts, and indeed institutions, that could support poets financially through publication and other less direct ways.

The Empire was enjoying the halcyon days of Pax Britannica, at the vanguard of industrial progress, engaged in no major European war in the period 1815–1914, and having successfully brushed off the Chartists' demands for political reform. There would be a steady increase in suffrage throughout the century, but it was paced so that it did not to threaten the social order. Irish suffrage roughly paralleled this development, and this reflected the growing feeling that Ireland was no longer a colony in the sense that Fiji was, but more of a partner, and much public money was spent on raising the level and number of Irish schools. But, at several important historical junctures, Ireland would receive forceful reminders of its subordinate status.

The event of overwhelming importance in this period was the Great Famine of 1845–9. Not only did about one million people die of starvation and disease, but about one and a half million people emigrated (mostly to England and America). The Famine affected the poorer sections of the population, and these were for the most part Irish-speaking, including a considerable number in Dublin. As one economic historian remarks, although the language was in retreat by the 1840s,

> the number of Irish-speakers alive in 1845, somewhat over 3 million in Ireland and perhaps another 0.5 million elsewhere, was the highest ever.

But those who perished or emigrated were disproportionately Irish-speaking, and by 1851 the number of Irish speakers living in Ireland had fallen below 2 million. Neither O'Connellite nor Fenian brands of nationalism did anything to foster Irish, and by the time a more advanced nationalist ideology adopted the old tongue it was too late.[1]

Thus when the Gaelic Revival began its work at the end of the nineteenth century, it would have a significantly narrower conduit to Irish culture than other cultural-nationalist movements in Europe in the period. For instance, Finnish, Czech and Bulgarian nationalists could turn to large populations in both town and country in order to blood their idealisations with a living oral culture. Ireland, lacking this base, created what Samuel Beckett would later call 'the Victorian Gael': a person for whom the Gaelic past was a kind of hobby or scholarly pursuit, and who deliberately suppressed those aspects of Gaelicism which conflicted with Victorian morality.

But these 'Victorian Gaels' had positive aspects also, as can be seen in the figure of Samuel Ferguson, who brought a greater scholarly exactitude to the study of ancient Irish literature, demanding more stringent standards of translation and interpretation. There was also an important ecumenical side to the project. Scholars, critics, poets and writers of different political persuasions – ranging from Unionist to radical nationalist – could meet amicably on the ground of antiquarian research.[2] They had different aspirations for their work, as we shall see, but they did not let those aspirations affect the integrity of their research. A consequence of this was that the fruits of antiquarian labour carried out by a Unionist could quite easily be used for nationalist arguments. Already in the poetry of J. J. Callanan, we saw how translation, or at least proximity to the Gaelic original, affected the idiom of original work in English. The increase in antiquarian activity in the second part of the nineteenth century, and its greater dissemination through institutions like the Royal Irish Academy and the Irish Archæological Society, as well as through popularising writers like George Sigerson, Sir William Wilde and his wife, Jane Elgee (Lady Wilde), meant that it became easier for poets to incorporate old Irish material – it themes, its images, its idioms – in their own work.

This Gaelicisation of Anglophone poetry in Ireland has a further context. In 1973, Austin Clarke wrote that 'it is not usually recognized that the predominant poetic influence in Victorian Ireland was that of Tennyson and, in consequence, our own poets, before the literary Revival, were provincial'.[3] William Allingham and Aubrey de Vere (1814–1902) were Tennyson's friends, and wrote in the lucid mode of the English poet, clearing their idiom of many of the archaisms of Romantic expression, but his influence is evidenced even in work that is more Gaelic in theme. Tennyson was the pre-eminent poet of his age and when he turned to Arthurian Romance as subject for a long poem, first with 'Morte d'Arthur' in 1842, and then more extensively in the 1850s, it was an unprecedented event which set a new direction in taste.[4] Previously, the mythology of England was the occasion for brief lyrics, whereas religious, philosophical or classical themes were thought more fitting for longer works. Like *Lalla Rookh*, *The Idylls of the King* (its first instalment published in 1859) has not stood the test of time, but like Moore's poem it was extremely influential in its day. Tennyson's choice of theme must be put in the context of the imperial triumphalism of its era, and his intention indeed was to be an apologist of empire, much in the same fashion as Virgil. Poets, like other artists, do not worry about the political provenance of a technique if it can profit them, and there was little difficulty in transferring this approach to Irish material. This duly happened in the decades that followed. There was Samuel Ferguson's *Congal* (1872), which we shall come to presently. Denis Florence MacCarthy (1817–82) wrote 'The Voyage of St Brendan', a poem which brings together much of the lushness of Romantic landscape description with early Christian themes, and another long poem, 'Ferdiah' (1882). Even Aubrey de Vere's long poem *Inisfail* (1861) can be considered as part of this tendency, as it narrates key episodes or dramatic situations in the Irish past in an effort to explain the present state of affairs. And, perhaps most successfully, we can see the fruits of Tennyson with an Irish twist in W. B. Yeats's *The Wanderings of Oisin* (1889).

The list of these long poems charts the lead-up to the Literary Revival, in which Irish writing in English came of age. The first poet we will look at, however, has nothing to do with this narrative, and for this reason, perhaps, it has taken his work a century and a half to come to light.

The publication of the *Selected Poems of James Henry* (2002), edited by Christopher Ricks, had all the look of a Mangan-esque hoax. One of the blurbs on the back cover puts the matter thus: 'James Henry turns out to be a very Ricksian (and Beckettian) poet: skeptical, atheistical, even blasphemous . . . [Ricks] has discovered a poet he could almost have invented, so much does he find there the movement of his own mind and the pitch of his own voice.' As Ricks notes in his introduction, none of the standard works of reference for Irish literature or culture list him. Yet he did exist; more importantly, his writings also existed (most of them self-published), and they are cached among the rare books of research libraries like Trinity College Dublin (Henry donated several of his books to this library). Ricks's edition is that uncommon thing: a literary discovery. Moreover, reading the original publications of Henry, one realises that

Ricks could easily have trebled the length of his selection without any drop in the quality of the poetry.

Henry was born in Dublin in 1798, the son of a woollen draper. He entered Trinity College in 1814, winning a gold medal in Classics in 1818. He left with the degree of MD in 1832 and practised as a physician in Dublin until 1845. He charged only five shillings as a fee, considerably below the going rate, as he said that a doctor's opinion was not worth more (he also supplied his patients with medicines free of charge). The unusual gesture catches something of Henry's independence of mind, a quality that would become apparent in his poetry. As he put it in one poem:

> I follow not the rhymer's trade;
>   To please, I have no zest;
> My verse is by mere instinct made,
>   Like bee's cell or bird's nest.
>
> To please himself, Correggio drew;
>   To please myself I write;
> Applaud or not, as ye think fit,
>   My verse is my delight.[5]

In 1845, he inherited a large amount of money which enabled him to stop practising as a physician. From then on he devoted himself to research on Virgil, preparing his large commentary entitled the *Æneidea*, as well as to poetry. His research entailed much travel between the libraries of Europe and he undertook most of it on foot with his wife and daughter, and then, after the death of his wife, with only his daughter. J. P. Mahaffy, in his obituary, remarked that 'seventeen times they crossed the Alps on foot, sometimes in deep snow, and more than once they were obliged to show the money they carried in abundance, before they were received into the inns where they sought shelter from night and rain'.[6] He wrote many poems which described those journeys in detail, as well as occasional poems about various places and historical personages associated with them.

The article on Henry in the *Dictionary of National Biography* devotes most of its attention to Henry's work as a classical scholar, and generally speaking his poetic reputation still lags behind. A brief introduction to a subject such as a country's poetry over two centuries should follow, not change, the general outlines. These few pages on Henry are an exception because his discovery was so recent. Though he was a civic-minded patriot, healthily critical of the British Empire, he did not care in the least about the emergent Irish nation, and his poems present a world more various and vivid than Moore, Callanan, Mangan,

Ferguson or Allingham could ever have imagined. For that reason, standard accounts have omitted him.

Where Mangan is burlesque, Henry is witty, as in a poem like 'Out of the Frying Pan into the Fire', in which the poet has a nightmare in which he is interrogated briefly by his Maker and then sent tumbling down to hell (there are remarks in passing about the particularly good company there – 'Titus the good, and Cato and divine / Homer and Virgil'[7]):

> and a Proclamation
> Of Martial Law in Heaven was just being read
> When, in a sweat of agony and fear,
> I woke, and found myself in Germany,
> In the close prison of a German bed,
> And at my bedside Mr. Oberkellner
> With printed list of questions in his hand:
> My name and age and birthplace and religion,
> Trade or profession, wherefore I had come,
> How long to stay, whither next bound, and so forth;
> All at my peril to be truly answered,
> And upon each a sixpence to the State,
> Which duly paid I should obtain permission
> To stay where I was so long as the State pleased,
> Without being prosecuted as a felon,
> Spy, or disturber of the public peace.[8]

Henry avoids a punch-line of the kind that rhymed couplets would demand, but lets his blank verse wander off into the bureaucratic mazes of Mr Headwaiter. The further he goes into these administrative particulars, the more time we have to think about the parallel between the punishments threatened by religion and the punctilious enmeshments of the real world. The meticulous Mr Oberkellner is the butt of the joke, while the metaphor, like all good ones, cuts in several ways: hell will be nothing compared to bureaucracy; we are capable of imagining hell, because we can create bureaucracy; his innocence in Germany (he is not a felon, spy, etc.) is a type of punishment; or, simply, while hell is bad, at least there is no entrance fee. The tone and diction of this are noteworthy: the first is relaxed and intimate; the second is colloquial, even plain. It is almost as natural as speech (with that expert line-end: 'and found myself in Germany' – one can imagine the comic pause after the country is named, as the listener briefly equates hell with Germany).

Poems like 'Old Man' and 'Very Old Man' effectively dramatise the parallax that occurs between youth and old age. In 'Julian and Gallus, In the Castle of Macellum', Henry sounds this theme even deeper. Here is the poem in its entirety:

> *Julian*
> Like, as an egg's, life's two ends to each other:
> Blind, helpless, speechless, at one end we enter,
> Not knowing where we are, or whence we come;
> Blind, helpless, speechless, exit at the other –
> Who has come back to tell us why or whither?
>
> *Gallus*
> Lazarus, for one.
>
> *Julian*
> And what did Lazarus say?
>
> *Gallus*
> Nothing; seemed not to know he had been away.[9]

Julian the Apostate was brought up in Macellum, a remote estate in Cappadocia (now part of Turkey), and, as Roman emperor (361–3 CE), he was famed for his disdain of the Christian religion. The terse elegance displayed by Julian and his brother in the face of the brute facts of existence bespeaks courage. There is no consolation provided by God. Of course, Lazarus was hauled back into existence by the Son of God, but one cannot help but speculate that Henry, a medical doctor, is suggesting that Lazarus did not truly die. However, what is most important is Gallus's nonchalance, as he elides the personal pronoun in the final line. Many other poems in *Menippea* (1866) also explore the hypocrisy of religious belief as it is handed down from one generation to the next. In the same collection there is an argument between Adam and God, when the former draws attention to all the deity's inconsistencies, especially his tendency to talk in tropes that do not truly describe the world. God fluffs the answers, and then says he should obviously have put a bit more poetry into Adam's composition. Adam has the last word:

> It can't be helped now; but next time you're making
> A thing, like me, with an immortal soul
> – For I'm none of your dust, I'm bold to tell you,
> But an ethereal spirit in a case –
> 'Twere well you'd make him with sufficient wit
> To understand your flights of poetry,
> Or, if not, that you'd talk to him in prose.[10]

On the face of it, this dialogue is theological, but Henry, as we know, is an atheist, and the point of this surprising exchange is to puncture all the pretentions that Godhead is given by humanity.

There is also another very different strand in Henry's work: his peripatetic poems which describe his journeys around Europe in detail. Ricks excerpts from one of these in his selection: *Thalia Petasata, or A Foot-Journey from Carlsruhe to Bassano* (1859; the title means abundance dispersed or spread out, but Thalia was also the muse of comic and idyllic poetry). The journey takes the travellers over the Alps from Germany into the vicinity of Venice. It is a kind of diary put into blank verse: there are descriptions of the changing landscape, the receptions which he and his daughter receive in various inns along the way, his opinions on the qualities of beds in different countries, as well as on the positive and negative aspects of mixing with aristocracy. It does not lend itself to easy quotation as the pleasure of the poem resides in that fact that it goes nowhere, even as the travellers themselves definitely do go somewhere. There are no Wordsworthian 'spots of time', moments of spiritual revelation that act as anchors for the meditation. The only thread in the poem is the road itself and the tread of the travellers upon it. Here is Henry's description of exactly the kind of road he liked:

> I like a long, straight, narrow, dusty road –
> That is, in case it's neither very long,
> Nor very dusty, and in case it's thickly
> Planted on each side with tall, stately poplars
> Pyramidal, luxuriant, green and whispering,
> And not less than a hundred years old, each,
> And casting down, each, its delicious shade
> On the white, glaring dust, and, with its fellows,
> Forming a vista through which at one end
> Appears a steeple – not cocked on a church,
> Like peacock's feather on the hat of a fool,
> But on the firm ground built, and overtopping
> The church beside it by some half dozen stories –
> And at the other end the city's entrance
> With busy people passing in and out,
> And overhead, between the poplar tops,
> A narrow stripe of blue, Italian sky,
> From town to steeple stretched like a blue ribbon.[11]

One receives far too much detailed information to the imaginary question: 'What kind of road do you like, Mr Henry?' It is like someone taking five minutes to explain how they like their egg boiled (the egg being done in three). The first line here would suffice. Henry is not to be brooked. But by the fifth line we see with what passion the description is made, born of many hours on roads, and deep affection for the metamorphoses of landscape and weather. This is an idyllic landscape (though Henry is also good elsewhere on depicting its dangers), that takes pleasure in the way that the poplars shade the traveller and arrange the sky above him. Henry does not interrogate the countryside to reveal the Romantic sublime; he is content to stay with exact description and achieve his effects through that.

Henry has no place in the canon of Irish poetry established by Yeats when he named 'Davis, Mangan, Ferguson' as its leading exponents in the nineteenth century. He is a rare type of poet in the nineteenth century for the exact, yet luxurious, plainness of his vision, his humour, his independence, his lack of moralising and his intellectualism. His diction is stringent and direct, occasionally edging over into prose, but most often it is refreshing for its lack of archaism and energetic colloquial delivery.

One of Samuel Ferguson's sympathetic critics, Peter Denman, has described him as 'at once the most innovative and the most unoriginal of Irish poets',[12] and to explain this contradiction is to explain much of Ferguson's significance for Irish poetry in the nineteenth century. He was innovative because he transformed the treatment of old Irish material, demanding greater precision and less nationalist ideology in its translation. He brought a large store of antiquarian knowledge to bear on his own translations and treatments of old Irish material. To complicate the picture, he was a Unionist and he thought his work valuable because it would clearly present the Irish and their history to an English audience: only through mutual recognition could the Union be strengthened. He was unoriginal because the poetry he wrote remained at the dullest and most conventional level of Victorian verse. Only when occasionally the syntax or tone of the original Irish materials breaks through the translation does something more interesting occur; but even that is usually just awkwardness, and does not bear comparison to the way in which J. M. Synge would twist English to catch the rhythms of Irish speech in his plays. Or as Gréagóir Ó Dúill put it in his excellent study of Ferguson:

> Ba mhinic ag Ferguson gan a bheith róchinnte dá dhearcadh féin i leith charachtar agus imeachtaí na seanscéalta lena bpléadh sé. Ba scoláire uasal AnglaÉireannach é, ba Ultach iarPhreispitéireach cúnantach, ba náisiúntóir é agus é ar tí a rá ó am go chéile gur cheart an ceangal le Sasana a bhriseadh – ba thrí phearsa in aon fhile é.[13]

Ferguson was born into a middle-class Presbyterian family in Belfast in 1810 and attended the recently established Royal Belfast Academical Institution before training as a barrister in London, and then at Trinity College, Dublin. In 1832 he published work in *Blackwood's Edinburgh Magazine*, and this bridge between Belfast and Scotland would prove important in years to come. The stereotype of the Irish Protestant is as landowning gentry, or what is referred to as the Anglo-Irish Ascendancy. Although Ferguson would later marry into this class (his wife was Mary Catherine Guinness, whom he was drawn to because of the fine way she sang the songs of Moore, according to Ó Dúill[14]) and he would often publish in the *Dublin University Magazine* (the Ascendancy mouthpiece), he never fully identified with their attitudes towards Irish culture. He deeply loved the country and the people, even while he condemned the radical movement for independence. Ireland should not be a colony of Britain's, but rather a partner, and he envisaged Dublin as a centre of intellectual excellence to equal the Scottish Enlightenment of the eighteenth century. (His practice as a barrister kept him in close contact with the north of Ireland, which necessarily meant Scotland also.) During the 1840s, so disgusted was he by Britain's treatment of Ireland that he helped found the Protestant Repeal Association.

His first major publication was a long, swingeing review of James Hardiman's collection of translations, *Irish Minstrelsy, or Bardic Remains of Ireland* (1831), which appeared in the *Dublin University Magazine*. At the end of the review, Ferguson provided some alternative translations of those covered in Hardiman's book, and this engagement with Irish culture set him on his future path. However, in the 1840s he struck up an association with the *Nation*, and was friendly with one of its founding editors, Thomas Davis (also a barrister). When Davis died in 1845, Ferguson wrote perhaps one of his finest poems memorialising his dead friend:

> I walked through Ballinderry in the springtime,
>   When the bud was on the tree,
> And I said, in every fresh-ploughed field beholding
>   The sowers striding free,
> Scattering broadcast for the corn in golden plenty,
>   On the quick, seed-clasping soil,
> Even such this day among the fresh-stirred hearts of Erin
>   Thomas Davis, is thy toil![15]

Employing different landscapes to feature different aspects of Davis's personality and achievement, Ferguson provides an affectionate and flattering portrait. He stops short, however, at praising Davis's radical nationalism ('But I grieve not, eagle of the empty eyrie, / That thy wrathful cry is still'[16]).

Ferguson was involved on an informal level with the work of the Ordnance Survey, which I described in the previous chapter. This would have further alerted him to the importance for Irish poetry of the tradition of *dinnseanchas*, which connects stories and folklore to particular places in the Irish landscape (*dionn* means eminent or famous place, and *seanchas* means lore). The tradition goes back as far as the last centuries of the first millennium CE. Through this method the landscape becomes a mnemonic for history, and so provides a further support for the oral culture. Along with the *aisling* tradition, which I discussed in the last chapter, *dinnseanchas* proved important for translations into English also. Landscape description took on a crucial role because, arguably, the actual land of Ireland – its rivers, mountains and forests – was the same land that Fionn MacCumhaill and other heroes once coursed over. (Although it should be noted that Ireland was almost completely deforested by the end of the seventeenth century.) The *dinnseanchas* tradition would prove important to twentieth-century poets also, such as Yeats, Clarke and Kinsella.

Although Ferguson was well represented in anthologies around the mid century, his first important book publication did not come till 1865, *The Lays of the Western Gael*. It was a long book which comprised several different modes – lyrics, translations as well as his own poems based on Irish material. One of the well-known pieces was 'The Welshmen of Tirawley' and its conclusion gives a good idea of the Unionist twist that Ferguson could give his material. The tribes of Burke and Barrett represent the erring native stock, and the *ollúna* (wise men) said how it was not

> Till the Saxon Oliver Cromwell,
> And his valiant, Bible-guided,
> Free heretics of Clan London
> Coming in, in their succession,
> Rooted out both Burke and Barrett,
> And in their empty places
> New stems of freedom planted,
> With many a goodly sapling
> Of manliness and virtue;
> Which while their children cherish,
> Kindly Irish of the Irish,
> Neither Saxons nor Italians,
> May the mighty God of Freedom
>   Speed them well,
>   Never taking
> Further vengeance on his people of Tirawley.[17]

The dig that Ferguson gets in with the reference to 'Italians' reminds readers that Roman Catholicism is no more native to the country than the Saxon. As the title of the book indicates, there are long poems such as 'The Tain-Quest',

'The Abdication of Fergus Mac Roy' and 'The Healing of Conall Carnach', which deal with some of the oldest materials of Irish legend, and indeed of European legend. The first of these relates not only some of the action, but also the difficulties of the transmission of the tale from generation to generation. The Gaels lose their poem, the *Táin*, and, we are told, 'songless men are meet for slaves'.[18] The fragment that remains is used as the basis for florid fictions, and thus the Gaelic heritage is corrupted:

> So it comes, the lay, recover'd once at such a deadly cost,
> Ere one full recital suffer'd, once again is all but lost:
> For, the maiden's malediction still with many a blemish-stain
> Clings in coarser garb of fiction round the fragments that remain.[19]

One consequence of this is that the antiquarian scholar himself becomes a sort of hero, ranging through the past, distinguishing fiction from true fragment, as though wrenching out a wedge of fashioned Greek marble from a neo-classical façade.

The major dialectic that runs through all of Ferguson's work is the contrast between advanced civilisation and savagery. It was not simply that he, as a Victorian gentleman, represented the first, and the Irish represented the second: he admitted that England itself had savage beginnings (along with a crude and repugnant literature), but these were purified and strengthened to their present triumphant form in the British Empire. There was no reason why the same could not be done for Irish culture. Time and again he refers to the 'repulsive', 'vulgar' and 'repugnant' aspects of Irish language and culture; but these are adduced not to denigrate Ireland and its past, but rather to show what must be done in order for the country to flourish. To further this cause, he himself endured first the scorn and then the neglect of English critics, even though he attempted to make his own work touch at various points with Tennyson's in the *Idylls of the Kings*.

His major late work is *Congal* (1872), a long poem based on the materials in *The Battle of Dun na n-Gedh and the Battle of Magh Rath*, which had been published in 1842. The events of the poem lead up to the Battle of Moyra in 637 CE, in which Congal, a pagan chieftain from Ulster, does battle with Domnal, the Christian high king, because of a supposed slight. Such a tale of military conflict in Ireland cannot but have raised the suspicion of an allegory of the latter-day situation. It is to Ferguson's credit, then, that it is difficult to draw any firm parallels between his contemporary period and that of the poem, although Peter Denman is surely correct when he says that 'the final more moderate search for the restoration of "Law and Justice, Wealth and Song" corresponds very accurately to what he desired for Ireland. These were precisely what he felt to be threatened by the centralised indifference to and ignorance of the Irish situation and heritage.'[20]

Congal, in the end, is killed by a fool (as he had been informed in a prophecy), and before he dies he is vouchsafed a vision of Ireland, and especially Dublin Bay:

> He looking landward from the brow of some great sea-cape's head,
> Bray or Ben-Edar – sees beneath, in silent pageant grand,
> Slow fields of sunshine spread o'er fields of rich, corn-bearing land;
> Red glebe and meadow-margin green commingling to the view
> With yellow stubble, browning woods, and upland tracts of blue; –
> Then, sated with the pomp of fields, turns, seaward, to the verge
> Where, mingling with the murmuring wash made by the far-down surge,
> Comes up the clangorous song of birds unseen, that, low beneath,
> Poised off the rock, ply underfoot; and, 'mid the blossoming heath,
> And mint-sweet herb that loves the ledge rare-air'd, at ease reclined,
> Surveys the wide pale-heaving floor crisped by a curling wind;
> With all its shifting, shadowy belts, and chasing scopes of green,
> Sun-strown, foam-freckled, sail-embossed, and blackening squalls
>   between,
> And slant, cerulean-skirted showers that with a drowsy sound,
> Heard inward, of ebullient waves, stalk all the horizon round . . .[21]

The description is protracted as Ferguson is reminding readers of what Dublin once was, and still to a large extent was in his time. The sweetness and richness of the flora and arable crops salve the warrior's spiritual wounds as he prepares to depart life. It is not an exaggeration to say that Ferguson imagined different factions reconciled by such a vision (as William Allingham did a few years before).

Congal is interesting to consult in its original publication as the book truly comes alive in its notes, which comprise 84 closely printed pages out of 236 (the poetry is more generously spaced). The notes gather a huge amount of antiquarian material which Ferguson often puts in a wider European context. Many academic debates are commented upon and judgement is meted out. They are written with much more verve and variety of tone than the poem itself and they make the reader regret that Ferguson did not write a prose book on the issues of Ireland and antiquarianism.

Denman comments that 'Ferguson's importance lies . . . in the fact that, for successive generations of Irish writers, from Gavan Duffy and *The Nation* anthologisers on through Yeats and Æ to Clarke and Kinsella, his work provided a necessary precedent.'[22] Indeed, Yeats's tribute a few months after Ferguson died was resounding in its praise:

> The author of these poems is the greatest poet Ireland has produced, because the most central and most Celtic. Whatever the future may bring forth in the way of a truly great and national literature – and now that the race is so large, so widely spread, and so conscious of its unity, the years are ripe – will find its morning in these three volumes of one who was made by the purifying flame of National sentiment the one man of his time who wrote heroic poetry . . .[23]

Yeats wrote this when he was only twenty-one years old, and the force of the passage is due not only to the daring of young genius: we are also witnessing the Literary Revival coming into being. In the next two decades it would emerge into its full strength. Every new literary or artistic movement not only has to promise innovation and change, but it has to change our ideas of tradition. Ferguson, at the time of his death, was a neglected poet; by designating him a great poet, Yeats gives value to the course that he and others had launched themselves upon. Of course, Yeats might well be describing Thomas Davis, so close does his talk of 'National sentiment' take Ferguson to Young Ireland. It elides his Unionism as well as the degree to which Ferguson found the Irish material, in its unrefined state, barbarous and repugnant.[24] Nevertheless, the general drift of Yeats's eulogy is accurate in identifying Ferguson's ultimate value: he brought Irish material closer to the Irish, and thus made the foundations of the emerging literature firmer. As Ó Dúill remarks, he also was the first person to realise that English as spoken in Ireland could be a huge literary resource, and this would be capitalised on by Yeats himself, Douglas Hyde, J. M Synge and many others.[25]

William Allingham befriended Alfred Lord Tennyson in 1851 and over the years that followed he was a frequent guest at the Poet Laureate's house. At this period, Tennyson was the foremost poet of his age and their relationship never progressed beyond that of master and acolyte. If Allingham had not worshipped Tennyson, he would not have accepted with equanimity the several snubs dealt him by the elder poet. Allingham faithfully recorded these in his diary and they make for uncomfortable reading. He recognised Tennyson's superiority to him as a poet, in both fame and achievement, and he was willing to swallow his pride in exchange for proximity to him. There are only a couple of exchanges on the subject of Ireland, but they are illuminating. Tennyson is ill informed on the subject, but that does not prevent him expressing trenchant opinions, anti-Irish in tendency. As for Allingham, elsewhere he would sometimes refer to the native Irish, implying that he and his family – although they had lived in the country for over two centuries – did not belong to that group. But when faced with Tennyson's attitude, he immediately feels the smart and his response demonstrates that he is indeed more native to the island than he would admit. Tennyson had the habit of making remarks like: 'Couldn't they blow up that horrible island with dynamite and carry it off in pieces – a long way off?', and Allingham tries to alert him to the historical reasons for its being horrible, many of which lay blame with the British. Tennyson enthusiastically admits how shabbily the Irish have been treated, but remains unmoved by Allingham's arguments: 'That was brutal! Our ancestors *were* horrible brutes! And the Kelts are very charming and sweet and poetic. I love their Ossians and their Finns and so forth – but they are most damnably unreasonable!'[26] On the face of it, Allingham is merely being objective and Tennyson explosively provocative (an inversion of the stereotypes that Tennyson uses to describe the English and Irish), but one can also sense how Tennyson is careful not to insult Allingham personally by aligning him directly with the Irish. The pattern repeats in their other few exchanges on the subject of Ireland. It demonstrates an instinctive knowledge on both sides of the complexities of Allingham's position as an English poet who was Irish.

Allingham was born in the village of Ballyshannon in Co. Donegal in 1824. The place is situated where the River Erne debouches into the Atlantic and it was an important port for many centuries. The area was settled by the English in the early seventeenth century and Allingham's family arrived there in this period. His childhood memories of the village would become one of the most important elements of his poetry. After working in a bank for a short while, Allingham became Customs Officer at the village. He arranged a transfer to a customs office in Lymington in 1863, so that he could be nearer to Tennyson, and more generally to London literary life (he also befriended Thomas Carlyle and Dante Gabriel Rossetti). His first collection, *Poems* (1850), contained what would later become the popular anthology piece, 'The Fairies':

> Up the airy mountain,
> 　Down the rushy glen,
> We daren't go a-hunting
> 　For fear of little men;
> Wee folk, good folk,
> 　Trooping all together;
> Green jacket, red cap,
> 　And white owl's feather![27]

For all the cuteness of this, there is an edge of condescension (what kind of man would be prevented from hunting by 'little men', especially when so bizarrely dressed?). But the poem is important as it demonstrates how fairies and Irish mythological material can be made palatable to a wider audience: a middle-class

English child can be dandled on a knee to this rhythm and told stories about fairies without sinking into the antiquarian morass that surrounded Ferguson's poems. Allingham, to his credit, is not content with this, and explores a more sombre register as the poem progresses:

> They stole little Bridget
>> For seven years long;
> When she came down again
>> Her friends were all gone.
> They took her lightly back,
>> Between the night and morrow,
> They thought that she was fast asleep,
>> But she was dead with sorrow.
> They have kept her ever since
>> Deep within the lake,
> On a bed of flag-leaves,
>> Watching till she wake.[28]

The ballad tradition has a great capacity for dealing with gruesome subject matter (here child mortality) in a jaunty and sometimes humorous fashion. Allingham uses this so well that these lines could almost be passed off as part of an anonymous folk ballad. (Early in his career, Allingham used to write ballads to old airs and have them printed and distributed anonymously.) The poem ends with the repetition of the first verse (quoted above), and this time our perception of these 'wee folk, good folk' is significantly altered. Celtic sweetness is laced with the smallest dash of violent menace.

Allingham's engagement with the ballad tradition led him to edit *The Ballad Book: A Selection of the Choicest British Ballads* (1865), and in the introduction he describes the complex process by which folk material is brought past the *cordon sanitaire* of modern polite literature:

> These narrative songs (some derived from ancient times and foreign countries, some abridged from the long metrical romances, some of new invention) were composed, not without genius in the best, by unlearned men for popular audiences; and passing from mouth to mouth and generation to generation of singers and reciters, dull and clever, undergoing numerous alterations by the way by reason of slips of memory, personal tastes, local adaptations and prejudices, additions, omissions, patches, and lucky thoughts, and on the whole gaining in strength in the process, came in a later day into the baskets of literary collectors, were transferred into the editorial laboratories, there sifted, mixed, shaken, clarified, improved (or the contrary), no one can ever tell how much, and sent at last into the World of Books in a properly solemn

shape, their triviality duly weighted with a load of antiquarianism, and garnished with fit apologies for the presentation of such 'barbarous productions' to 'a polished age like the present,' and assurances that those high literary personages, the 'ingenious' Mr. This and the 'elegant' Mr. That, whose own poems are so justly, &c. (read now, forgotten), have given some countenance to the venture.[29]

There is a healthy suspicion here of the antiquarians and the arbiters of literary taste, as well as an awareness of the hybrid nature of ballad material. It is also a helpful passage to bear in mind as it indicates that Britain, like Ireland, was discovering its folk past, and this shift in British taste made the Irish material all the more welcome, especially when presented by an ambassador as urbane as Allingham.

Allingham's own ballad-poems added a further element to make them even more hybrid: Victorian morality. One poem is about a girl who 'a maid again I can never be, / Till the red rose blooms on the willow tree.'[30] She has been deflowered by a man who now ignores her. She considers throwing herself in the river, like a fallen woman in Dickens, but scruples: 'Sweet Lord, forgive me that wicked mind! / You know I used to be well-inclined.'[31] The awkwardness of the rhyme is perhaps due to the presence of Allingham's prudishness that is so out of place in a ballad. But it would be too easy to dismiss Allingham as a Victorian prude; elsewhere he displays a beguiling dexterity with sexual symbolism:

> One evening walking out, I o'ertook a modest *colleen*,
> When the wind was blowing cool, and the harvest leaves were falling.
> 'Is our road, by chance, the same? Might we travel on together?'
> 'O, I keep the mountain side' (she replied), 'among the heather.'[32]

Two verses on the poet says that 'Now I know the way by heart, every part, among the heather.'[33] Allingham must have been aware of the innuendo of these lines, which is a stock device in ballads, and it is noteworthy that he does not balk at it.

Allingham's major work was, however, not in the lyric mode, but was a long poem that combined social realism and poetic narrative. *Laurence Bloomfield in Ireland* (1864) is the story of an Anglo-Irish landlord who returns from education in England and the Grand Tour to his estate in Lisnamoy, an Irish place that is made as generic as the realist mode will allow. He faces multiple difficulties: the incomprehension of his Anglo-Irish neighbours when he tries to introduce new methods, both of farming and treatment of tenants; the resistance of the landlord's agent, who exploits the gap between the apathy of the landlord and the desperation of the tenant; and nationalist agitation against landlords. The hero is a reformer who treats his tenants fairly and they respond favourably to his enlightened methods. The narrative moves with a fair clip that is reminiscent of Alexander Pushkin's novel in verse, *Eugene Onegin* (1833); another important predecessor closer to home was Elizabeth Barrett Browning's *Aurora Leigh* (1857). Although the general vision of the poem is blandly eirenic, in its local details there is a refreshing bite. Here is Allingham's description of one of Bloomfield's neighbours:

> Finlay, next landlord (I'll abridge the tale),
> Prince of Glenawn, a low and fertile vale,
> No fool by birth, but hard, and praised for wise
> The more he learn'd all softness to despise,
> Married a shrew for money, louts begot,
> Debased his wishes to a vulgar lot,
> To pence and pounds coin'd all his mother-wit,
> And ossified his nature bit by bit.[34]

His depiction of the Catholic peasantry is condescending and occasionally it resembles antebellum pro-slavery propaganda from the American South. The Irishman, like the Negro, needs a master and prospers under his guidance:

> Moreover, if the Kelt be rash and wild,
> Quick, changeful and impulsive as a child,
> He looks with somewhat of a childlike trust
> To those above him, if they're kind and just;
> Be tender to his moods, allow a whim,
> No surly independence lurks in him;
> Content with little, easy to persuade,
> The man who knows him speaks and is obey'd.[35]

Passages like this made it difficult for some literary historians to admit Allingham into the pantheon of Irish poetry proper.[36] He wishes to assure the English reader that the true Irishman, if treated well, will be an adornment of the Empire, and not the thorn in its side. Allingham could write lines like these because over six decades had passed since the last important Irish revolution, and nearly as much time again would pass before 1916. As for nationalist agitators, they are shown to be self-seeking perverters of the good Irish peasant, little better than criminals. His treatment of the Catholic Church is more accurate as he depicts it as sympathetic to the Catholic poor, but complicit with the British powers-that-be. Bloomfield himself is au fait with advanced antiquarian research on Ireland, and Allingham implies is that he is a better custodian of this culture than the Catholic 'natives'.

The dramatic action of the poem revolves around the murder of Pigot, the landlord's agent, by the Ribbonmen, a group of radical nationalists. One young Catholic tenant of Bloomfield's, Neal Doran, is being drawn into this group, but the young landlord's fair treatment of his parents persuades him that he should retreat from this line of action. For its conclusion the poem cuts to several years later when Bloomfield is blissfully married and a successful landlord, with Doran the trusted manager of his estate. There is a prospect of the landscape, viewed by Bloomfield and his wife, in the final pages of the poem which is similar to the vision of Ireland at the end of *Congal.* The two Unionist poets, Ferguson and Allingham, in this way express their love and benevolent wishes for Ireland.

In 1870 Allingham left his job at the Customs, and launched upon the free-lance literary life. He became editor of *Fraser's Magazine* in 1874, and this, along with his friendships with the leading men of the day, ensconced him at the heart of the English literary establishment. Allingham died in England in 1889 and his remains were buried in Ballyshannon. The social realism of *Laurence Bloomfield in Ireland* – balanced, sympathetic, by times humorous and acerbic – remained a resource untapped by Irish poets in the decades to come. They had other business to conduct.

Chapter 3

Revival

*Douglas Hyde, Katharine Tynan, Ethna Carbery, Emily Lawless,
Eva Gore-Booth, Padraic Colum, Susan L. Mitchell,
Francis Ledwidge, J. M. Synge, Oscar Wilde*

The two decades between 1890 and 1910 were not very eventful in Anglophone poetry. After the magnificent achievement of the Romantics, with Tennyson and Arnold in their wake, English poetry was guttering in the *fin de siècle* (Thomas Hardy would publish his first collection of poetry as late as 1898). As for matters Stateside, Walt Whitman had died in 1891, his reputation still not firmly established in his native land, and the extent and significance of Emily Dickinson's poetry had yet to be discovered: this left a clear stage for lesser lights such as Edgar Lee Masters and Edwin Arlington Robinson. Thus when a young, talented American poet looked around him for exemplars in 1908, he turned to French poetry, not English, so that he could explore new structures and themes. The poet was T. S. Eliot, and, along with Ezra Pound, he would become a leading exponent of what is loosely referred to as Modernist poetry. This work was formally experimental and intellectually demanding: poetic voice was fragmented and often macaronic; the poems ranged widely in European cultural history, and often farther afield; many readers felt that their chaotic structures reflected the confusions of the age, especially in the period after the Great War.

Pound remarked about this period of innovation, '[t]o break the pentameter, that was the first heave',[1] and this gives some idea of the disruption that Modernist poetry entailed. The Modernists' radical experiments with language and form invited comparison with the paintings of Picasso and Braque, and it was supposed that their work expressed most directly the spirit of the age, in short, expressed the spirit of modernity. Western civilisation was perceived to be in decline – its religious and cultural values fragmented, its politics in turmoil – and only those poets who were prepared to smash open the staid forms of traditional verse would be able to catch something of this change in their poetry. Eliot's *The Waste Land* (1922) employed a variety of voices and indeed languages with hardly any explanations to connect them, and this difficulty, so Eliot implied, was somehow the only adequate response to the age. His advocates spread the idea that those who were unable to confront such confusion were likewise unable to face the complex reality of their own age. This was connected with a further important element of Modernist literature: deracination. To express this complex reality, the poet could not be 'rooted' in his home culture, but had to be a homeless cosmopolitan, floating through different cultures and languages.

Where Modernism appeared avant-garde, poetry in Ireland seemed to be turning back to the past, while generally maintaining the forms and tones of Victorian poetry. This was part of a larger movement referred to as the Irish Literary Revival: long decades of antiquarian labour now bore fruit in a popular movement that touched many areas of life in Ireland – from farming to the fine arts. There was increased interest in the Irish language, Irish dance, Irish stories, songs and poems. Irish cultural nationalism fostered intense debate about Ireland's status within the Union, and many of the leading members of the Rising of 1916 were active in the Revival organisations. One strand of this movement, the Irish Irelanders, advocated cultural (and later economic) self-sufficiency, viewing with suspicion any foreign elements to be found in Irish literature, whether written in Gaelic or English. Well into the twentieth century, the Modernist movement would be viewed as an affair of rootless cosmopolitans (neither Eliot nor Pound lived in the country of his birth), whereas many poets of the Revival, to put it roughly, were interested in expressing the 'blood-music' of the Irish race.[2]

However, the opposition of Modernism and Revival is a false one. John Hutchinson discusses the ways in which modernity was an integral part of the Revival movement:

> Despite its Janus aspects, cultural nationalism creates the basis of national development in two respects. First, by highlighting the dynamic aspects of the native past, it has enabled modernizing groups to harness traditional symbols to their purposes. Secondly, by stressing the indigenous sources of Western progress, it has provided a powerful critique of attempts to impose a single model of development on world societies.[3]

In general terms, both Modernist and Revival poets were engaged in a radical revision of tradition, in the hope that this would lead to new prospects for culture, the first in an international context, the second in Ireland. By the mid 1930s Eliot was emphasising the importance of indigenous culture, and already agreeing with the idea of 'blood-music' expressed by some Revivalists.

Of course, many policies, religions and æsthetics agree on fundamental concepts: the devil is in the detail. But even here we see that, in Irish poetry, the

Revival introduced many methods which were germane to Modernism. First, the Revival was a bilingual cultural phenomenon: it stressed the limitations of the English language for expressing certain aspects of Irish national character and thus changed literary idiom in order to accommodate these. The poetry was not as brilliantly polyglot as Eliot's, but even the introduction of one other language (and indeed typeface) into Revival texts raised some of the same points as Modernist poetry: the limits of the Victorian poetic mode, its questionable theological consolations and more generally the problematic nature of tradition. Moreover, much of the work of the Revival involved translation from an oral tradition – which lacked a standard orthography and standard versions of stories or songs – into English print culture. Whereas eighteenth-century translators attempted to mould these fragments into new unities in English, now the tendency was to leave the fragments as they were found in the original. Readers were thus alerted to how difficult it was to convey the national spirit from one language to another. It is less difficult to translate Dickens into French than it is an Irish farmer-bard into English because Dickens is translated from the language of one advanced European country to another – there will be greater proximity between terms for social classes, institutions and urban spaces – whereas the farmer-bard will have to be translated literally into another world. Despite some local successes, neither J. J. Callanan, James Clarence Mangan nor Samuel Ferguson was ever able to find the right pitch for their Irish material in an English literary idiom: this would be the greatest achievement of the Irish Literary Revival.

The best illustration of these issues is Douglas Hyde's *Abhráin Grádh Chúige Connacht / Love Songs of Connacht* (1893). Hyde collected the lyrics of these songs from peasants in various parts of Ireland, and in one case, in America. Sometimes he collated versions, and sometimes he provided several versions of the same song; sometimes he tried to explain the obscurities of the songs, and sometimes he left them as they stood; in all cases the originals were to be found on the facing page, along with the commentary in Irish. 'The Paustyeen Finn, or the Fair-Haired Childeen [*sic*]' is a good example of the strange poetic texts that were produced by his labours. The first three verses describe how a man's sister, who is the fair-haired child, is to be taken away from him by a menacing figure; and he resolves to dress up in her clothes to foil the attempt. Then, in the verses that follow, the poem becomes a love poem about the *paustyeen*, and the speaker is now her lover:

> ᵹꞃáꝋ Le m'ᴀnᴀm í, ᴀn páꞃⱅín ꝼíonn,
> ᴀ cꞃoïꝋe 'ꞃ ᴀ h-ᴀnᴀm ᵬeiꞇ ꝼáiꞃᵹⱅe Liom,

ᴅá ċíċ ɠeaᴌa maṗ ḃᴌáċ na ᴅᴄom
's a píob maṗ an eaᴌa ᴌá máṗᴄa.

nuaṗ ᴅ'éṗiɠ ṗí aṗ maṗoın an páṗᴄín ḟıonn,
'a ċuıṗᴌe na ɠ-caṗaᴅ cṗéaᴅ ᴅeunṗaṗ ᴄu ᴌıom?'
'a ṗıúṗ' aṗ ṗa mıṗe, 'ᴄaḃaṗ ᴅ'aᴄaṗ aṗ ḟaıᴌᴌ,
's má ċoɠṗuıɠeann ᴄu aıċṗıṗ ᴅo ṗɠeuᴌ ᴅó.

caᴅ ᴅo ḃ'áıᴌ ᴅaoıḃ mo ċṗoċaᴅ ṗá 'n b-páṗᴄín ḟıonn,
a'ṗ ɠuṗ aṗ mo neaṁ-ċoıᴌ ᴄuɠᴄaᴅ mé ann,
ní éıɠın ᴅ'á n-aıṁ-ᴅeoın ᴅo ṗınne mé ann,
aᴄᴄ ᴌe ᴌán-ċoıᴌ a h-aᴄaṗ 'ṗ a máᴄaṗ.

The love of my soul is the Paustyeen Finn,
Her heart and her soul to be squeezed to me,
Two breasts, bright like the blossom of the bushes,
    And her neck like the swan on a March day.

When she rose in the morning, the Paustyeen Finn,
'O pulse of the friends, what wilt thou do with me?'
'O sister,' said I, 'take your father on an occasion
    And if you choose tell him your story.'

Why do you wish to hang me for the Paustyeen Finn?
And sure against my will I was brought into it.
It was not violence against their wish I did there
    But with the full consent of her father and mother.[4]

It is difficult to know what is going on in the song: as is clear from the entire text of the poem, the girl seems at one moment to be a sister and the next a lover, and not both at the same time. Hyde says that 'it is probable that there are two songs mixed up in this one', and goes on to remark that 'if these old songs had been collected a hundred or a hundred and fifty years ago, together with the stories that belong to them, these great gaps would not occur in them, and they would not be so broken up and so unintelligible as they are now . . . Alas! it is an incredible loss.'[5] The inconsistencies of this one song come to stand for the present fragmented state of Gaelic language and culture. To read the text and confront its difficulties is to contemplate the fate of the Irish language and people in the preceding centuries. That is a story of loss and sadness, but the fragmented and inconsistent text also possesses a peculiar strength of its own: there is a fluidity of speaking voice and dramatic situation that is strange to English poetry. The translation exists not just as a relic, but also as an elliptical, sensuous and forceful poem, and these were qualities which English poetry no longer possessed in the nineteenth century.

Even the title of Hyde's book is striking – and this is by accident as it was envisaged as part of a larger project entitled *The Songs of Connacht* – as it connects the idea of love with a province more usually associated with desolation. Many of its inhabitants settled there after they were displaced by Planters in the seventeenth century, and were thus condemned to subsistence farming of the most desperate kind; also Connacht suffered severely during the Famine because the land was poor and rocky. Yet here was a collection of love songs of great sweetness, and, to compound the point, Hyde remarks that 'there is no sort of song amongst the peasantry more plentiful than they':[6]

> ceó meala lá reaca, aп coillτiŏ ouba oaпaiʒe
> a'r ʒráŏ ʒan ceilτ aτá aʒam ouiτ a báɱ-cɲɲ na nʒeal-
> cioc,
> oo com reanʒ, oo beul τana, a'r oo cúilin bi car mín,
> a'r a céao-reaпc ná τɲéiʒ mé, ar ʒuп ɱéaouiʒ τu aп
> m'aicio.

A honey mist on a day of frost, in a dark oak wood,
And love for thee in my heart in me, thou bright, white, and good;
Thy slender form, soft and warm, thy red lips apart,
Thou hast found me, and hast bound me, and put grief in my heart.[7]

The strong internal rhyme in the last line is bad (arguably this is where substandard Victorianism is creeping back in), but the first three lines are beautiful, managing to breathe life once again into the old lovers' talk of lips, softness and slenderness. This is achieved by the strange syntax, mainly by the way the first line determines the trajectory of all that follows, and this is taken directly from the Irish. As Robert Welch remarks:

> In order to achieve an English translating style which would correspond
> to Gaelic idiom, Hyde adopted the English speech of the Irish country
> people, itself enriched with the lingering shapes of Gaelic idiom and
> syntax. Such a fusion allowed him quite an extraordinary degree of
> linguistic latitude, in phrasing, syntax, even in imagery, so that his prose
> translations of Irish verse, in the *Love Songs* and elsewhere, have
> something of the strangeness, delicacy and daring later to be found in
> Synge.[8]

Hyde also had a fine gift for presentation of the poems, interlarding them with a prose text that seems like the voice of an old *seanchaí* sitting by the fire. Gone is the antiquarian academic apparatus of notes that Ferguson employed; and yet Hyde has been judged a better scholar than Ferguson.

Of course, the sub-Victorian mode persisted in poetry of the period (one is frequently and floridly *consoled* by poets in the face of loss), but this was not the whole story, and the Literary Revival released many new forces in Anglophone poetry. There was a higher level of knowledge about Irish mythology and history than at the time when Moore wrote, and several poets were able to marry his degree of mellifluousness with more exact accounts of myths and stories. For instance, Katharine Tynan (1861–1931) in her second collection of poetry, *Shamrocks* (1887), achieved exactly this. The long opening poem, 'The Pursuit of Diarmuid and Grainne', is delivered in a suave, honeyed idiom:

> But for my Grainne – all her dusk hair flowing
>   Framed the sweet face as night doth frame a star;
> Proudly she heard the song and music going,
>   Her gaze as one who mused on things afar.
>
> Her face on the long throat was like a lily:
>   She drooped, then straightened, with a sudden scorn
> In the great stormy eyes; anon grown chilly,
>   She shivered, for the old night waned to morn . . .[9]

The book is dedicated to William Michael Rossetti and Christina Rossetti, and this is an instructive connection. It indicates the degree to which the Literary Revival learned from the Pre-Raphaelites and their followers how to write about historical and mythological subject matter for a modern audience. Tynan's technique makes Gaelic material more acceptable to an English ear; it is less crabbed and wilfully difficult than Ferguson. It is also worth noting that the book has no notes, only press notices for Tynan's previous collection, and publisher's advertisements of other books. This is the moment when Gaelic material becomes commercially viable. Tynan in her later career drifted away from Irish material to write more conventional poems about Catholicism, the joys of motherhood and the changing of the seasons; her most important title in this mode is *The Wind Among the Trees* (1898), and her influence on Yeats is clear in the title of his collection, *The Wind Among the Reeds*, published the following year.

There were other modes of Revival poetry. Ethna Carbery (1866–1902), with Alice Milligan, founded the *Shan Van Vocht*, a nationalist literary and political journal, in Belfast in 1896, and it had a wide distribution, especially in America. (The Ulster Literary Revival was a cultural phenomenon distinct from that which was taking place in the south.) In 1902, she published her only collection of poems, *The Four Winds of Eirinn*. Most of her work is of negligible value and combines Christian with Celtic motifs. But at her best, she wielded her Irish materials with a fierce energy, as for instance in 'Rody M'Corley', or below:

> I am Brian Boy Magee!
> And my creed is a creed of hate;
> Love, Peace, I have cast aside –
> But Vengeance, *Vengeance*, I wait!
> Till I pay back the four-fold debt
> For the horrors I witnessed there,
> When my brothers moaned in their blood,
> And my mother swung by her hair.[10]

The violence of this, the marvellous harnessing of hatred by the metre, reminds us of Yeats at his most forceful. It also indicates that the Revival was not simply a hobby for the bourgeoisie, but occasionally drew upon darker currents of national feeling.

Although Emily Lawless (1845–1913) employed almost exclusively Irish subject matter for her writing she disagreed with the main political aspiration of the Revival writers: she did not believe the Irish capable of self-governance. Her reputation as a novelist has overshadowed her considerable achievement as a poet in the collection *With the Wild Geese* (1902). The first poem is voiced by Ireland as she considers her sons scattered around the world in the wake of the Battle of Aughrim in 1691: 'She said, "God knows they owe me nought, / I tossed them to the foaming sea, / I tossed them to the howling waste, / *Yet still their love comes home to me.*"'[11] There follow poems about, among others, episodes in the Battle of Fontenoy, during the War of the Austrian Succession, when an Irish brigade excelled; then the book skips back to deal with episodes in the Desmond Rebellion in the sixteenth century; and there are several lyrics set in the Aran Islands in which Lawless meditates upon the people and landscape. The successes and desolation of Irish history are faced unflinchingly and her technique is spare and precise. She is too interested in history to be concerned about mythology, and this emphasis sets her apart from other poets of the period. It would not be until Richard Murphy's *The Battle of Aughrim* (1968) that a similar approach was taken to Irish history as poetic material.

Tynan and Carbery, along with other poets such as Lionel Johnson, Joseph Campbell, Padraic Colum, George Russell, James Stephens and F. R. Higgins, followed the poetic templates forged by W. B. Yeats. Lawless, as we saw above, did not. Eva Gore-Booth (1870–1926) was fixed in a different frame by Yeats in 1927 in the poem 'In Memory of Eva Gore-Booth and Con Markievicz': 'The light of evening, Lissadell, / Great windows open to the south, / Two girls in silk kimonos, both / Beautiful, one a gazelle.'[12] Eva is the gazelle, and Yeats goes on to describe her thus: 'I know not what the younger dreams – / Some vague Utopia – and she seems, / When withered old and skeleton-gaunt, / An image of such politics.'[13] Gore-Booth's political and cultural involvements were much more complex than Yeats admits, and his poem is inaccurate in its assessment of her subsequent career. She wrote a pioneering work of feminist theology, *A Psychological and Poetic Approach to the Study of Christ in the Fourth Gospel* (1923); she was an acclaimed poet and dramatist; and she was a leading trade-union figure and suffragette. Most of these aspects of her life have been brought to light again with the publication of volumes IV and V of the *Field Anthology of Irish Writing* (2002), and a selection of her poems was included in Éilís Ní Dhuibhne's anthology, *Voices on the Wind: Women Poets of the Celtic Twilight* (1995).

Occasionally her theological and trade-union interests are reflected in her poetry; an example of the former is 'To C. A.' and a stronger example of the latter is 'The Street Orator'. She also made use of Irish mythology, but in a strikingly different way from the other poets of the period. Queen Medbh, a key figure in the *Táin Bó Cuailnge*, who leads the men of Connacht against Ulster, was the subject of many of Gore-Booth's finest poems. For many Revival writers, mythology provided a magical other world that was diametrically opposed to mundane reality; for Gore-Booth, the mythological figure of Medbh leads her back to that everyday world. She tells a tale of

> How a great Queen could cast away her crown,
> The tumult of her high victorious pride,
> To rest among the scattered fir-cones brown
> And watch deep waters through the moonlight glide.[14]

Cowardly figures, for Gore-Booth, were people who were incapable of living in reality, as for instance the title figure of 'The Anti-Suffragist':

> They brought her forth at last when she was old;
> The sunlight on her blanchèd hair was shed
> Too late to turn its silver into gold.
> "Ah, shield me from this brazen glare!" she said.[15]

Several critics have referred the to way that she brings the theme of lesbianism into Irish myth, and certainly 'The Vision of Niamh' expresses the love between women with tenderness and delicacy:

> For thee Maeve left her kingdom and her throne,
> And all the gilded wisdom of the wise,
> And dwelt among the hazel trees alone
> So that she might look into Niamh's eyes.

No sorrow of lost battles any more
In her enchanted spirit could abide;
Straight she forgot the long and desolate war,
And how Fionavar for pity died.

Ah, Niamh, still the starry lamp burns bright,
I can see through the darkness of the grave,
How long ago thy soul of starry light
Was very dear to the brave soul of Maeve.[16]

This does not openly express lesbian love, but like a lot of gay poetry of the nineteenth and twentieth centuries it tactfully gestures towards it; such a moment demonstrates the diverse uses to which Irish mythological material was put by Revival writers.

Where Hyde's book conveyed something of the excitement of Irish fragments, George Sigerson (1836–1925), in *Bards of the Gael and Gall* (1897), presented a historical survey of Gaelic poetry, from the earliest Milesian settlers (which were, in fact, a later mediæval invention) to the contemporary period. The poetry is varied in form and theme, and it exceeds the usual conception of 'Celtic' poetry – rich imagery, wild stories, unrestrained emotions, etc. He showed how the work displayed both an austere restraint and almost always technical prowess. His long and erudite introduction placed the achievement of Gaelic poetry in a broad context and concluded by remarking that 'to the student of European literature it is essential to know the literature of a nation which, when Rome had fallen, held the literary sceptre of Europe for three centuries'.[17] The anthology made clear the extent to which Irish poetry had been influenced by classical literature in the Middle Ages. Here then was a tradition, perhaps not as important, varied and vital as that of the English language, but a tradition nevertheless.

As T. S. Eliot remarked, writers of genius force us to rearrange the canon in their wake. Sometimes they do this violently, sometimes they do it with a slow subtlety, but for the most part this work takes place within one language. The tradition which Sigerson presented to Irish readers, however, had been translated, and this introduced a further factor into negotiations. Issues of linguistic competence arise, and after that of translation theories. These can pose obstacles, but they can also send a writer surging forward with new unexpected energy. As we will see in the case of Yeats in the next chapter, these issues can even profoundly affect a writer with no knowledge of the source language. It is important to note, though, that this process does not *convey* the spirit of Ireland from one language to another, i.e., from Irish into English; this is not simply a resurrection or recuperation. For all the excellent antiquarian work that preceded the Revival and continued into the next century, this is an act of imaginative creation. The greatest betrayal of that imaginative force, and what eventually rendered the Revival legacy progressively obsolete in the next century, was its institutionalisation. It was not until the political upheavals of the Troubles in Northern Ireland in the last three decades of the twentieth century that poets found a way to reinvigorate these images and themes.

Another important aspect of the Revival was its dependence on funding and audiences outside Ireland. Finance flowed in from expatriates in America, and England provided homes, incomes and an audience for many Irish writers of the period. Revival literature was not purely Gaelic, but was profoundly affected by these other *loci*, and many critics of Irish literature still have difficulty absorbing this fact. As recently as 1995, Declan Kiberd remarked that 'the Irish writer has always been confronted with a choice. This is the dilemma of whether to write for the native audience – a risky, often thankless task – or to produce texts for consumption in Britain and North America.'[18] It is important to examine the assumption behind this: the natives read texts in a vaguely organic way, while readers abroad 'consume' books that are little better than industrial products. In the last chapter, I said that William Allingham, a poet deeply rooted in the English literary scene, was one of the first to handle Irish folklore in a fashion that made it interesting to a wider audience (including a wider audience in Ireland). The same is true of Yeats, as we shall see in the next chapter. One of the primary reasons for the success of the Revival was the recognition by some of its exponents that the English language and the English people were not inimical to Anglophone Irish literature, but were in fact the necessary condition for its existence. William Morris, and more generally the Arts and Crafts Movement, created a cultural atmosphere that was amenable to the elements of Irish mythology in the new literature as it offered contact with pre-industrial reality. This is an index of the degree to which the Literary Revival – for all of Brian Boy Magee's talk of vengeance – was in harmony with important tendencies in English culture of the time. (Indeed several Revival poets lived most of their lives in England, for instance Nora Hopper Chesson (1871–1906) and Lionel Johnson (1867–1902). Both wrote conventional poems which romanticised Ireland's past and, in Johnson's case, made vague threatening gestures towards England. He was not as bad as Carbery at her worst, but neither could he equal her furious best.)

A further important aspect of the Revival was the figure of the Irish peasant. Edward Dunsany was not alone when he expressed the following thought in 1914:

> I have looked for a poet amongst the Irish peasants because it seemed to
> me that almost only amongst them there was in daily use a diction
> worthy of poetry, as well as an imagination capable of dealing with the
> great and simple things that are a poet's wares. Their thoughts are in the
> spring-time, and all their metaphors fresh . . .[19]

The habit began in the last decade of the nineteenth century when two Trinity
professors designated the language and literature of Ireland as degenerate; the
Revivalists then had to assert the purity of Irish and all things associated with
it. As P. J. Mathews states, 'It is this moment, then, which marks the beginning
of the idealization of the Irish-speaking peasant as a noble and pious character
enriched with a pure folk imagination.'[20]

A poem like Padraic Colum's 'The Plougher' exalts this figure till he takes on
heroic, almost god-like, proportions: 'Earth savage, earth broken, the brutes,
the dawn man there in the sunset, / And the Plough that is twin to the Sword,
that is founder of cities!';[21] and the tone of the poem continues rising in pitch
from here. Cynics suggested that in order to assess Revival works, they should
be tested for PQ ('peasant quality'). This deification of the Irish peasant was the
reason for the uproar when Synge's *Playboy of the Western World* was performed
in Dublin in 1907 – the igniting spark was provided by a reference to a shift
(underclothing) – which required the theatre to call in the Dublin Metropolitan Police. A writer in the *Freeman's Journal* remarked that one of the play's
characters 'makes use of a word that no refined woman would mention, even
to herself'.[22] This provoked a mordant response from Susan L. Mitchell (1866–
1926), in her *Aids to the Immortality of Certain Persons Charitably Administered*
(1908):

> Oh no, we never mention it, its name is never heard –
> New Ireland sets its face against the once familiar word.
> They take me to the Gaelic League where men wear kilts, and yet
> The simple word of childhood's days I'm bidden to forget.

The poem concludes by begging Gaelic Leaguers and Sinn Feiners to listen to
her as she begs for

> The right to mention once again the word of other days,
> Without police protection once more her voice to lift –
> The right to tell (even to herself) that she still wears – a shift![23]

Unfortunately, the good sense of Mitchell and her like did not win out in Irish
society in the years subsequent to the establishment of the Free State in 1922,
and the Victorian Gaels, in mohair and chasuble, lorded it over the twenty-six
counties.

In the passage quoted above Dunsany is introducing the work of Francis Led-widge (1891–1917), who was born in Slane, Co. Kildare, and worked as a labourer in several different jobs. Although involved with nationalist organisations, in 1914 he went to fight Germany in the Royal Inniskilling Fusiliers, as part of Kitchener's army. It was only after he came into contact with the work of Yeats and Katharine Tynan that he began to incorporate motifs from Irish mythology in his poetry, and to no great effect. He is best remembered as a nature poet of an etiolated Keatsian variety: his poems display technical facility and have a narrow thematic range, much like the Georgian poets in England at this time. Both his poetry and the way he found his death recall the English poet Edward Thomas (1878–1917), but he suffers from the comparison: whereas Thomas was a successor to Keats, Ledwidge is only his epigone. A poem such as 'Desire in Spring' displays his strength and weakness; here are its concluding lines:

> And when the sunny rain drips from the edge
> Of midday wind, and meadows lean one way,
> And a long whisper passes thro' the sedge,
> Beside the broken water let me stay,
> While these old airs upon my memory play,
> And silent changes colour up the hedge.[24]

The rhythm and rhymes are crisp and lightly handled, the observation is sharp and detailed, and finally he refrains from a Victorian conclusion (i.e., he neither moralises nor consoles) in favour of an image, along with an unusual usage ('colour up'). However, this is essentially an ornamental poetry that is never cathected by any larger forces, whether of nature, politics or human emotion.

The poems of J. M. Synge (1871–1909) are in the same pastoral mode as Ledwidge's but they are more successful and, despite their small number, they represent one of the finest achievements in poetry during the period of the Revival. Because he revolutionised the idiom of European drama and because his plays catalysed some of the most important debates of the Revival, his poetry, which is more or less conventional, has commanded little interest. The poems are extremely short, concise and limited in theme: for the most part they talk of love and nature, the eternal stalwarts of poetry. But there is a terse, strong sensuousness in them that is absent from Ledwidge's poems. Here is 'Samhain':

> Though trees have many a flake
> Of copper, gold, and brass,
> And fields are in a lake
> Beneath the withered grass;

> Though hedges show their hips
> And leaves blow by the wall
> I taste upon your lips
> The whole year's festival.[25]

Samhain, the old Celtic festival, was celebrated on 1 November to mark the beginning of winter. Rose-hips are found in the bare hedges, and their tart, red pulp – wrapped tightly in a shining skin – morphs at the end of the poem into the lips of the lover; this is a good example of rhyme carrying much more than a mere identity of phonemes. The first part of the poem shows the way that nature shuts down slowly as winter approaches; and the last two lines blow this wide apart, as Synge makes a different motion of time collide against that of the seasons – and the whole year is recuperable by one kiss. This is a festival, in Wallace Stevens's words a blaze of summer straw in winter's nick. The poem 'In Glenasmole' also makes different ideas of time collide. The speaker remarks that this was the valley where Oisín, the mythical hero, grew suddenly old; but because Synge is now with his lover, his years fall away.

Synge's best work – both drama and poetry – was written after his several stays on the Aran Islands at the turn of the century, and critics over several generations have emphasised this strongly as it consolidates one of the most valued ideas of the Revival: that the spirit of Ireland resides in those parts of the country least touched by England. Their opinion is expressed eloquently by Declan Kiberd:

> His years of writing in Paris had yielded nothing but morbid and
> introspective works; but the discovery of Aran, and the challenge to
> project its life to the world in English, signalled his discovery of himself
> as a writer. The English in which he had tried and failed to express
> himself in those Paris writings had been mannered, weary and effete;
> only when that language was vitalized by contact with a 'backward' oral
> culture did it offer him the chance of real self-expression.[26]

As with the previous passage from Kiberd, there is a contrast here between metropolitan and cosmopolitan experience (enervating) and Irish experience (invigorating): those writers who choose the latter, choose correctly, in his view. The nationalism of the argument blurs, rather than clarifies, the contours of Irish literature (for instance, he has signal difficulty bringing Samuel Beckett into line with his narrative). Yet it would be wrong to deny the general rightness of this as a description of Synge's development as a playwright. His poetry, however, offers other indices, for instance, 'On a Birthday':

> Friend of Ronsard, Nashe, and Beaumont,
> Lark of Ulster, Meath and Thomond,
> Heard from Smyrna and Sahara
> To the surf of Connemara,
> Lark of April, June, and May,
> Sing loudly this my Lady-day.[27]

The slightness of this poem, its pure existence as exclamation, is its main virtue. But it also presents an insidious argument in its rhymes. The first two are macaronic: Thomond and Connemara are two Irish place-names that have Gaelic roots, the first meaning 'North Munster' and the second 'the Conmacne people of the sea'; Beaumont is 'fine hill' in French and Sahara is the Arab word for desert. Synge makes foreign places and their languages harmonise with the native radical. This is not a rejection of 'weary and effete' foreign places and languages, but a reminder of how integral they are to Irish experience. The lark's song, like literature, belongs to no one country or nation. Just as the line between Modernism and the Literary Revival is not so clear as it once seemed, so too does a poem like this beautifully blur the edge of Ireland.

Another fine poem is 'A Question', which emerges, as so many of the others, out of a lovers' dialogue.

> I asked if I got sick and died, would you
> With my black funeral go walking too,
> If you'd stand close to hear them talk or pray
> While I'm let down in that steep bank of clay.
>
> And, No, you said, for if you saw a crew
> Of living idiots, pressing round that new
> Oak coffin – they alive, I dead beneath
> That board, – you'd rave and rend them with your teeth.[28]

There are small imperfections along the way (the inversion of the second line; 'That board' in the last line is superfluous, an expletive phrase inserted for the rhythm – if the last line concentrated only on the woman's attack, it would be better) which remind us that Synge's first *métier* was not poetry, but the poem still beautifully expresses the vanity, tenderness and violence of love.

The case of Oscar Wilde (1854–1900) is somewhat similar to Synge's, as his reputation as a dramatist and prose-writer has overshadowed his poetry. However, one is not so tempted to protest as in the case of Synge. Wilde was a suave and elegant stylist and many of his poems display little more than his facility. (Several, such as 'Le Panneau' and 'Les Ballons', were written as merely decorative pieces for women's magazines.) But the writhing eroticism of 'The

Sphinx' catches much of the sensual carnival of the *fin de siècle*, and his final long poem 'The Ballad of Reading Gaol', is a terse, pathetic complaint about the harshness of the penal system as well as a meditation on the violent aspects of love.

Wilde stands before the Revival, but he provided Yeats with hospitality in London when the younger poet was establishing himself in the metropolis. This chapter has, for the most part, tried to assess the poetry of the Irish Literary Revival with scant reference to Yeats. But Yeats was its *sine qua non*, and its greatest poet. The next chapter is devoted in its entirety to his work.

Chapter 4

W. B. Yeats

The poetry of W. B. Yeats is both the culmination of the nineteenth century and the unsurpassed achievement of the twentieth; he is at once a bridge from the minor achievements of the preceding decades to the major works of Irish poetry and their greatest instance. Through him Irish poetry learned to confront modernity and found new ways to configure the relations between literary works and nationalist ideology. Yeats marshalled the major elements of nineteenth-century culture – translation from the Irish, antiquarianism, the influence of English Romanticism and the Arts and Crafts Movement, the tensions for an artist between an English audience and his Irish provenance – and employed them in the creation of some of the best poems in the English language. He drew together figures as diverse as Mangan, Davis and Ferguson and crafted their legacy into an Irish poetic.

Yeats transformed himself from a *fin de siècle* poet to a poet, who if not a Modernist himself, certainly set the pace for Modernism through his connections with Pound, and to a lesser extent Eliot. Along with Robert Frost, Paul Valéry, Rainer Maria Rilke, he demonstrated that twentieth-century poetry, in order to be truly of its time, need not rid itself of traditional poetic devices. Nevertheless, while spurning most Modernist innovations he paid close attention to them, and some critics argue that Pound and especially James Joyce affected the development of Yeats's later poetry and critical thought. Edna Longley has remarked that 'Irish poetry often refuses to recognise its English dimension; while English poetry overlooks its Irish debts, such as the centrality of Yeats.'[1] She goes on to argue that one of the reasons for this is that we consider Modernism, with its radical poetic experiments, as central to twentieth-century poetry. In consequence poets who continue to write in traditional forms look somehow obsolete. And yet, she says: 'the more traditional team makes a formidable bunch. Headed by Yeats, so often inaccurately co-opted for Modernism despite his clear protestations, it contains Hardy, Frost, Thomas, Owen, Graves, Auden, MacNeice, Douglas, Larkin, Heaney, Mahon. Again, what these poets say about poetry should be central to academic syllabuses, displace a few Modernist pundits.'[2]

The profound political changes that Ireland underwent from the turn of the century to the establishment of the Free State are linked in complex ways to Yeats's development; his work engaged with these and to an extent created them. During the last decade of the nineteenth century, he was ever careful to avoid militant issues, but this changed in the twentieth century, as his poems intervened directly in political matters – commenting, deploring, instructing – such as the riots surrounding *The Playboy of the Western World*, the debacle of the Hugh Lane bequest and land agitation near Coole. In his early career he was reviled by nationalists at home, and yet was their greatest advertisement in America, and in more subtle ways in London. As he moved into the twentieth century, however, he became increasingly distant from radical nationalism; the deep ambivalence of 'Easter, 1916' reflects this. Political issues are not extraneous to the poetry, but lie at its very heart. Yeats, while arguing in favour of tradition over individualism, made his own poetic autobiography the history of his country. (As an index of this, the finest biography of the poet was written not by a literary critic, but a historian, R. F. Foster.)

If W. B. Yeats did not lead the Revival in Ireland, then he was certainly at the centre of most of its debates. As I remarked in the previous chapter, the phenomenon of the Revival embraced a dizzyingly wide range of activities – from farming co-operatives to the study of bardic metres – but perhaps the major element was the Irish language. From the 1890s to the end of his life, Yeats came under strong attack for his ignorance of Irish (he could neither speak nor read it), and this draws attention to the paradox at the centre of his poetic achievement: his poetry, at least in the first three decades, proclaimed its profound connection with the country, and yet he could only get at this material through interpretation and translation. R. F. Foster reports a comic moment from the court proceedings that followed the disturbances in 1907 when Synge's *Playboy of the Western World* was first performed (and when Yeats, here referred to as 'this Irish dramatist', was perhaps better known as a theatre-man than as a poet):

> WBY gave evidence in court that Béaslaí [one of the agitators in the Abbey] '"had addressed some words to me in Irish." "Were they complimentary or the reverse?" "I am sorry to say, I understand no Irish."' (*Evening Telegraph*, 30 Jan. 1907). 'What an instance of National topsey-turveydom in the picture of this Irish dramatist, this authority on the ways and speech of the Western peasant, standing sick, silent and ashamed when addressed in Irish,' remarked a contributor to the newspaper.[3]

But Yeats had to make that connection because he saw Irish culture as an important refuge from modernity, which for him, as for many others, stood for individualism, industrialism, blinkered rationality, disrespect for tradition, irreligiousness and philistinism. He believed that the remnants of the pre-modern were still extant, and could be reached through reading or meeting with 'Indian and Japanese poets, old women in Connaught, mediums in Soho, lay brothers whom I imagine dreaming in some mediæval monastery the dreams of their village, learned authors who refer all to antiquity'.[4] In 'Irish Witch Doctors' (1900) he tells of how he managed, after great trouble, to meet an old healer. The suspense is built up over several pages, until at last Yeats and his companion corner him: 'We reached the cottage amid a storm of wind, and the door was cautiously opened, and we were let in. Kirwan was sitting on a low stool in a corner of a wide hearth, beside a bright turf fire.'[5] This is the thrilling moment of contact, when Yeats steps across the barriers of culture and learning, from one civilisation to another, and connects with what is racy of the Irish soil and also with what amounts to a living critique of the modern world. Kirwan sits arguing with Yeats about ailments, cures and how the fairies influence these. Yeats knows that he will be mocked for believing such hocus-pocus. But he also knows that such mockery emanates from a Victorian culture that was itself in deep crisis as it could not reconcile its belief in science with religious belief. He is beautifully disdainful of such criticism, and he does not waver once in his purpose, remarking that he escaped 'disfiguring humour.'[6] He continued to search out more such old men and women in Connaught and to attend more séances in Soho.

Kirwan speaks only Irish and Yeats only English; they have an interpreter. Yeats would claim that Gaelic culture, in such interviews and through research, could be transferred to English, and made available to monoglots like himself. Thus his poetry makes its claim to Irishness. At the same time, Yeats knew that he owed his 'soul to Shakespeare, to Spenser and to Blake, perhaps to William Morris, and to the English Language in which I think, speak and write, that everything I love has come to me through English; my hatred tortures me with love, my love with hate'.[7] Irish criticism and Irish people in general have been reluctant in the twentieth century to make such an admission, even while generally failing to engage with Irish-language culture. To admit that our writers owe more to the English tradition than to the Irish original seems a type of treason. As I remarked before, it is only so if we restrict that tradition to England. Gaelic culture influenced Yeats deeply, as it did other Irish poets writing in English; but that influence must be calibrated against the deeper influence of the literary tradition of the language they wrote in.[8]

Yeats was born in Sandymount, Dublin, in 1865. Two years later, his family moved to London, where they would remain for thirteen years, with frequent trips back to Co. Sligo, where the family of Yeats's mother still lived. He would continue to commute between England and Ireland to the end of his life, reflecting one of the major dynamics of Yeats's creative life. From 1880, his schooling was in Dublin, first at the Erasmus Smith High School on Harcourt Street, and then at the Dublin Metropolitan School of Art, and not Trinity College, Dublin, which most Anglo-Irish Protestants attended (a social class which Yeats's father had pretensions to). In 1885 he began to publish his first poems, and already we see the establishment of what would prove lifelong interests. There was, firstly, esotericism, an enthusiasm which he shared with his friend Æ (the esoteric name adopted by George Russell (1867–1935)). Secondly, in the same year he became friends with John O'Leary, a Fenian who had endured imprisonment for seditious writings. He was an extremely cultured man, and Yeats often showed him drafts of poems, listening carefully to his advice. Yeats came to these interests – and sustained them – through friendships, and friendship would remain perhaps Yeats's most important means of intellectual development throughout the rest of his career.

Moderate nationalism along with the occult were now established as central to his imaginative life; there was one more element to come. In 1887 the family moved back to London and there Yeats met the English poet William Morris. But Morris was more than a poet; he was also a craftsman, designer and socialist who had been influenced by the writings of John Ruskin. This led him to resist the industrialisation of British society, and produce designs for furniture and fabrics that reflected the taste and production values of the mediæval era. As early as 1834, Thomas Carlyle expressed his despair at the increasing mechanisation of the world: 'To me the Universe was all void of Life, of Purpose, of Volition, even of Hostility: it was one huge, dead, immeasurable Steam-engine, rolling on, in its dead indifference, to grind me limb from limb. O, the vast, gloomy, solitary Golgotha, and Mill of Death!'[9] Such dissatisfaction would spread through Victorian society, insidiously undermining the work of progress and empire. Morris's lifework is one such result. In the 1880s, Morris's Arts and Crafts Movement had wide appeal, and this helps us see that although Yeats would rail against the values he associated with Victorian England, he himself was a quintessential product of that milieu. His exploration of Celtic mythology was fuelled by the extensive antiquarian work that had been underway in Germany, France and Ireland in the previous century, but it is questionable whether he would have engaged upon it without the example of Morris, as well as of Matthew Arnold in *On the Study of Celtic Literature* (1867). Celticism, as a result, was extremely fashionable in English literature at the end of the nineteenth century. (It is also worth noting that Morris's Kelmscott Press would later provide the model of the Cuala Press, established by Yeats's sisters.) This is not to question the seriousness of his interest in Celticism, but rather to indicate its complex provenance. In London during this period he fell under the spell of Maud Gonne, an Englishwoman who supported radical Irish nationalism. Her passion for Ireland combined with Yeats's passion for her would prove crucial to his poetry over the next thirty years. Through Gonne, Yeats came to write love poetry that had national resonance.

Of Yeats's diverse enthusiasms and commitments in this period, Foster comments that 'his interests and involvements ricocheted off one another, driven by a number of consistent motivations. One was sexual frustration; another, professional ambition. These everyday impulses could – and did – drive him to produce unexpectedly exotic effects. Above all, he needed to belong to organizations and, once attached, to shape them into the image he desired.'[10] One of the important organisations was the Rhymers Club in London, which Yeats was involved with in the years 1891–4. This loose grouping of *fin de siècle* poets included Arthur Symons, Oscar Wilde, Ernest Dowson and Lionel Johnson. They provided a crucial link to French Symbolist poets such as Paul Verlaine and Stéphane Mallarmé. Another important occupation was his editing of William Blake, the Romantic poet, who profoundly criticised the religious and political beliefs of his age. At the same time, he was drawn increasingly towards Dublin cultural politics and he founded the National Literary Society in Dublin, with John O'Leary as President. With the death of Charles Stewart Parnell in 1891, the main currents of Irish nationalism turned away from parliamentary action to the cultural sphere, and at the time when Yeats was coming into his force. As the century drew to a close, Yeats joined with Lady Augusta Gregory (1852–1932) and Edward Martyn to found the Irish Literary Theatre. In 1904, with Gregory and John Millington Synge (1871–1909) he established the Abbey Theatre. Perhaps the most important episode in this period was the Abbey's production of Synge's *Playboy of the Western World* in 1907, when Yeats defended the play against nationalists who could not accept the amoral depiction of Gaelic speakers from the Western seaboard. The native speakers of Irish who lived a simple life beside the Atlantic were important guarantors of Irish culture: whereas the east of the country had been Saxonised, the west had remained untouched, or so the ideologues of nationalism believed.

The publication of the volume *Poems* in 1895 fixed an image in the public mind that would endure for decades, occasionally serving to annoy the elderly poet. It collected the narrative and lyrical poems which had been published in *The Wanderings of Oisin and Other Poems* (1889), and also the plays *The Countess Cathleen* (1892) and *The Land of Heart's Desire* (1894). This last is about how Mary Bruin is called away, or wishes for, a land far from the cares of the real world. It is a realm of the spirit and beauty. The crucial moment comes when the fairy child and Father Hart are fighting for the soul of Mary: 'FATHER HART. By the dear Name of the One crucified, / I bid you, Mary Bruin, come to me. / THE CHILD. I keep you in the name of your own heart.'[11] This tension between institutional religion and the desire of the individual heart would be refigured by Yeats in his later work as a tension between the demands of modernity and the desire to maintain tradition. He would later inveigh against such individualism, but here as yet he is not tempered with the knowledge of its dangers. Although the fairies represent an ancient mythology of the land, their main attraction is that their social structure is vaguely feudal and not that of an institution like the Catholic Church, whose aim, in Yeats's view, was to serve the middle class. They offer an escape from this, and by extrapolation, from the grids of business and rationality.

The long narrative poem 'The Wanderings of Oisin' deals with the moment in Ireland's past when the country shifted from Celtic mythology to Christian belief, as the hero of the poem recounts the adventures of the Fianna to the newly arrived St Patrick. Most of the poem dwells on Oisin's adventures with his fairy bride, Niamh, in the Land of Faery. The verse is as densely ornate as a Pre-Raphaelite painting, and its compound adjectives and long lines are reminiscent of Ferguson; these dense verbal textures have the effect of slowing down Yeats's narrative. 'The Wanderings of Oisin' tells a story less in the manner of a novel, or a narrative poem like *Eugene Onegin*, than in the manner of an arras – heavy, mediæval and moving only to the slightest extent.

While the lyric section of *Poems* is as uneven as many of Yeats's subsequent collections, it contains some of the poems that would guarantee his fame, among them 'The Lake Isle of Innisfree', 'The Pity of Love', 'Who Goes with Fergus', 'The Man Who Dreamed of Faeryland', 'The Stolen Child' and 'To Ireland in the Coming Times'. Many draw on the antiquarian research into Irish mythology that had attracted Ferguson also; the latter's results, as we saw in chapter 2, were not outstanding, but the material had been primed well, and was now waiting for its master-builder. Like Ferguson, Yeats recognised the significance of place and the Irish landscape in general, as these offered a concrete connection with the heroic stories of Irish warriors of the past. Indeed some places in Yeats's own Sligo, where he spent part of his childhood, crop up regularly in the old legends. Another connection was offered by old witches such as Kirwan: as we saw, Yeats searched out those people who still believed in the Little People in the machine-age of the nineteenth century, for they offered him a revolutionary world-view. Through them he could learn to see the world as something other than Carlyle's horrific steam-engine. Yeats's themes might have seemed infantile to some Victorian readers, but there was no lack of serious purpose:[12]

> Where the wandering water gushes
> From the hills above Glen-Car,
> In pools among the rushes
> That scarce could bathe a star,
> We seek for slumbering trout
> And whispering in their ears
> Give them unquiet dreams;
> Leaning softly out
> From ferns that drop their tears
> Over the young streams.
> *Come away, O human child!*
> *To the waters and the wild*
> *With a faery, hand in hand,*
> *For the world's more full of weeping than you can understand.*[13]

This kind of material provided the basis for children's literature – for instance, Charles Kingsley in his fey *Water Babies* (1863) or, later and with more of an edge, J. M. Barrie in *Peter Pan* (1904). As I remarked in chapter 2, William Allingham had already shown how fairy stories could be used in poetry. Yeats is clearly indebted to Allingham, but even in such an early poem, written when he was twenty-one, and spoken by the fairies who wish to tempt a child away from its home, he outstrips him easily. First, there is a deft humour (that pools should be categorised according to whether or not they can bathe a star; that the fairies' occupation should be giving trout 'uneasy dreams'). And second, although he employs the same jaunty rhythm of Allingham, he is able to modulate the voice into a tone that is much more piercing and plaintive, as we can observe here in the italicised refrain. It is as though in the refrain the fairies speak with their full supernatural force and insight into the workings of nature. They cease to be jolly, wee folk with green jackets, red caps, and white owl's feathers, and rise up to display their sorrow, their beauty and as well a menace much more impressive than that of Allingham's fairies.

The difference between Yeats and Thomas Moore is in precisely this menace. Yeats was distant from militant nationalism and only came to understand its power – both mythic and pragmatic – after the Easter Rising of 1916. However, we can see a parallel between the intellectual intensity that he brought to folk materials and the growing determination of certain Irish agitators to confront England as an equal, and not as errant child. No English writer of the late nineteenth century realised the profound power offered by such 'children's tales' – not even Thomas Hardy and George Eliot, who were both acutely attuned to the rhythms of the English countryside and its traditions. It is noteworthy that when Irish folklore and mythology was used for children's literature in Ireland, for instance by Patrick Pearse in his school, St Enda's, and Padraic Colum in *The King of Ireland's Son* (1916), it was a way of priming young men to fight against the British.[14] The British themselves had a large library of derring-do to make boys into soldiers, but none of these had anything to do with tales of English fairies.

Terence Brown emphasises the importance of Irish place-names in *Poems*; their use implied that the imperial language, 'instead of being a language which extended its influence as if inevitably and by divine right throughout an ever-widening empty or cleared space of geographic and political manifest destiny, English found itself halted and transformed, by the names and mythic sites of a small west of Ireland region'.[15] One index of this is the title of Yeats's first book, originally *The Wanderings of Usheen*, and then *The Wanderings of Oisin*, as he rejected the spelling more phonetically suited to an English reader and adopted the new Irish orthography. Of course, over the many centuries of its development into a world language, English has profited from being 'halted and transformed' in precisely such a fashion. As Brown shows, Yeats was keenly aware of the impact of such a shift on an English readership.

In the poem 'To Ireland in the Coming Times', Yeats creates his canon of nineteenth-century poets ('Davis, Mangan, Ferguson') and orders the reader in the following terms:

> *Know, that I would accounted be*
> *True brother of a company*
> *That sang, to sweeten Ireland's wrong,*
> *Ballad and story, rann and song . . .*[16]

For all his railing against empire, the imperative form would prove a favourite device in his poetry to come. Again, it manifests a magisterial adult force, pitched in defiance of the British yoke. But Yeats is also explaining his position to fellow Irishmen who perhaps might mistake him for a West Briton. Although he might not speak Irish, he displays his credentials by using a word like 'rann', which is the Irish for 'stanza'. Yeats nails his colours to the mast, but his green is not just of one shade. Two couplets on from the nineteenth-century triumvirate of Davis, Mangan and Ferguson, we read:

> *For the elemental creatures go*
> *About my table to and fro,*
> *That hurry from unmeasured mind*
> *To rant and rage in flood and wind;*
> *Yet he who treads in measured ways*
> *May surely barter gaze for gaze.*[17]

First, the lines express Yeats's belief in the power of poetic tradition and the pointlessness of experiment: by relying on tradition, the poet borrows strength and can take on great themes, whereas without its support he remains a solitary individual facing the modern tide. Second, the lines introduce a strange bestiary into nationalist iconology, and not, it must be said, a bestiary that gained much purchase. It is difficult to say what exactly those 'elemental creatures' are. However, the lines demonstrate Yeats's determination to connect his occult interests with his nationalist agitation. Here he obliquely insists that séances, tarot and divination are not just ways of getting in touch with your aunt who recently passed on or enjoying a bit of chit-chat with Napoleon, but are a means to contemplate, on the most profound level, matters of history, personality and culture. The grandest expression of this tendency would come with the publication of *The Vision* in 1925, an esoteric prose work which tried to codify human types and historical eras. It is not a work that has had any influence on the occult tradition nor has it helped many thinkers to understand history more clearly, but Yeats's work on the book with his wife was a preparation for his finest poetry, which I will deal with in the next section.

The Wind Among the Reeds (1899) consolidated but did not extend the achievement of *Poems* (1895). *In the Seven Woods* (1903) included the play *On Baile's Strand*, but there was only a small number of poems. Outstanding among them was 'Adam's Curse', a meditation on female beauty, ageing and the work of the artist. The poem marks an important development of Yeats's range: it is realistic in its depiction of three people sitting in a room talking and there is no Celtic mist and nothing is 'dew-blanched'. The new spareness of delivery has the paradoxical effect of intensifying the lyricism, not enervating it. This is the mode that Yeats would build on in the years ahead. The reason for his declining poetic output was his involvement in theatre business. (Selina Guinness remarks that 'Adam's Curse' is the first modern conversation poem, and this might have been caused by his work in the theatre.[18]) *The Green Helmet and Other Poems* (1910) also showed a small harvest, but it did contain 'No Second Troy', a poem which marked the beginning of his re-assessment of the Irish nationalist cause. It indicts the lack of heroism in contemporary nationalism, as the poem 'September 1913' later would; but it also praises Gonne for her nobility. Whereas in the 1890s, his love for Gonne drove his involvement with the issue of Ireland, now Yeats develops his theme by uncoupling Gonne from Ireland.

His political instinct was proved wrong when the first Republic of Ireland was called into existence by Patrick Pearse and other signatories on the morning of 24 April 1916. There followed a bloody week of fighting in Dublin, and the unconditional surrender of the revolutionaries. Ireland's betrayal of the Empire at a time when the latter was fighting for its existence in the trenches of

Europe was punished with the execution of the leaders. This shocked many Irish people who had previously been happy under British rule: they were suddenly alerted to their colonial position as a subject people, not as true partners in the Empire. Yeats wrote 'Easter, 1916' between May and September of the same year (although he did not publish it until 1920, and in book-form not until 1921 in *Michael Robartes and the Dancer*). He pays a moving tribute to the heroism of the leaders while also questioning the sense of their actions. Despite this reservation, Yeats the realist proclaims that nothing can ever be the same again. If he had been wrong-footed by the Rising, he was accurate in his subsequent prognosis. In 1922, the Irish Free State was declared, which would prove the beginning of the end of the British Empire, as became clear to the world in 1947, when India gained independence.

Responsibilities (1914) contains several poems of importance, among them the above-mentioned 'September 1913', but it is the penultimate poem, 'A Coat', which reveals most starkly Yeats's position as both poet and cultural figure. With a handful of other figures, he had spearheaded the Literary Revival; he had brought their work and his own to international audiences (some of those audiences still know nothing of his subsequent poetry); his thought and his words had shaped a new generation in Ireland, and it was slowly but surely being acknowledged that he was a living classic. His work is described as 'a coat / Covered with embroideries / Out of old mythologies', and then he turns and dismisses it with shocking *sprezzatura*: he says, let the epigones have it; but for himself 'there's more enterprise / In walking naked'.[19] At around this time, Yeats had embarked on the first of a long series of autobiographical writings, and he was becoming conscious of ways in which the story of his own life included that of his era. In 'A Coat' he goes further and makes his stylistic changes resonate on a national level. The rhyme of 'coat/throat' is noteworthy (he describes the coat as covering him from 'heel to throat', which is not idiomatic English). However, Yeats is not straining for his rhyme: that the coat goes right up to the throat suggests strangulation. The image of the embroidered coat is also hieratic – Yeats as high priest of the Revival, intoning his ranns and songs. The last three lines are an amazing movement from resignation to resurgent power. That is the note for the decades to come.

The year 1916 was tumultuous in Yeats's personal life as well as for Ireland. He proposed marriage to Maud Gonne and when he was rejected, he began discussing the possibility of marriage with her daughter, Iseult. He had passed fifty, was childless and becoming aware of the importance of lineage and the maintenance of tradition. Whereas in his earlier work the nation was the fundamental unit of social and cultural meaning, Yeats now turned to the family, believing that it is impossible to have a strong polity and flourishing arts without long generations of men and women who were honourable, proud and educated. In 1925, he described the Irish Protestant Ascendancy and his own relation to it: 'I am proud to consider myself a typical man of that minority. We have been a great stock. There are few more famous stocks in Europe. We are the people of Burke and of Swift, of Grattan, of Emmet, of Parnell. We have created nearly all of the literature of modern Ireland and most of its political intelligence.'[20] More particularly, he turned his attention to his own family history, insisting not quite accurately that they had never been of the merchant class (this last was considered ignoble by him). This pride in family connects with an important æsthetic belief: that the poet should not try to be original, but rather he should give himself over fully to poetic tradition. As he wrote in an essay of 1937: 'Talk to me of originality and I will turn on you with rage.'[21] Any artist whose work does not emerge from his stock, his family, who tries to deny his own history and become *déraciné*, can be of little worth. Such a belief would become much debased in the work of younger poets who were overawed by Yeats (F. R. Higgins would later talk of the 'blood-music' of the race[22]), but it only served to quicken and broaden the elder poet's imagination. The passage above is taken from a speech on the issue of divorce. The Irish Free State banned it and Yeats deplored this, as indeed he deplored the way that successive Irish governments kow-towed to the Catholic Church in the 1920s and 1930s.

In August of 1917, Yeats importuned Iseult Gonne for her hand; unsuccessful, he proposed marriage the next month to a young Englishwoman George Hyde Lees and they were married in October (Ezra Pound was the best man). Despite his precipitate manœuvring, his choice proved an inspired one: Hyde Lees was a gifted linguist, passionately involved in the occult, and had a keen appreciation of Yeats's imaginative as well as practical requirements. Soon after their marriage they embarked on long sessions of automatic writing, during which, Yeats believed, they were in contact with the spirit world. It cannot be doubted that her presence by his side profoundly influenced and enabled the great creative work of the last period of his life. The next year they moved into a Norman keep in Ballylee, Co. Galway, located near Lady Gregory's Coole Park. Although they would return to the tower over the succeeding years, the life of the Yeatses was for the most part peripatetic, moving between Dublin, Oxford, London and the Mediterranean littorals of France and Italy. In 1919 and 1921, a daughter and son were born to them.

After the establishment of the Free State in 1922, Yeats became a Senator for six years, and moved into an old Georgian house on Merrion Square, near the Dáil. (During the early hostilities, Anti-Treaty forces fired a few shots through his windows.) Through his choice of house, he identified himself even more strongly with the 'great stock' of the Anglo-Irish Ascendancy. In the remaining sixteen years of his life, he was bedevilled by long illnesses, but he also made a long lecture tour in the USA, conducted two affairs (two and half, if one includes the lesbian Dorothy Wellesley) and was briefly involved with Blueshirts, the Irish fascist movement (he was a great admirer of Mussolini). He passionately pursued his interest in the occult and in Indian mysticism, promoting the work of a thinker such as Shri Purohit Swami. He was also an adroit and relentless polemicist in newspapers and political speeches. The habits of a lifetime were not to be broken.

Despite all this activity to come, the overriding tone of *The Wild Swans at Coole* (1919) is crepuscular and retrospective, nowhere more so than in the title poem. It is nineteen years since the poet first saw these swans in the demesne of Lady Gregory, and the constancy of their beauty contrasts with his decline, both physical and imaginative. This is the tone up to the third stanza. Then in the final two stanzas, Yeats's attention is drawn to the life of the swans independent of his own story, as he follows them in his mind's eye: 'Passion or conquest, wander where they will, / Attend upon them still.'[23] Already at this stage, the poet's imagination is beginning to revive and lift slowly into the air. The poet might indeed discover that the swans have flown away, as he remarks at the end of the poem, but the final stanza talks of mystery, beauty and delight, not of abandonment and despair. Moreover, the question of the stanza indicates that Yeats still wants to know where beauty and mystery are to be found, that he will not be satisfied without these things. The poem also deals with a central tension in the late work: the conflict between the poet's old age and his great hunger for mystery, delight and beauty.

Other important poems in the book include the elegies for Lady Gregory's son, who was killed during World War I; foremost of these is 'In Memory of Major Robert Gregory', in which he is praised for, among other things, the way he painted the landscape of the west of Ireland.

> We dreamed that a great painter had been born
> To cold Clare rock and Galway rock and thorn,
> To that stern colour and that delicate line
> That are our secret discipline.[24]

The repetition of the word 'rock' is noteworthy: Yeats associates the rough, desolate landscape with the people who live there, and by the last two lines quoted here, it is impossible to say whether the 'colours' and 'lines' are those of the canvas or the actual land. There is a variation on this theme in 'The Fisherman' in the same collection, where Yeats conjures up a man of the west, who has this 'secret discipline' of the land. But Yeats also admits that he is a man 'who does not exist, / A man who is but a dream'.[25] The admission that the farmer-peasant of the Gaelic Revival does not exist comes near the very end of the poem; only four lines remain. Most other poets would slow-fade after such a deflationary tactic; Yeats, however, rallies more powerfully again, crying out: 'Before I am old / I shall have written him one / Poem maybe as cold / And passionate as the dawn.'[26] There is a pleasing exactitude to the description of the dawn as 'cold'. The adjective also indicates the reserves of control which Yeats brings to the business of passion. In our age, we associate passion with an abandonment of form, control and, more generally, tradition; for Yeats, passion could only be properly expressed through these structures, otherwise it was only a worthless expression of individuality.

Michael Robartes and the Dancer, although it contained the above-mentioned 'Easter, 1916' (less topical than at the time of its original composition), as well as 'The Second Coming' and 'A Prayer for My Daughter', was not as substantial as the collection that followed, and no other single volume of Yeats is. *The Tower* (1928) takes as its central image the Norman keep in Ballylee, where Yeats lived sporadically during the 1920s, and especially during the War of Independence at the beginning of the decade.

The first poem, 'Sailing to Byzantium', expresses an old man's desire to leave his country because that country neglects 'monuments of unaging intellect'. However, even in the opening verse, it is clear that the speaker is half in love with what he leaves, namely the luxuriant description of the country's 'sensual music'.[27] He wishes to go to Byzantium and become a timeless work of art made '[o]f hammered gold and gold enamelling'.[28] Paradoxically, once he has reached that stage he will turn to look on all that he has left behind him, the whole world in which creatures are born and die. This tension between the desire for the world, with all its sensuality, violence and upheaval, and the timeless certainty of great art continues throughout the book. Throughout *The Tower*, as in 'Sailing to Byzantium', the division is constantly and profitably made unclear, for instance, as artists and architects are called in to design great houses, and thus commemorate power of the most worldly kind. The family is the zone for Yeats in which history and timelessness meet and interact: families, even the greatest, are at the mercy of history, and yet, if successful over several generations, they can create 'monuments of unaging intellect'.

The next poem, the title poem, is the first of three major sequences, each of which combines lissom shifts of speed with lapidary utterance. They are Pindaric odes, each section of which employs a different stanza form and thus enables changes of tone and angle of approach, much like those of John Dryden. Yeats's adaptation of the form also encourages the poet not to resolve an antimony (as, say, at the end of a Shakespearean sonnet), but to let it resonate through ever more various structures. Having happily settled as a serene gold bird on a bough in Byzantium, Yeats at the very beginning of 'The Tower' dismisses such satisfaction with disdain. His utter disgust with his state explodes across the opening lines, punctuated by apostrophes to his own heart. He goes on to say that he never had a more 'excited, passionate, fantastical / Imagination' as he does now.[29] After this outburst in the first section, the poet is left walking back and forth on his tower. It is as though Yeats knows he must move out of himself in order to escape the pressing question of old age and passion; he must transcend his individuality and enquire of the tradition of the place where he stands. He begins with an amusing if macabre anecdote, and then recalls the story of a girl who was celebrated in a song. This leads him to consider the relation between song and reality, as we are told that the fame of the girl's beauty reached such proportions that one man was drowned as a result of it. Yeats glosses:

> Strange, but the man who made the song was blind;
> Yet, now I have considered it, I find
> That nothing strange; the tragedy began
> With Homer that was a blind man,
> And Helen has all living hearts betrayed.
> O may the moon and sunlight seem
> One inextricable beam,
> For if I triumph I must make men mad.[30]

By moving to Homer, Yeats broadens the terms to include the relations between myth and history. Common sense sees history as the hard facts that would upset the good stories of myth. But he goes further and reminds himself how myth can change those facts and influence the course of history. Already here the antimony between the moon (read: imagination, myth, poetry, occult knowledge, Byzantium) and the sun (reality, history, practical matters, civil war in Ireland) has been resolved: they must become 'One inextricable beam'. His poetry must not try to abscond to Byzantium, but neither must it forgo Byzantine dreams when it faces the pressing issues of the day. It is a tall order, and Yeats never finds an Olympian mode in which to express this tension in a balanced permanent way, but rather he frets back and forth, now calm, now enraged, now lecherous, now magisterial, as in the last section of the poem:

> It is time that I wrote my will;
> I choose upstanding men
> That climb the streams until
> The fountain leap, and at dawn
> Drop their cast at the side

Of the dripping stone; I declare
They shall inherit my pride,
The pride of people that were
Bound neither to Cause nor to State . . .[31]

These trimeters demonstrate the stunning clipped control of late Yeats: they
are impassioned, yet consummately restrained; they express disdain, pride and
love; they are concerned with inheritance and the transmission of certain moral
and cultural values; and they connect these values with the landscape of Ireland.
Witness the way he *declares* in the sixth line here. The line break creates a pause;
a more diffident speaker or poet would not have the nerve for such a pause, but
Yeats keeps the pause because, in part, he wants you to know that he has the
nerve to stare you down as you wait for exactly what it is he wishes to declare.
In that moment, you realise that the substance of the sentence is not primarily
about inheritance, etc., but is that proud stare itself. If you meet the stare of
this person, then there is a kind of community, a kind of conversation through
the generations.

At the end of the poem he recapitulates the worst aspects of ageing and
death, and even worse: 'The death of friends, or death / Of every brilliant
eye / That made a catch in the breath'.[32] The first line here is conventional,
but the next two are extraordinary for the way they show that the life of the
intellect and the life of the body are inextricable. This gasp of sudden realisation, or perception, is a touchstone of late Yeats. (Many of his poems in this
period pivot around the word 'suddenly'.) But even such terrible losses, the
poet tells himself, will '[s]eem but clouds of the sky / When the horizon fades;
/ Or a bird's sleepy cry / Among the deepening shades'.[33] These closing lines
of the poem are far removed from the enraged old man of the first section.
They heal that anger, offering as consolation the idea that the shades deepen
because of man and because '[d]eath and life were not / Till man made up the
whole'.[34]

The house is the central image of 'Meditations in Time of Civil War', which
follows 'The Tower'. In the first part, Yeats considers 'Ancestral Houses' and the
way that great families maintain themselves. He is also preoccupied with the
relationship between political violence and the grace of art, believing that they
are interdependent. Hence the beautiful surprise of lines like these:

Some violent bitter man, some powerful man
Called architect and artist in, that they,
Bitter and violent men, might rear in stone
The sweetness that all longed for night and day,
The gentleness none there had ever known . . .[35]

By the end of the third line here we must expect something truly awful to follow; after all, one does not think of sweet or gentle things 'rearing' like this, just ugly heads, or more violent and bitter children. Yeats knows that we want to think that our great art has nothing to do with the battlefield or the dirt of politics (at one stage, he liked to think it himself), and considers that a terrible naivety. The beautiful things depend on power and violence, and Yeats wishes to harness something of that power and violence in his own poetry, not repudiate it. Hence, when he turns to his own house in the next section and considers all the wars and violence that took place in the 'tumultuous spot', he is exulting in them. In the third section, 'My Table', he considers a mediæval Japanese sword that was given to him. The sword had been in the family of Junzo Sato for five centuries, and so it connected with Yeats's belief in family tradition; and that the sword's business is to kill people in defence of that family's honour makes it even more alluring. In 'My Descendants', family history is placed against the backdrop of cosmic history, as he wonders what will remain of his own stock; his ultimate consolation is in the stones of the house.

However implicit violence is to the beauty of an ancestral sword, Yeats is still unprepared for the real thing when it appears at his door. Thus in section five, a soldier talks jovially of murder and violence 'As though to die by gunshot were / The finest play under the sun'.[36] The sun here is the mark of utter realism: there is no cooling shade or consolation of myth, there is just the awful actuality of dead young soldiers carted off down the road. In other moments, Yeats admires such robust courage, but when confronted with the actuality, he retreats, envious, back to his chamber in the tower. Once there, he sees that Ireland's present conflict echoes with conflicts in other places and times. He wonders if his retreat to art is escapist, a mere sign of his failure to effect change in the world of men. The evidence of the poem itself is that his art is not escapist, and so one cannot quite believe the final lines of the poem: 'The abstract joy, / The half-read wisdom of dæmonic images, / Suffice the ageing man as once the growing boy.'[37] This is suggestive of the alchemist tinkering with his alembics, blithely ignorant of a war raging all about him. There is no such 'abstract joy' in Yeats's own art, which confronts the issues of power, violence and politics head on.

The same trauma of contemporary violence haunts 'Nineteen Hundred and Nineteen'. Yeats thinks back to the earlier decades of the Irish Revival when it seemed that political change could be effected by cultural means alone. But the violence ran out of control, and that becomes a verdict on all the previous work that was carried out by Gregory, Synge, Hyde and Yeats himself:

> Now days are dragon-ridden, the nightmare
> Rides upon sleep: a drunken soldiery
> Can leave the mother, murdered at her door,
> To crawl in her own blood, and go scot-free;
> The night can sweat with terror as before
> We pieced our thoughts into philosophy,
> And planned to bring the world under a rule,
> Who are but weasels fighting in a hole.[38]

The important image here is that of the dragon: it conveys the vast terror of the time, unanswerable by any one man. The final lines are full of self-reproach: the penultimate line grandiosely indicates their past plans, and the ultimate line undercuts those plans with savage wit. Yeats's lithe handling of the structure of the sequence is immediately apparent in the next section, as we see the terrible dragon transformed on the stage into 'A shining web, a floating ribbon of cloth' moved by dancers. The violence is absorbed by art, permitted to move through it, much as Yeats himself admitted it into his poem, with all its fury, in the first section. The process of mythologisation has begun again: he does not make violence turn tail, but rather turns it into a tale, which will be interrupted only when violence breaks out again. There is no further consolation than this.

If the expansive grandeur of Yeats's art is on display in the three sequences at the beginning of the book, his epigrammatic wit is apparent in the three briefs lyrics that follow. For instance 'Youth and Age', for all its straightforwardness, depends upon a rich complexity and sharp observation. The first two lines are voiced with the pomposity of old age, as the elder, established poet condescends to his younger self; the stock phrase of the second line suggests that the young Yeats did most of the oppressing and not the world. But there is nothing pompous in the last two lines, as the poet understands that his fame is but the prelude to death. What is also remarkable about the lines is their psychological perceptiveness, the way they translate a social gesture into a more fatal situation.

'Leda and the Swan' is another brief poem, here about the rape of Leda by Zeus in the form of a swan. The sonnet asks whether the woman, at the moment of congress with the god, possesses something of his knowledge and power. Does she catch a glimpse of the terrible history – the fall of Troy and all the havoc among the Greeks – that will unfold from their coupling? Yeats is preoccupied with precisely such historical knowledge (in large part, the work on *A Vision* was an attempt to obtain it) throughout his later work. Whatever knowledge and power the god has in 'Leda and the Swan', it cannot be disentangled from his violent act, and Leda can only know these at the moment of contact with him. This apprehension echoes in the next poem I will discuss.

'Among School Children' is an extremely dense meditation on some of the same issues. Yeats separates the stanzas (of *ottava rima*) with Roman numerals and several of them could stand as independent lyrics, much like the components of the long sequences at the beginning of the book. The complexity of the poem is not so much in the individual sections (although there are some passages that are hard to understand), but rather it resides in their relations with each other. In the first section Yeats tells about his visit to a new model school in his role as a Senator. The nuns answer his questions kindly and the children seem to be prospering, though Yeats is doubtful about the value of democratic education for all. He is also a little uneasy with the figure he himself cuts, 'A sixty-year-old smiling public man'.[39] In the second section he thinks of a 'Ledæan body', a woman who has coupled with a god, and played a role in a grand national tragedy. She shared her grief with the poet, and that brought them together, almost as close as man and wife. In the third section, he recalls that this Ledæan body was once a child too, and he wonders if the small girls he sees in the Waterford school could have anything in common with her. In the fourth section, he thinks of the Ledæan body's old, gaunt appearance now. At this point his recollection of the Greek myth and his own past goads Yeats ever so slightly: it challenges him to live up to his own past, to create or recognise such mythical force in the present moment. He hesitates, but then dismisses the scruple, preferring to 'show / There is a comfortable kind of old scarecrow'.[40]

At this stage, the setting of the school is dropped completely: he has decided to maintain the social role given to him, and thus cannot be further provoked into thought or passion by its elements. However, the poem is only at the halfway mark. The next two sections, or stanzas, consider two different aspects of the cycle of life and death. In the first, Yeats imagines a mother who sees her newborn son at the age of sixty. In its starkest terms, the thrust of this verse is: what is the point of life? What can such a mother be told? There is nothing particularly remarkable about such a question; what is important is the intensity of the interrogation, and the refusal to accept a platitude as an answer. In the sixth section he considers the answers provided by Plato and Pythagoras, and summarily dismisses them in the closing couplet, as if to say, 'Bah! What did they know who ended up as old men also?' The seventh section suggests that images provide a consolation when faced with the futility of human existence. There is no answer to the question that he posed earlier; the images are merely delusions of varying power. Eventually however, because of their static nature they mock all of men's enterprise (they are not as captivating as living beauty, and later they merely remind us how much beauty has been lost).

Having rejected the philosophy of the Greeks and the images also, Yeats finds ultimate consolation in an idea of human labour that is intellectual, imaginative and physical all at once. If you search for meaning in philosophy, the life of your senses will pass you by: you will accept words and their larger structures in place of the day, the sun, your body's feelings. If you accept the iconography of religion, similarly you avoid the brute facts of existence. What is left to Yeats is this:

> Labour is blossoming or dancing where
> The body is not bruised to pleasure soul,
> Nor beauty born out of its own despair,
> Nor blear-eyed wisdom out of midnight oil.
> O chestnut tree, great rooted blossomer,
> Are you the leaf, the blossom or the bole?
> O body swayed to music, O brightening glance,
> How can we know the dancer from the dance?[41]

The second, third and fourth lines here refer to the philosophers and the wor-shippers of images. The two questions that conclude the poem are of note because of the way they are not and are rhetorical. Primarily they indicate that it is impossible to distinguish the leaf, the blossom and the trunk from each other – the tree is all of these things at once – and at the moment of the dance we cannot separate the dancer from the dance. Secondarily, however, they remind us that Yeats is in fact interrogating these phenomena, even though he knows such an activity is pointless. Such ambivalence is everywhere in the book, and resolved nowhere. The achievement of *The Tower* is that it lets such contrary forces flow through its structures.

The late grand style having been established in this book, the collections that followed were *The Winding Stair and Other Poems* (1933) and *A Full Moon in March* (1935); in 1938 the Cuala Press published *New Poems* and in 1939 *Last Poems and Two Plays*. Among the most important poems of this period number 'In Memory of Eva Gore-Booth and Con Markievicz', 'Blood and the Moon', 'Coole Park, 1929', 'Coole and Ballylee', 'Vacillation', 'The Gyres', 'Lapis Lazuli', 'The Municipal Gallery Re-visited', 'Under Ben Bulben', 'Cuchulain Comforted', 'The Statues', 'A Bronze Head', 'The Circus Animals' Desertion' and 'Politics'. In several of these he elegises people who were close to him, and because of their importance to national life in Yeats's lifetime, his poems become a means of contemplating the recent history of the country. The question of stock remains to the fore, together with the house as guarantor of a family's continuance. 'The Statues' changes significantly his idea in 'Among School Children' that images are mockers of man's enterprise, and he acknowledges more warmly their shaping power in history. In 'The Municipal Gallery Re-visited' he sees himself, his friends and his era projected on to canvas, and this becomes an occasion to repeat some of the ideas in 'The Tower'. Several of the poems forcefully reject what he refers to as the 'filthy modern tide',[42] and 'A Bronze Head' relishes the thought of apocalypse, as he wonders if there is anything 'left for massacre to save'.[43]

Perhaps most touching of all is 'Politics', often positioned as the last poem in the *Collected Poems*, which has the elder poet listening to the talk of international politics, and simply stating that he cannot concentrate on such matters when all he wants is to have his youth back and embrace the beautiful girl who is standing nearby. He is an 'Old lecher with a love on every wind', as he described one of his alter-egos elsewhere.[44] What is so alluring about the poem is that it says little more than my paraphrase here. It is utterly simple, demanding none of the complex intellectual responses necessary when reading, say, 'The Tower', and yet its poignancy depends on our knowledge of the majestic, difficult poems which preceded 'Politics'. It is dashed off with nonchalance and style, expressing in a straightforward manner what was said with troubled brilliance elsewhere.

Yeats published his *Collected Poems* in 1933 and for many years before this he had been engaged in the revision of his early poems, making some of the vaguer, gentler passages or phrases more vivid and forceful. Thus the first line of 'The Sorrow of Love' in its original publication in 1891 referred to 'The quarrel of the sparrows in the eaves', whereas the version published in 1933 has 'The brawling of a sparrow in the eaves'.[45] First, a brawl is much more physical and uncivilised than a quarrel, and, second, that there is only one sparrow suggests greater strength in a single feisty bird than in the aggregate chatter of a greater number. The rest of the revisions to the poem are even more profound, affecting its basic meaning: the earlier version stresses the strength and consistency of the earth, whereas the later one essentially paraphrases the passage quoted above from 'The Tower': '[d]eath and life were not / Till man made up the whole'. Not every poem was subjected to the same revisions as 'The Sorrow of Love'; nevertheless, because the standard edition for decades was based on the 1933 *Collected Poems*, for most readers all of Yeats is late Yeats. The situation could hardly be improved.

Modernist is not the most accurate adjective for the Anglophone poetry of Yeats's period (I noted at the outset that Yeats did not wish to think himself 'modern' in such terms), but it is hard to escape it. One of the frequently stressed aspects of Modernism is the deracination of many of its writers. This obviously does not fit Yeats's early work, and it does not describe his later work either. His thoughts on the nation differed greatly from those of the rest of the country in the last two decades of his life, but the nation remains the crucial framework. We glimpse Yeats's ideal nation in the last section of 'The Tower' in that fellowship of 'upstanding men'. A year before his death he developed this idea further:

> I write with two certainties in mind: first that a hundred men, their creative power wrought to the highest pitch, their will trained but not broken, can do more for the welfare of a people, whether in war or peace, than a million of any lesser sort no matter how expensive their education, and that although the Irish masses are vague and excitable because they have not yet been moulded and cast, we have as good blood as there is in Europe.[46]

In evidence here is his disdain for a democratic polity that promotes universal literacy. It also expresses the same deep desire for rootedness that is to be found in the work of many European thinkers and artists in that period. His radical ideas of nation and blood kindred led him to join the Eugenics Society in England, and he was one of its more extreme members. *On the Boiler* (a short prose book) is a fascist text. The difficulty for many admiring readers of Yeats is that its ideas are central to his late poetry; only through energetic and intense wishful thinking can one separate *On the Boiler* from the poems.

In the same piece of writing (which was published after his death in 1939), he remains preoccupied with the question of the language of Ireland, for that is also connected with the will he drew up at the end of 'The Tower': 'If Irish is to become the national tongue the change must come slowly, almost imperceptibly; a sudden or forced change of language may be the ruin of the soul.'[47] He remained aware of the questionable status of Anglophone literature in Ireland: it had achieved much, but he consistently implies that it would be much better if it were in Irish. The greatness of Yeats's achievement has meant that the next generation of Irish poets in English had to confront his legacy, and either engage with it (MacNeice) or succumb to it (Clarke, Kavanagh, Colum, Higgins, Campbell . . .). But it was infinitely preferable to have to struggle with such a predecessor than to have to face the language question with the same awful intensity that Yeats did, and establish an Anglophone Irish poetic tradition more or less from nothing.

Chapter 5

Wild earth

Padraic Colum, Austin Clarke, Patrick Kavanagh,
Louis MacNeice

The achievements of the Irish Literary Revival were beyond dispute: in the genres of drama and poetry, there now existed works that commanded the attention of the Anglophone world and beyond. These works, in different ways, all attempted to express some national essence, some spirit that could not be found anywhere else on the planet. It would be fair then to assume that the generation of writers that followed would find the going easy, as they could, with confidence, expand the themes and audience that Yeats, Synge and Gregory, among others, had established. Many Irish poets of the generation after Yeats refused to embrace the challenge of Modernism, preferring instead to follow the instructions laid down by their great forebear: 'Cast your mind on other days / That we in coming days may be / Still the indomitable Irishry.'[1] Blanaid Salkeld (1880–1959), although she began in an archaic sub-Yeatsian mode with her collection *Hello, Eternity!* (1933), quickly embraced a kind of hectic futurism in some of the poems of her next book, *The Fox's Covert* (1933). But she is something of an anomaly, and an unsuccessful one at that. For many poets, the idea of national continuity expressed by Yeats was compelling. It contains an idea of 'rootedness' that is at odds with Modernism, a preference for the homespun over homelessness. The world may indeed have been falling apart, but that was all the more reason to assert and maintain the cultural integrity of Ireland. Poets such as F. R. Higgins (1896–1941) and Joseph Campbell (1879–1944) prosecuted exactly this programme.

These are broad historical strokes, and, as always in literature, the more interesting writers escape such stark contrasts, while the epigones are left to exemplify general tendencies. By way of introduction, I want to look at an outstanding poem by another of those Revivalist epigones. Padraic Colum (1881–1972) spent much of his working life outside Ireland and so was particularly prone to romanticisation of his homeland. Many of his poems are but dutiful reworkings of Revival motifs and manœuvres; and even in his late work of the 1960s, we see these elements alive and well, as he interrogates the Irish landscape for traces of ancient mythology. But 'A Poor Scholar of the Forties' from his first collection, *Wild Earth* (1909), offers a good deal more than nationalist sentimentality. The 'Forties' refers to the 1840s, a period of dire poverty and starvation in Ireland as well as nationalist agitation. The scholar teaches Latin and Greek in the hedge schools, he is accused by a Young Ireland activist of being deaf to the call to arms, and his work is viewed as irrelevant to the national struggle. The scholar dismisses this criticism and answers the Young Irelander, explaining the deeper, longer relevance of his profession: 'Years hence, in rustic speech, a phrase, / As in wild earth a Grecian vase!'[2] This incandescent line is also the last line of the poem. The scholar refuses the imperatives of nationalist ideology – as voiced by the man from the Young Ireland organisation – in favour of a cosmopolitanism that embraces the European cultural inheritance. This does not make him 'rootless'. The scholar does not dream of leaving Ireland to work in a European metropolis; rather he wishes to root classical culture in the 'wild earth' of Ireland and perhaps create an Ireland that exceeds nationalist ideology. Colum's poem also harmonises with the later classical preoccupations of Eliot and Pound, as they searched ancient mythology for *pointes d'appui* when facing what Eliot referred to as contemporary chaos. Moreover it was Padraic Colum who introduced one of the most radical of all Modernist works to an American audience when he wrote the preface for the American publication of the Anna Livia Plurabelle section of James Joyce's *Finnegans Wake*. He called it 'epical in its largeness of meaning and its multiplicity of interest'; and some pages later he said that Joyce, 'the most daring of innovators, has decided to be as local as a hedge-poet'.[3] This oblique reference to his own poem bears out Terence Brown's point that 'the Irish Literary Revival in its nationalist context was contiguous with modernism rather than merely concurrent';[4] it is possible to speak of even a common purpose between Colum and Joyce, despite different means.

Of the three poets that I will be mainly dealing with in this chapter, Austin Clarke (1896–1974) is perhaps the most conventionally Revivalist. Clarke was born in Dublin. His first book, *The Vengeance of Fionn* (1917), consisted of a long poem reworking the story of Diarmuid and Grainne from Irish mythology; much of its diction and delivery were close to the work of Samuel Ferguson. Peter Denman has remarked that 'although the strong Gaelic presence in his work harks back to the middle ages and earlier, his vision has its immediate origins in nineteenth-century antiquarianism and the accompanying vogue for medievalism'.[5] In 1921 he moved to England, where he made a living as a reviewer and became involved in verse drama. In the mid 1920s, his interest moved from Irish mythology to early Christianity in Ireland. Clarke greatly admired the art and learning of the Irish church of that period, and in this sense it played the same role as the Grecian vase in wild earth did for Colum:

it offered an idea of Ireland different from the one prevailing in Clarke's time. In the early days of the Free State, the Catholic Church was consolidating its position as perhaps the most important institution in the country, socially and politically. Few would seriously consider appending the adverb 'culturally' in the last sentence, as Irish Catholicism discouraged cultural initiatives which exceeded nationalist ideology. Clarke was dissatisfied with this status quo, and indeed he lost his position in University College Dublin in 1921 when it was discovered that he had married in a registry office and not a church. By attending to what he refers to as the 'Celtic-Romanesque' period, Clarke was able to plumb the past of his own nation and its engagement with Rome. The title poem of *Pilgrimage and Other Poems* (1929) offers a fine example in this mode:

> Grey holdings of rain
> Had grown less with the fields,
> As we came to that blessed place
> Where hail and honey meet.
> O Clonmacnoise was crossed
> With light: those cloistered scholars,
> Whose knowledge of the gospel
> Is cast as metal in pure voices,
> Were all rejoicing daily,
> And cunning hands with cold and jewels
> Brought chalices to flame.[6]

Before discussing the thematic aspects of this passage, I would like to remark on the use of rhyme. At first glance there is none, but on closer inspection, one sees a pattern of assonantal chimes (rain/place, fields/meet, etc.). Clarke is adapting the Irish *deibhí* rhyme to English.

In 'Pilgrimage', ecclesiastical spaces are not shuttered away from the land, but flow within it as merely one more part of nature. The sacred place of the monastery of Clonmacnoise is a meeting place for the weather and the products of the hives. The scholars might indeed be 'cloistered', but their cloisters are 'crossed / With light'. When the chalices flame forth, they do so both with the fire of religious revelation, but also with the naturalness of the sun. His preoccupation with the landscape had begun already during the phase of work, and he describes the experience in his memoir, *A Penny in the Clouds* (1968): 'The discovery of our own mythology and epic stories by the poets of the Irish Literary Revival excited my imagination and I cycled with delight to many places associated with legend and enchantments – from the Glen of the Madmen in County Kerry to the Twelve Pins of Connemara and the Poisoned Glen in Donegal.'[7] Landscape becomes a way to make the alien worlds of ancient heroic cycles and early Christianity closer to contemporary experience. At a stretch, one could imagine that some *genius loci* in, say, Clonmacnoise had endured the centuries of change and was still available to the contemporary tourist with a literary or historical bent. Clarke, like Ferguson and Yeats before him, and Kinsella and Heaney after him, expends much imaginative energy on landscape description, as though this guarantees the authenticity of the work. For all of these poets, as many others, had as their grand theme the story of Ireland, and they were aware that their explorations of its past had resonances for their own times. Many of Clarke's poems begin with landscape description, as though this would ground his imaginative fictions of life in Ireland a millennium or more ago; however, in most cases, those descriptions remain the height of the poems' achievement.

It is too easy to challenge Clarke's fictions: their tone, as in 'Pilgrimage' above, is solemn and strained; as cultural criticism they are too self-consciously ornamental to have much force. Observe the conclusion of 'Pilgrimage':

> on a barren isle,
> Where Paradise is praised
> At daycome, smaller than the sea-gulls,
> We heard white Culdees pray
> Until our hollow ship was kneeling
> Over the longer waves.[8]

The speakers hear the hermits, or Culdees, praying on the small island and there is something poignant about their prayers sounding over the Atlantic like the cries of gulls; and Seán Ó Ríordáin would later use a similar image to join Christianity and the Irish seascape ('Mar bhí lucht Aifrinn ag teacht thar farraige ón mBlascaod'[9]). But when the last two lines of the poem say little more than that the pilgrims' ship was departing, one realises that the whole point of the poem was simply to describe early Christian prayer in the Irish landscape. No further imaginative pressure is exerted.

Clarke returned to Ireland in 1937 and published only one book of poems in this decade, *Night and Morning* (1938). This book, along with some of the inclusions in his *Collected Poems* (1936), announced Clarke's new interest in satire and public comment. His targets were for the most part easy (the Catholic Church was a particular favourite), and his execution shoddy. Here he is on the founders of the Free State:

> They are the spit of virtue now,
> Prating of law and honour,
> But we remember how they shot
> Rory O'Connor.[10]

The death warrant of Rory O'Connor had been signed by Kevin O'Higgins, the Minister for Justice and External Affairs, along with that of seventy-six other anti-Treatyites in 1922–3; he was executed lawfully under the Special Powers Act and to my knowledge no historian has suggested that O'Higgins acted from dishonourable motives. Good satire requires not only a good rhyme, but a mordant thought to go with it. Clarke has only the rhyme, and in most of his other satirical poems, he does not even have that. Of the satire of this period, Alan Gillis remarks on Clarke's paradoxical position: on the one hand he is extremely critical of the Irish Free State and on the other he cannot see beyond its ideological structures.[11]

Clarke did not publish another full collection until *Ancient Lights* (1955). A prolific period followed with the publication of *Too Great a Vine* (1957), *The Horse-Eaters* (1960), *Flight to Africa* (1963), *Old-Fashioned Pilgrimage* (1967), *The Echo at Coole* (1968) and *A Sermon on Swift* (1968), among others. This late flowering also included several long poems such as *Mnemosyne Lay in Dust* (1966) and *Tiresias* (1971). Clarke won many new admirers during this period, but, as Gregory Schirmer has remarked, attention was

> focused chiefly on the poems that were coming out at that time, and so tended to neglect the earlier work, especially *Pilgrimage* and *Night and Morning*. This meant that those who praised Clarke's poetry of the 1960s and 1970s failed to see that, for all its variety, it grows out of the same struggle with religious prohibition documented in *Pilgrimage* and *Night and Morning*, and has as its center the same humanistic vision that informs Clarke from beginning to end.[12]

This is formulated as reproach, but it usefully emphasises the fragmented nature of Clarke's œuvre. First, there are the chronological gaps, and, second, and more importantly, there are the scattered themes and methods: it is all too easy to apprehend its disparate parts without an idea of how they fit together. Schirmer places the blame with readers; a less indulgent critic would place it with Clarke himself.

Mnemosyne Lay in Dust is an autobiographical poem about Clarke's stay in a mental asylum when he was twenty-two (he employs the pseudonym of Maurice Devane). The story recounts the protagonist's retrieval of his memory (Mnemosyne is the goddess of memory, as well as the mother of the muses), and eventual release back into the city of Dublin. The poem is by times melo-dramatic, tender, carnivalesque and contemplative. However, once again it is difficult to make sense of the poem in the context of Clarke's œuvre: the self's loss of memory does not resonate with larger issues of national remem-brance and revival. Whereas American poets such as Whitman, Ginsberg and

Graham can make stories about themselves be also about their country, Clarke cannot. Of course, autobiographical poetry need not necessarily be political also, but this lack draws attention to its failure even as pure autobiography. Although writing forty years after the event, Clarke still has no distance on it, as evidenced by the hackneyed neo-romantic language he uses to describe the trauma ('Unconsciousness became the pit / Of terror. Void would draw his spirit, / Unself him'[13]). His prose memoirs are more engaging documents.

Perhaps the only successful long poem by Clarke is *Tiresias*, which recounts the life of the Theban prophet, as he changed from man to woman and back to man again in order to satisfy the curiosity of the gods whether, in the sexual act, there is 'greater bliss as woman or man'.[14] The poem is suffused with Mediterranean light and its sensuousness extends from dashing fauve colour-work to open treatment of sexuality. In *Mnemosyne Lay in Dust*, Clarke hints that his incarceration was in part due to sexual frustration, and throughout his career he had difficulty in dealing with sexual matters. In part this was due to repressive censorship measures, but also because Clarke was, in Beckett's phrase, a 'Victorian Gael'. It was only during the late 1960s that he threw off such scruples and wrote openly about sex (his second memoir, *A Penny in the Clouds*, is forthright about his sexual liaisons), and more generally about the body. Feminist critics would complain a decade later that Irish male poets transform female bodies into objects for ideological purposes, and that these representations have little connection with women's real experiences. But in *Tiresias* the female body is presented neither as agit-prop for nationalist ideology nor as titillation. One notable passage has a girl exploring her sexual organs, and this is follows by her mother's reaction to the daughter's first *menses*: she refers to it as shame, but she is unembarrassed by the conversation.[15]

In the second section of the poem Pyrrha recounts how she found herself before a shepherd's 'bothy',[16] which is an Irish turf hut. The word is anomalous in a poem set in the Greek world of North Africa, and it is the smallest indication from Clarke that his celebration of sexuality is not alien to the Irish context. Indeed the word nestles in his text much like a Grecian vase in wild earth, its presence suggestive of other Irelands beneath the monolithic stele of Catholic philistinism that had triumphed in the new state.

As I remarked in chapter 3, one of the most important elements of the Literary Revival was the Irish peasant. Yeats, in 'The Fisherman', conjures such a noble Irish peasant, nevertheless admitting that he is but a dream; lesser writers did not scruple to mention this. As was tirelessly pointed out after the Revival, these representations of Irish peasantry were confected by people who were separated from their subjects by class and religion. Colum might pass muster by these criteria, but Yeats, Synge, Æ and Gregory did not. Clearly 'peasant quantity', as opposed to the quality, had to be increased.

In December 1931, the required dosage arrived on the doorstep of Æ in Rathgar in the figure of a twenty-seven year-old man from Monaghan, who really was a farmer and who had written some exquisite lyrics about farming life which Æ had published in *The Irish Statesman*. What would such a walking bundle of authenticity have to say to the Revivalist salons of Dublin? Would he confirm their every intuition or would he wreak havoc as Frankenstein's monster did in the life of his maker? For no matter which answer it would be, he had come at their calling; he was, in part, the creature of their making. We will let his biographer, Antoinette Quinn, take over the story:

> Kavanagh set off to visit [Æ] a week before Christmas . . . He was
> apparently acting on impulse, since he did not inform Æ of his intended
> arrival. Lest the sage doubt his rural authenticity or need for patronage,
> he decided to wear his shabby old work clothes for the visit instead of
> dressing up in his Sunday suit. Since his appearance was unmistakably
> countrified, his adoption of the guise of a Syngean tramp was, as he later
> realised, quite unnecessary. To exaggerate his peasant persona still
> further, Kavanagh decided to walk the sixty-odd miles to Dublin, rather
> than travel by train or bicycle, though it was the depths of winter and the
> journey took the best part of three days . . . He was deliberately acting
> the part of a 'country gobshite', 'pretending' instead of behaving
> 'honestly, sincerely'.[17]

This displays an admirable seriousness of purpose: he is indeed in possession of real peasant quality, or 'PQ', which was the waggish shorthand for this ingredient, but he carefully manipulates this Irish archetype which was at the centre of so many debates in the period.

Patrick Kavanagh (1904–67) was born in Inniskeen, Co. Monaghan, the son of a cobbler and farmer. He left school in his early teens to help out on the farm, and schooled himself in the craft of verse. His first full collection was *Ploughman and Other Poems* (1936). It contained 'Inniskeen Road: July Evening', and other excellent lyrics from this period include 'Shancoduff' and 'Plough-Horses'. The poems give reports from everyday farming life, but also Kavanagh expresses his distance from the life around him, because he is a poet. While the local lads and lasses go to the dance-hall, he enjoys a solitary splendour: 'A road, a mile of kingdom, I am king / Of banks and stones and every blooming thing.'[18] There is a pun on 'banks' (one thinks of the sense in which the Bank of England is chartered to the crown), and an even sharper pun on 'blooming'. This is at once an expression of joy in the natural world and a dismissal of it ('blooming' as synonym for 'bloody'). The play on this word encapsulates much of Kavanagh's subsequent career: he would write poems of celebration of the natural world, whether it be found in Monaghan or beside a canal in Dublin, but he would also squander many of his years satirising and attacking certain Irish writers and social values.

In 1938 he published *The Green Fool*, a winsome autobiographical book about farming life, and he would go over this material again for his novel *Tarry Flynn* (1948). These books were written to make money, but they also served the deeper literary purpose of sketching out the hinterland behind the brief lyrics of farming life. It was as though Kavanagh realised that these in themselves were not enough to sustain a reputation; and it was also becoming clear that as a poet his work was extremely uneven. All the more reason then to have the support of prose.

In *The Great Hunger* (1942), Kavanagh attempted to marry his lyrical and narrative gifts in a long poem about Patrick Maguire, a middle-aged farmer obliged to look after his ageing mother. His society treats as obscene all expressions of sexual desire and he realises that he has been robbed of the best years of his life. Kavanagh mocks idealisations of the peasant, while showing that the reality is altogether grimmer. The poem's detailed discussions of family and property relations savagely blow apart the last of Revival pretentions about the Irish peasant. As Quinn remarks: '*The Great Hunger* exposes a nation-wide conspiracy of lies, secrecy and silence: a false paradisal perception of Irish country life sponsored by post-colonial chauvinism and national economic expediency, and enforced by a combination of religious precept and a cautious, thrifty, small-farm ethos.'[19] Kavanagh would later and with insight condemn the poem as 'underdeveloped Comedy': certainly the *saeva indignatio* at the consensus in Irish society that perpetuated these problems, along with the poem's demand that the reader pities Maguire, leave room for little else.[20] The method of the poem has been loosely described as Modernist, and Kavanagh claimed that he was influenced by *The Waste Land*. It is perhaps closer to a book like Edgar Lee Masters's *The Spoon River Anthology* (1915), which depicts life in a small American town with realist accuracy and irregular rhyme and metre. Nevertheless, the mere fact that Kavanagh wished that the poem be considered Modernist indicates an aspiration to surpass the traditional lyric.

In the mid-forties to the mid-fifties, Kavanagh devoted much of his energy to satire, but, first, he lacked the technical facility necessary to make these poems convincing, and, second, he simply wasn't as intelligent as Pope or Dryden. Most of his work in this line is a monotonous complaint that he has been badly treated by the world at large. As Quinn incisively remarks of one of these poems, 'Kavanagh does not succeed in making a credible moral issue of out middle-class Dublin's failure to include him among its favoured charities.'[21] His egotism obtrudes elsewhere also. For instance, the long poem 'Lough Derg', written in 1942 but unpublished until 1971, is about the place of pilgrimage which also appears in poems by Denis Devlin and Seamus Heaney, and begins like this:

> From Cavan and from Leitrim and from Mayo,
> From all the thin-faced parishes where hills
> Are perished noses running peaty water,
> They come to Lough Derg to fast and pray and beg
> With all the bitterness of nonentities, and the envy
> Of the inarticulate when dealing with an artist.[22]

This is awkwardly done, as the bitterness and envy of the nonentity attach themselves to the speaker, rather than to those described. In its wake, one can trust nothing of what Kavanagh says – not his prolix analyses of the Irish character, not his condescending tenderness, not his histrionic self-deprecation at the poem's conclusion – because we feel that all is distorted by egoism. The critic Ron Callan once remarked that it's interesting to compare Kavanagh's poetry, marred by egotism, with that of Whitman and his scions for whom egotism, or egoism, made their work expansive, generous and inclusive. Arguably, the small handful of outstanding poems by Kavanagh are the occasions when his ego is in abeyance: what is revealed is a sombre landscape with human figures balanced against the forces of nature and history, wry and aware of their lot.

Kavanagh defined his approach as 'parochial' and he contrasted it favourably with 'provincialism'. For him a provincial was someone who defers in matters of artistic taste to a higher, and distant, authority – most often a few coffee-houses and pubs in a capital city; whereas a parochial writer knows that his own 'mile of kingdom', though it is in the back of beyond, is just as authoritative in matters of art as the metropolitan centre. The distinction animates one of Kavanagh's finest poems, the sonnet 'Epic', in which the speaker begins by claiming that he has lived through great events. One would expect subsequent mention of statesmen and world wars, but by the third line we see that the speaker is referring to faction fights about some 'half a rood of rock' in a small country village. The onset of World War II is dismissed in passing: 'That was the year of the Munich bother.'[23] Kavanagh is in control of the subtle threads of expectation and surprise, and his irony dares the reader to disagree with him. There is the slightest hint of smugness in this dismissal of world events, a smugness which was occasionally visible in Irish public life during the war. The volta, or turn, in the final lines of the sonnet, however, introduces a new tone of seriousness, as the speaker confides that actually he himself was beginning to think that all these local rows were of no significance. But then he hears the distant voice of Homer whispering to him: 'I made the *Iliad* from such / A local row. Gods make their own importance.'[24] The speaker was drifting towards provincialism, but is retrieved from the brink by another 'parochial' writer, the father of European literature.

In March 1955, Kavanagh was diagnosed with lung cancer and underwent surgery to combat it. He convalesced in the following months, and spent many hours sitting idly by the Grand Canal enjoying what was a particularly good summer for Ireland (his bronze statue is seated on a bench there now). He subsequently wrote poems that express his sense of gratitude for surviving and his joy in the everyday world. Kavanagh figured this as something of a breakthrough, but as Quinn points out, the Canal Bank sonnets merely continue a strand of his poetry that had been present from the earliest period.[25] In poems such as 'Lines Written on a Seat on the Grand Canal' and 'Canal Bank Walk', as well as others like 'Kerr's Ass', 'In Memory of My Mother' and 'Come Dance with Kitty Stobling', Kavanagh balances the demands of his ego with those of his surroundings; there is also a détente in his inner conflict between city and country. Kavanagh had made his name and life in Dublin city as a poet of the countryside, and he was aware of the equal dangers of nostalgia for and vilification of his rural home. In several of these poems, the country and the city interpenetrate each other in an eirenic way: thus as he sits in the midst of the metropolis, he sees 'a barge . . . bringing from Athy / And other far-flung towns mythologies'.[26] Neither country nor city is preferred: they are mutually dependent and mutually enriching.

Kavanagh's achievement is restricted to a handful of poems which anthologists of two generations have agreed upon. Exploring his work outside this number is a dismal experience. Nevertheless, these few poems were extremely influential in the decades to follow: for the likes of Seamus Heaney and John Montague, they sanctioned rural realism as poetic theme; but more generally, they instituted a poetry of personal anecdote and everyday observation which, boosted by the popularity of Confessional poetry from the United States, flooded the magazines and slim collections. It was not a happy legacy, as few of these poets could equal Kavanagh at his best. Necessary to this development was a consensus that Kavanagh was a poet of the first order, an opinion which few readers outside Ireland have shared. He provoked important cultural debate in his time, although he was unable to follow his provocations with arguments of substance. However, his achievement, though small, looks set to endure.

So far there have been only small fragments of Grecian vases to be found in the wild Irish earth. Clarke and Kavanagh both chafed against the tenets of the

Revival, but ultimately remained within its sphere of influence. I placed Colum's poem at the head of the chapter mainly to accommodate Louis MacNeice, because of the three poets considered here he was the one who most successfully flew the nets of the Revival and confronted the achievement of the Modernist poets. His friendships with W. H. Auden and Stephen Spender positioned him with the avant-garde in English poetry: here were young men who wished to express what it was like to be in the modern world, as opposed to rural life in Ballyrush or Gortin.

While such statements somewhat journalistically catch something of the reception of MacNeice, they must immediately be qualified with the precision of real journalism, as MacNeice himself would be the first to object to such broad characterisation. To fly the nets of the Revival is not to abandon Ireland. And although MacNeice spent all of his working life in England his ties to the country remained central to his poetry. One must avoid the simplifications of Revival thinking, as evidenced for example by Austin Clarke in his *Poetry in Modern Ireland* (1961), which mentions MacNeice briefly as having 'achieved rapidly a reputation as one of the leaders of the English advanced group which was so active in the years before the war';[27] this figures MacNeice as a flash in the pan, beside Revivalist poets such as Joseph Campbell and Lyle Donaghy, both subsequently and justly consigned to the oblivion of literary history. Peter McDonald, whose study of MacNeice is subtitled 'A Poet in His Contexts', explains that several contexts are necessary to interpret his poetry, and, unfortunately for his posthumous reputation, those contexts are usually considered independently of one another:

> It could be plausibly maintained that the difficulties from which MacNeice's reputation has always suffered have their origin in his poetic violation of certain canonical (and contextual) norms: a 1930s poet who insisted on his Irishness; an Irish-born poet who lived most of his life in England. In one case, he seems to threaten the critical elevation of Auden as a poet representative of both a generation and a time; in the other, he appears to undermine the stability of an orthodox notion of national 'identity'.[28]

As a poet he is uninterested in nationalist ideology; but at the same time he does not try to make himself a rootless cosmopolitan. When he uses Irish material in his poetry, he does so like a true native, that is, as someone who does not have to proclaim his *echt* Irishness to the world, but takes it for granted in backgrounds, gestures, turns of phrase. Equally, he is an English poet for the same reasons, and to omit either of these contexts is to reduce his achievement.

MacNeice himself argued the issue of 'roots' when he confronted critics of Auden's removal to America:

> Some people do go so far. It is argued by extremists, most of whom have never crossed the Atlantic, that no Englishman – no English writer anyway – 'can' change countries like this; it was all right, perhaps, for Henry James and Eliot to come this way, but no English writer can go that way and get away with it. This looks to me like sheer nonsense. Of course, it is hard to write where you have no 'roots', but because it is hard it may be all the more worth doing. We have had plenty of 'rooted' writing; the individual artist may have soon to dispense with 'roots' (in this narrower, local sense), just as the world must sooner or later dispense with national sovereignty. This question of roots is a question of degree: few of us believe the diehards who think you must stick to your own parish, fewer of us than formerly think that it is good for a small country like Ireland to attempt a cultural autarchy.[29]

It is of note that although he is dealing with the matter of England, America and Auden, his thinking drifts back to the Irish situation, raising issues of his own self-definition.

MacNeice was born in Belfast in 1907 and was raised in Co. Antrim. His was father was a Church of Ireland rector and his mother, who was from Connemara, died when he was seven. From an early age, Ireland was a place where he returned from English schools for the holidays; at Marlborough College he became friendly with Anthony Blunt, the future art expert and traitor. He studied Classics and Philosophy at Oxford, and after graduating worked as a Classics lecturer at the University of Birmingham in the years 1929 to 1936. British intellectuals were becoming enamoured of Marxism at the time, but, as his biographer, Jon Stallworthy, points out, MacNeice's stay in Birmingham brought him closer to the working classes than his peers ever were.[30] Perhaps this discrepancy between what he saw around him in the industrial city and the theories produced by his friends made MacNeice suspicious of Marxist ideology, and indeed of any ideology whatsoever. An urbane reasonableness animates his poetry and his prose (his selected journalism is a classic of the genre); and indeed sometimes restricts it. Terence Brown calls this 'a sceptical vision' (in his 1975 book of the same name), in the positive sense meant by a philosopher like George Santayana, whereby man avoids totalising structures of meaning and belief in order to remain open to the richness of experience.

The poems of his first collection, *Blind Fireworks* (1929), published when MacNeice was in his early twenties, were designated as 'juvenilia' by the editor of MacNeice's first *Collected Poems*, and so it is perhaps fairer to view *Poems* (1935) as his proper début. 'Train to Dublin' contains something of his anti-ideological manifesto (a rich oxymoron): 'I will not give you any idol or idea, creed or king, / I give you the incidental things which pass / Outward through space exactly as each was.'[31] The outstanding moments of the book are when he describes those moments of human experience that are not reducible to political or religious meaning. They are attractive for MacNeice precisely because they escape ideology. This is the opening of the poem:

> Our half-thought thoughts divide in sifted wisps
> Against the basic facts repatterned without pause,
> I can no more gather my mind up in my fist
> Than the shadow of the smoke of this train upon the grass –
> This is the way that animals' lives pass.[32]

History, as a grand Hegelian mechanism encompassing the lives of individuals and political structures, haunted the poetry of the 1930s; MacNeice here dwells on a very different type of time, one that streams out unstructured and dream-like. Thoughts are not shaped into orotund conclusions, but remain hanging unfinished in the air, leaving MacNeice a little like a cloud in pants, to use Vladimir Mayakousky's expression. Of course, this is an æsthetic ideology in itself, and it is an extremely limited one. There is a world of facts that cannot be bent into the shapes necessary for theory or precept. This leaves the poet with the repetitious work of celebrating the 'everyday', whatever that is. Increasingly MacNeice saw the 'everyday' as a panorama of mechanistic events, and in his mid-career this left him with bleak prospects indeed.

But before this moment arrived, MacNeice wrote *Autumn Journal* (1939), considered along with the work of his last two collections to be the height of his achievement. It is a long meditative and descriptive poem which describes the run-up to World War II, especially around the time of what Kavanagh called 'the Munich bother'. I remarked above on MacNeice's suspicion of grand abstractions: the challenge then was how to avoid them when dealing with one of the most abstract areas of human activity – international politics. McDonald comments that for MacNeice 'the political good resides in individuals rather than in *the* individual',[33] and this has profound implications for his method in *Autumn Journal*. Rather than speak of how world events impinge on the life of nations, MacNeice set out to say with precision and balance how these events impinge on him. It is a gambit, as the poet risks egotism at a time when millions are in danger. But MacNeice avoided this pitfall through careful description. Derek Mahon has remarked on his 'extraordinary visual and tactile sense of the period', and that for MacNeice, 'the surface *was* the core. Like Horace, he was *profoundly* superficial.'[34] Just as Colum's scholar was only interested in Grecian beauty when it touched the wild earth of Ireland, so too MacNeice wants to know what the newspaper headlines mean in his particular patch of the world; if he can extrapolate from that to say something of larger import, then good, but that must not be achieved through any distortion of the weather, the tints, the flitting feelings, of everyday life during one fateful autumn. Thus the poem opens with a setting:

> Close and slow, summer is ending in Hampshire,
>> Ebbing away down ramps of shaven lawn where close-clipped yew
> Insulates the lives of retired generals and admirals
>> And the spyglasses hung in the hall and the prayer-books ready in the pew
> And August going out to the tin trumpets of nasturtiums
>> And the sunflowers' Salvation Army blare of brass
> And the spinster sitting in a deck-chair picking up stitches
>> Not raising her eyes to the noise of the 'planes that pass
> Northward from Lee-on-Solent. Macrocarpa and cypress
>> And roses on a rustic trellis and mulberry trees
> And bacon and eggs in a silver dish for breakfast
>> And all the inherited worries, rheumatisms and taxes,
> And whether Stella will marry and what to do with Dick
>> And the branch of the family that lost their money in Hatry . . .[35]

Nothing could be further from war and war's alarms than this drowsy, luxurious landscape, but this is MacNeice's point: the complacency that is palpable in Hampshire is also palpable in Britain's timorous and improvident foreign policy, as Neville Chamberlain (who would die a year later in Hampshire) gave in to Hitler's demands for a greater Germany. The passage is weakened by the last lines, as MacNeice conjures up stock characters to emphasise his point. This is a crude move for both a journal writer and a journalist, and is tantamount to inventing one's sources. What was earlier expressed with nuance is pounded out now in large-point sans-serif. The lines also point to the poem's central weakness: it is often crushed by the grand abstractions that MacNeice is so wary of. It is as though their weight was too much for MacNeice's imagination.

For MacNeice *condescends* to the facts of everyday life: he can only appreciate them insofar as they are fugitive from ideology and abstraction; they do not have value for him in themselves. And during this particular period in European history, the everyday facts and personal feelings are pitiful and almost worthy of contempt. His main theme then is not the integrity of everyday experience, but rather how it doesn't give in to the big abstractions. To be fair to MacNeice, he lavishes his condescension as much on himself as on the Stellas and Dicks; nevertheless it is a limiting perspective and there is not sufficient imaginative pressure exerted against the pressure of events. Further sections of *Autumn Journal* tease out the Yeatsian binary of metaphysics and mundanity, wax nostalgic about lost love, consider the war headlines as they come in, recall a visit to Spain before the Republican government came to grief, inquire about the meaning of Europe's common Greek and Roman culture and subsequently about the English educational system. In section XVI he also considers the matter of Ireland, asking:

> The land of scholars and saints:
>   Scholars and saints my eye, the land of ambush,
> Purblind manifestoes, never-ending complaints . . .
>   . . .
> Why do we like being Irish? Partly because
>   It gives us a hold on the sentimental English
> As members of a world that never was . . .
>   . . .
> Put up what flag you like, it is too late
>   To save your soul with bunting.[36]

The last statement echoes with what Tomás Ó Duinnshléibhe said about the loss of the Irish soul. Observe also the no-nonsense tone of this: here is a man who is not going to tolerate any fine-sounding words. It is as much a reaction against Yeats as it is against Ireland. The shifting mode of address is also of note. While he employs the first-person plural in the middle passage, by the time we get to the last (which is taken from towards the end of the section), MacNeice has disentangled himself from his country and his countrymen and addresses them from across the channel.

In 1941, he began working for the BBC, where he remained until his death in 1963. He wrote and produced radio plays, as well as broadcasting travel pieces and reportage. The poetry he wrote up to the mid 1950s has few advocates, but many critics view the final collections – *Visitations* (1957), *Solstices* (1961) and *The Burning Perch* (1963) – as his finest. What differentiates this work is MacNeice's new awareness of the way death was suddenly speeding towards him. In these poems, childhood memories are telescoped into adult experience and the poet flounders to make chronological sense of what is happening to him; yet MacNeice expressed that confusion with consummate poetic control. This is often done by employing the tone and techniques of parable, as Edna Longley remarks.[37] In 'The Slow Starter', the poet receives advice – as a child, as a young lover and as a young man embarking upon his career – that he should take his time and all will come to him. Each receives a verse of its own, and then in the final and fourth verse, there is a terrible realisation:

> Oh you have had your chance, It said;
> Left it alone and it was one.
> Who said a watched clock never moves?
> Look at it now. Your chance was I.
>   He turned and saw the accusing clock
>   Race like a torrent round a rock.[38]

The violence of the closing image is intensified by the rhyming couplet (of the other stanzas, only the first is also closed with a rhyming couplet). Perhaps the best poem in this mode is 'The Taxis', in which the speaker gets into successive taxis during his life, and each time he seems to have accrued extra persons, who remain invisible to him, but not to the taxi-drivers. The final driver indicates that MacNeice has reached the end of the line:

> As for the fourth taxi, he was alone
> Tra-la when he hailed it but the cabby looked
> Through him and said: 'I can't tra-la well take
> So many people, not to speak of the dog.'[39]

The 'tra-las' accompany the poem all the way through and this jaunty counter-point increases the sense of dread. As the ballad rhythm breaks into the everyday remarks, it suggests the way in which humans – no matter how elegant their 'half-thought thoughts divide[d] in sifted wisps' – are ultimately shaped by the grim verities that ballads often assert.

MacNeice died of pneumonia in 1963, his health much weakened by years of alcoholism. In the decades ahead he would prove influential to Northern Irish poets such as Michael Longley, Derek Mahon and Paul Muldoon, and precisely because of the hybridity that McDonald discusses: for these later poets, that MacNeice had so many contexts, and so many in common with their own, made him a central figure, and his mark is to be found in their poems and their criticism up to the present time. There were other Northern Irish poets of the same period, such as W. R. Rodgers (1909–61) and John Hewitt (1907–87), who played lesser tutelary roles: these were valued not so much for their achievement, which was of a lesser order than MacNeice's, but simply for the fact that they had existed. Ranging more widely, we see that there was a large range of poets who wrote one or two excellent poems but whose careers never came to fruition. Some of these poems had a brief afterlife in anthologies published in the 1960s and 1970s, others not even that. Patrick McDonogh's (1902–61) 'Over the Water', Sheila Wingfield's (1906–92) 'A Tuscan Farmer', John Hewitt's 'I Write for My Own Kind', Donagh MacDonagh's (1912–68) 'The Hungry Grass', Valentin Iremonger's (1918–91) 'This Houre Her Vigill' and Rhoda Coghill's (1903–2000) 'Flight'. As emblem of these, I give Maurice Craig's (b. 1919) 'Love Poem' in full:

> Flowers upon your lips and hands,
> The gentle movement of your breast:
> I have remembered these in lands
> Where I was but a passing guest.
>
> Strange, to have seen so long before,
> Reflected through each flaw and fault
> This inlet on the sunlit shore
> Where sweet water meets the salt.[40]

The poem, along with several excellent ones by the same author, slipped out of memory for decades, and Craig went on to become Ireland's foremost architectural historian.

But perhaps the greatest achievement of the poets who came after the Revival was that they familiarised the idea that Irish poetry did not necessarily have to depend on the Irish language. Twentieth-century Irish poetry, for the most part, energetically tries to forget that Colum's poem is a kind of translation: who now recalls that the poor scholar of the 1840s would have spoken in Irish and not in English? What is the Irish for 'wild earth', for 'Grecian vase'?

Chapter 6

The ends of Modernism: Kinsella and Irish experiment

Denis Devlin, Brian Coffey, Thomas Kinsella, John Montague, Trevor Joyce, Randolph Healy, Maurice Scully

The publication of *The Oxford Book of Modern Verse* (1936) edited by W. B. Yeats seemed to provide official confirmation that Modernism in poetry had passed Ireland by. Although poets such as Ezra Pound and T. S. Eliot were represented in the book, they did not receive the coverage that their present reputations demand. Yeats had little understanding or sympathy for this new movement in poetry, which was radical in its formal experiments and more ambitious in its themes than much of the Georgian poetry in Britain at the beginning of the twentieth century. Yeats himself was able to bring traditional forms together with a thematic range to equal anything in Pound or Eliot, but while the Gaelic Revival released many disruptive forces into poetic idiom, in general Irish poetry in its aftermath was both thematically limited and formally conservative. Irish poetry in the mid century, then, reflects the depressed state of the culture, as well as the economic doldrums the country was going through.

The work of Denis Devlin does not upset this picture to a great degree, but it is an interesting exception, and, taken along with the work of Brian Coffey, shows the ways in which Irish poetry began to absorb the legacy of Eliot and Pound. Devlin was born in Scotland of Irish parents in 1908, and when he was twelve his family settled in Dublin, where his father ran a pub in which Michael Collins and his associates would often meet. Devlin attended Belvedere College nearby, and then University College Dublin, where he read English and French, completing his BA in 1929. For some years he considered and worked towards an academic career, but in 1935 he joined the Department of External Affairs. Postings to Rome, New York, Washington, Istanbul and London followed; the year before he died in 1959 he was appointed Irish Ambassador to Italy. His Washington appointment was particularly significant as it brought him into contact with Allen Tate and Robert Penn Warren, as well as the French poet Saint-John Perse, whom he would translate. Tate was one of the most important poet-critics in America at the time, and his admiration for Devlin's work opened up publishing possibilities for the Irish poet. More significantly,

Tate himself in his poetry and critical work was coming to terms with the legacy of Eliot, and his approach influenced much of the poetry of the 1930s and 1940s. Rather than continue Eliot's experimentalism, Tate turned back to the conventional forms of the poets whom Eliot praised in his criticism. He was also preoccupied with the legacy of the South (he was from Tennessee) but his regionalism never made him lose sight of the challenge posed by Eliot's *déraciné* collages of contemporary civilisation: for Tate, as for Eliot, regional and religious values were under threat from modernity.

The same pattern can be found in Devlin, but Tate, rather than instigating this, served as confirmation. Devlin throughout his career pondered the legacy of Catholicism and the particular form it took in Ireland. He placed this against a wider backdrop of European church history. But that international ken does not take away from the fact that he was, as J. C. C. Mays put it, 'self-consciously and proudly an Irish poet, though self-consciousness and pride are checked by self-possession and restraint'.[1] His intellectual range and ambition so obviously exceeded that of contemporaries such as Austin Clarke and Patrick Kavanagh that for many decades he was perceived as an internationalist whose poetry had little purchase on Irish experience; one can only accept this judgement if one agrees on an extremely narrow idea of what constitutes 'Irish experience'. Mays also reminds us that he is not an experimental poet – although he would often write free verse, he never abandoned rhyme and traditional metres.

'Est Prodest', published in Devlin's first collection, *Intercessions* (1937), is a meditation on the way that God is spread out through people.[2] The poem plays through the phases of agony and exaltation that such divine dispersal creates in humans. Devlin also concentrates on the shapes that are made by heaven on the earth, the way that divinity, being outside time, intercedes in the course of history, or as he puts it later, 'The charged rippling starfields / Murmur of holy cities': the ethereal creates patterns of human habitation and settlement. Divinity also affects the course of human speech as those phrases are 'twisted through other / Reasons'[3] in reflection of and reaction to Godhead.

The meditation has no reference to Ireland but in the title poem of his second and final collection, *Lough Derg and Other Poems* (1946), Devlin attends to the particular form of Catholicism in his native country: 'With mullioned Europe shattered, this Northwest, / Rude-sainted isle would pray it whole again.'[4] The poem is set in the present day, but also ranges back to the Middle Ages, and compares those freer and braver times with the contemporary situation. However, the sharp satirical tang of some of these passages (Ireland is described as 'doughed in dogma'[5]) is contrasted with a profound sympathy for the pilgrims, and in the final lines, after such wide-ranging meditations on the relations between divinity and national history, the poet turns to the person immediately next to him: 'and so, knelt on her sod, / This woman beside me murmuring *My God! My God!*'[6] The woman's supplication parallels Devlin's own desire for a life of the spirit unsullied by the degeneration he finds in the Ireland of his time, for it is to a Catholic god that Devlin ultimately prays. One of the important developments here from 'Est Prodest' is the particularity of the woman – in the earlier poem we only had vague 'Groups of men and women'. This attention to particulars comes through in Devlin's last major poem 'The Heavenly Foreigner' (written in the late 1940s and early 1950s), which remained uncollected at his death. The individual parts of this sequence are titled with the names of various European cathedral cities, such as Geneva, Dublin and Chartres. Some of these are associated with Celtic settlements and others with the evangelising work of Irish monks in Europe in the early Middle Ages. Devlin's religious preoccupation takes on a geographical aspect as he examines the way that God is dispersed through the cities and nations of Europe. The cathedral is an intermediary zone between the divine realm and the profane city spreading out around it. The poem's mode of address is decorous and elaborate in the tradition of the lyrics of courtly love. Its ambition is clearly equal to Eliot's *Four Quartets*, which surveys the spiritual history of England and America, but the achievement of 'The Heavenly Foreigner' is more disputable. As with much of Devlin's poetry, there is an uncertainty of tone, as the poet tries to marry the language of devotional and meditational poetry with that of satire. There are also many obscure patches in the poems, as Devlin makes transitions across a broad historical canvas; they arise not from the materials themselves but from Devlin's unsure handling of them. Yet his work can be seen retrospectively as a promise of poetry that deals with Irish experience against a European background, of poetry that is not restricted, as was arguably the case of both Clarke and Kavanagh, by journalistic and critical debates about the meaning of Irishness.

Devlin's name is often coupled with that of Brian Coffey (1905–95), with whom he attended university in the 1930s, and they are taken to be exponents of experimentalism in Irish poetry in the mid century. In Devlin's case, as I indicated, such a characterisation is wrong. Coffey on the other hand was drawn to the methods of Ezra Pound and the Eliot of the 1910s and early 1920s. Coffey's work is derivative of American Modernist poetry and can only be viewed as experimental if one's horizon is restricted to Ireland. He is also paired with Devlin because he spent the greater part of his life abroad, studying theology in Paris, subsequently teaching philosophy in the United States and mathematics at secondary level in England. This emigrant life is reflected most clearly and, it should be noted, most flatly, in his 'Missouri Sequence' (1962), where he abandons his usual more obscure idiom for direct autobiographical writing. In his longer poems, however, he has adhered to the Modernist device of the 'mythical method', whereby the poem is organised upon a template provided by ancient myth. So in *Death of Hektor* (1982), Coffey offers a swingeing account of nuclear civilisation through reference to the events in the Iliad. Coffey's apocalypse does not wait for humanity at the end of time, but rather is with it from its beginnings in Greek myth. The poem balances this gloom by concluding on a more positive note:

> And [Homer] gave us his Andromache lamenting
> like any woman victim of any war robbed of her world
> her husband her child her friends her linen her pots and pans
> the years it took to put a home together living against the grain
> of great deeds   her woman's life   in her heart
> much held fast   word hidden for all[7]

The passage is sonorous enough at the beginning but one of the problems here, as everywhere in Coffey, is the blandness and vagueness of the language (namely, the use of 'any' here and a cliché like 'the years it took to put a home together'). The myth serves only to make a sweeping statement about humanity. Indeed, it is difficult to see justification for the claims that Coffey is an experimental poet in any meaningful sense; certainly, bizarre punctuation and spacing of words do not in themselves constitute originality. So while Coffey adopted some of the earlier aspects of Modernist experiment, he himself did not extend them.

'Once the major excitements of the Revival were over,' writes Seamus Deane, 'there was inevitably a sense of disappointment and disillusion.'[8] The major Irish writers of the beginning of the century such as Yeats and Joyce were dead and the patriotic heroism of the Republic was transformed into bureaucratic zeal. F. S. L. Lyons remarked on the widespread 'frustration and cynicism' in Irish society in this period.[9] The achievements of poets like Kavanagh, MacNeice and Clarke were varied, but they were certainly of a second order compared with Yeats. As Ireland moved into the 1950s, there was a pervading sense, in both social and literary spheres, of living in the shadow of a great past. Exhaustion, boredom and resignation were the key signatures.

On to this scene emerged Thomas Kinsella. His work expressed these feelings, but in an exceptionally poised and disciplined way. Many of the poems in his first books employ difficult verse-forms and rhyme schemes, and the persona that narrates them has no illusions about the banality and drabness of life in the new republic. As Andrew Fitzsimons points out, they avoid the question of the nation; it is only later that this would become important for him.[10] The complex formal structures of art provide a foil for the boredom and confusion of the daily grind. He was born in Dublin in 1928, studied science at University College Dublin, without receiving his degree, and entered the civil service where he would eventually work as the secretary of T. K. Whitaker, the Minister of Finance. He retired in 1965 and from that point he held various teaching posts at universities, for the most part in the USA.

The 1960s saw the publication of what are arguably Kinsella's two best individual collections, *Downstream* (1962) and *Nightwalker and Other Poems* (1968). While many of these poems employ traditional poetic forms (such as *terza rima* in the title poem of *Downstream*), Kinsella is already coming to suspect the consolations of poetic form in the face of the chaos of history. The range of his vision is also beginning to broaden: whereas in earlier books the despair, boredom and exhaustion were often merely personal, in the collections of this decade he begins to survey Irish and European history, seeing there a panorama of violence and confusion. Kinsella begins to explore ways to represent these elements in his art on a formal level. In practical terms this entailed his gradual abandonment of rhyme and regular metre in favour of more Modernist collage forms, as is clear in 'Nightwalker', where he employs free verse with many disjunctions of voice and context.

In 1972 with the help of Liam Miller of the Dolmen Press Kinsella began publishing his new work through the Peppercanister Press from his home in Percy Place in Dublin. With its wide-ranging and varied material and techniques of collage, the Peppercanister series marks Kinsella's reinvention of himself as a Modernist poet in this period. It is worth remarking here that Kinsella's adoption of poetic techniques that were ground-breaking fifty years previously does not mean that he is an experimental poet. He only appears experimental in Ireland because of that country's overwhelming poetic conservatism. When compared to, say, the disjunctive strategies of John Ashbery, Susan Howe or Louis Zukofsky, Kinsella's work, in technical terms, becomes recognisable as a fine-tuning of Pound, the rough edges and swathes of tedium removed, leaving the central methods of medley and collage. Historically, such fine-tuning creates a very different dynamic. In the *Cantos* the rough edges and passages like the prolix disquisition on Chinese history, if little else, convey a sense of the risk and precariousness of the whole project, as well as its rejection of a poetic rhetoric that overmasters its material to such an extent that it cannot include all of history. Here Pound advocates the hard-edged æsthetic of Vorticism: 'The image is not an idea. It is a radiant node or cluster; it is what I can, and must perforce, call a VORTEX, from which, and through which, and into which, ideas are constantly rushing. In decency one can only call it a VORTEX.'[11] And the artists of this vortex happening in London in the 1910s 'cannot help bringing about changes as great as the Renaissance changes',[12] that is, will achieve a state of affairs in which 'the life of arts [will be] obviously and conspicuously intermingled with the life of power'.[13] Kinsella's belated adoption of Modernist collage carries no such charge, or excitement, rather it adopts a long-established poetic rhetoric. Pound's represents a strong rupture with tradition which is supposed to let 'process' come rushing in, while Kinsella's development in the late 1960s is a conscious choice of one pre-existing style (Modernist collage) over another (the well-made poem of Frost and Larkin, *et al.*). Questioned as to whether his translation work from Irish is an attempt 'to bridge [the] gaps, to regain contact with some kind of lost inheritance', he responds: 'It isn't. The gaps can't be closed. The most you can do is attempt to understand it, to put it in its place as a gap, as fracture, as rupture. The failure of these ideas is as important as any success. Significant experience has to allow for failure.'[14] This is as good a description of Kinsella's method in the Peppercanister Poems as any. Despite his avowal that our powers of representing the Irish tradition are bounded, we still appear very much in control of the gaps and fractures that appear within it: we do not endure or suffer them, we *deploy* them. Kinsella dismisses the idea of success contained in the dream of totality of representation, but subtly introduces another criterion of success, one that is still very much dependent on that dream: the presentation of a gapped or fractured totality.

What holds the Peppercanister Poems together, Kinsella hopes, is that in their variety and interconnectedness they comprehend 'how the whole thing' – all of national and personal history – 'works'.[15] The most important figure in the Peppercanister Poems is that of the artist. He (and it is always a he) is the one who can comprehend in one vision the history of his own self and the history of the nation, and is the main point of access to comprehension of 'the whole thing'. The politician figure, in his positive manifestation as John F. Kennedy, comes near this ideal, but the politician deludes himself that he is in control. Nevertheless, the assassinated Kennedy shows how murderous the 'beast' of history is; the adept who would face it must be strong. The politician in his negative manifestation (also inclusive of the Catholic clergy in Ireland), while perpetrating evil acts (for instance, the demolition of an important archæological site at Woodquay in Dublin to make way for civic offices) is never credited with the kind of historical awareness Kinsella ascribes to the artist.

It is Seán Ó Riada who first embodies this knowledge. Insofar as Kinsella wishes to connect the personal with the national, his own close friendship with Ó Riada was fortuitous. Here was a personal friend who was both a composer of national importance and whose main work was about the Irish nation. In *A Selected Life* (1972) and *Vertical Man* (1973) Kinsella concentrates on the way that Ó Riada's music configures the consciousness of a nation: 'That you may startle the heart of a whole people', and engenders visions 'of elements and things and beasts'.[16] Such a visionary passage contrasts strongly with the more realistic personal banter of his address to Ó Riada ('Would you care to share a queer vision I had?',[17] etc.). Here and elsewhere in the earlier Peppercanisters such passages link the personal with the larger panorama of national history. They describe another dimension of Jungian archetypes and locales – snakes, other beasts, desert scenes. But when we start to look closer at these Jungian archetypes, problems arise. What are these beasts symbols of? Which exact forces of historical change do they represent? This is never stated. Instead of helping us to gaze into the murky depths of national history and distinguish various agencies, the Jungian bestiary and locales only serve to heighten our awareness of the bravery of the poet in facing these things. And in the case of the artist we must ask, what exactly is the ordeal he undergoes when trying to comprehend history? It is clear that the politician who would change the course of a nation must face physical danger, but less clear in the case of the artist, especially one not living in a repressive regime.

In *One* (1974) the people of Kinsella's own nation are the invading foreign bodies, who come to an uninhabited land and set up their community there. This is a significant pamphlet because for the first time Kinsella sketches out the panorama of Irish history, from the founding of 'the oldest place' to his own childhood memories. Of course, there is a massive gap, or rupture, in the vision, and Kinsella, as we have seen, has been careful to point out how he wishes to incorporate such breaks in the national tradition into his work. But the idea of rupture itself presumes a prior unity – and we are left with a stronger sense of this unity than of fragmentation. The instalment is fifteen pages long in the *Collected Poems* and is divided into seven poems. Each poem relates a particular episode and between two of the poems there is a gap of many centuries. But the poems still connect, and if gaps and fragments do nothing else, they encourage the reader to imagine the total edifice of the past.

The first section, 'Prologue', is disjunctive: first there is the figure of a *seanachie* placed against a cosmic backdrop, and this refers directly to 'the Voyage of the First Kindred'.[18] This comes out of Kinsella's readings of the *Lebor Gabala Erinn* (The Book of Invasions), the old Irish text which relates the history of the country and the successive invasions it endured. Donatella Abbate Badin comments that 'the narration of the voyages in *Lebor Gabala Erinn* . . . merges with cosmogonic myths – Genesis and the story of Cessair's father, Bith, whose name means world'.[19] The next untitled section is a dream narrative in which a person wakes and goes forth eating small animals, and is full of sub-Joycean agglutinations ('whimswift', 'snapdelicious'[20]) and sub-*Four Quartets* prosaic musing ('But with the satisfaction / comes a falling off /

in the drive, the desire'[21]). The next section, 'The Entire Fabric', is as close as Kinsella has ever come to a revisionist approach to history, where history seems to be orchestrated by 'a man, sporting a striped jacket, / posed in confident quackery'.[22] This Mephisto figure would obviously like to make us the dupes of his spectacle, the one which he sets in action, and which follows straight after it in the two long poems which make up most of *One*, 'Finistère' and 'The Oldest Place'. These are remarkable poems in themselves, but within the context of the pamphlet and the Peppercanister Poems in general, they are *pointes d'appui* of Kinsella's meditations on the Irish nation.

Although narrated by one voice, they relate a collective experience: travel over the sea till a kind of promised land is found, settling and suffering great hardships, but enduring there so that it becomes 'the oldest place' of the title. There are several noteworthy aspects to these poems. First, although the speaker is Amergin, the first Irish poet, the voice sounds utterly contemporary. Kinsella, who in 1969 had already published a translation of the ancient Irish epic, *The Táin*, would have had no difficulty giving the poem an archaic surface, but he forgoes this:

> I steadied myself. 'Our Father . . .' someone said
> and there was a little laughter. I stood
> searching a moment for the right words.
> They fell silent. I chose the old words once more
> and stepped out. At the solid shock
> a dreamy power loosened at the base of my spine
> and uncoiled and slid up through the marrow.[23]

The effect is strange. On the one hand the seriousness of the voice credibly conveys the trauma of the group of people, but on the other its neutrality has the effect of disengaging it from its particular historical moment, many centuries in the past. The titters at the proposal of the 'Our Father' brings it almost to the contemporary moment in Ireland when the power of the Catholic Church is ebbing fast, and one implication of this is that the poem also relates the drama of Kinsella himself addressing the nation. That it is not just the relation of the Voyage of the First Kindred is confirmed by the speaker's statements of déjà vu: 'I had felt all this before',[24] 'Repeated memory / shifted among the green-necked confused waves',[25] although the precise implications of these are unclear. Could it be that it is the Mephisto figure again, unable to throw his voice all that much, hoodwinking us into buying the lie of Ireland's history? But the tone invites our credulity. The group gathers in one place, and the implication is that this is the source from which the Irish nation springs.

The kaleidoscopic use of lyric speaker is most apparent when moving from this poem to the next three. The title of the first, '38 Phœnix Street', is something of a jolt, its specificity contrasting strongly with what preceded it: that there is a street, that the street has a name, that the house has a number, all imply the existence of the larger structure of a nation with its cadastres and bureaucratic system, things that could not have been imagined by the First Kindred. These three poems in themselves are conventional family nostalgia, and it is only their position in the overall plan of *One* that allows the reader to pick up other signals from them. In one part of 'His Father's Hands', the child is told his family history going back as far as the eighteenth century:

> And some years before that time
> the Family came from somewhere around Tullow.
>
> Beyond that.[26]

These last two words, with an asterisk below the full stop, are like a vector pointing back to 'The Oldest Place', as flying buttresses suggest a vaulted roof which collapsed centuries before. Vast gaps in our knowledge of national history remain, but what endures is a strong sense of its continuity with more or less contemporary personal experience. The vector of 'His Father's Hands' meets with that of 'The Oldest Place' at some point outside the poem in the uninterrupted duration of national identity – something which Kinsella only intimates but does not describe. We are left in little doubt however that they do meet. The ease with which Kinsella appropriates the voices of the first colonisers confirms this. In the poem what fills this gap in collective memory is the land itself: the same place that Kinsella's family lives was also perhaps where megalithic builders laboured. Immediately following the asterisk above we have a landscape whose boulders have 'stabilized in menace'.[27] Kinsella's Ireland is not the golden island of earlier chauvinists: it is a violent place, subjecting its inhabitants to endless ordeals, with none of the consolations of romantic nationalism. But in his typology, the nation is something that lays such a great claim on our lives and identity that we are left with no other way of understanding ourselves. We are interwoven into the land itself, and to deny its deep rhythms in ourselves is a kind of hubris that is frequently associated with an Enlightenment rationality. This is particularly ironic given that the nation is more or less an Enlightenment ideology; such ironies, however, Kinsella leaves to the revisionists. The mocking figure that inducts us into the narratives of *One* may well be the conjuror of simulacra, but what cannot be gainsaid are the centuries of suffering and ordeal that are experienced in the one place: these are what ultimately binds the collective together and to the land.

Kinsella continues to publish further instalments in the Peppercanister series, but another of his major creative activities in the last few decades has been the revision and rearrangement of his poems, both in trade editions that gather together several Peppercanisters, and more importantly in the publication of his *Collected Poems* (the first by Oxford University Press in 1996 and the second by Carcanet Press in 2001). This is perhaps best exemplified by the changes that he has wrought upon 'Downstream', published in the eponymous collection in 1961. The poem began as *terza rima*, with a strong obvious allusion to Dante's *Inferno*, and in the most recent versions, Kinsella has tried to make that allusion weaker, both through typographic rearrangements and through excisions and changes in the rhyme scheme. Kinsella has stressed the importance of process and incompletion; 'Downstream', in its many versions, stands for this, and for a poet who has combined restlessness and scholarly exactitude, adventure and concerted and consistent effort throughout his career.

The pattern of John Montague's career is similar to Kinsella's in several respects, although the rhymes and stanzas of his first collections *Forms of Exile* (1958) and *Poisoned Land and Other Poems* (1961) were perhaps not as burnished as Kinsella's and the brief lyrics of these books were for the most part modest in their ambitions. They announce early on the theme of autobiography, and for much of his subsequent career he would use the episodes and figurations of his own life to explore his preoccupation with history; the books also contain some of his best love poems, a mode which would also continue to attract him. 'The Trout' gives us a restrained, delicate account of the poet watching a fish in a river:

> Flat on the bank I parted
> Rushes to ease my hands
> In the water without a ripple
> And tilt them slowly downstream
> To where he lay, tendril-light,
> In his fluid sensual dream.[28]

This tells of the poet's passage out of the human world into that of the fish: it is almost as if Montague's delicacy of observation allows him to apprehend something of the fish's dream, and this donates the hushed tone of the stanza. The poem ends with the speaker lunging, almost erotically, to whip the fish out of the river, and Montague expertly breaks the restraint, as passion and fear flare out: 'To this day I can / Taste his terror on my hands.'[29]

After these two books, Montague became preoccupied with ways to include larger stories within his poetry, especially that of the nation. Like Kinsella, he looked back to Modernist structures, especially those of William Carlos Williams and his epigones such as Robert Duncan and Charles Olson. He did not abandon the short traditional lyric as these Americans did, rather he learned ways to orchestrate it into larger patterns, as well as fit it in collages with other discourses, such as historical accounts, newspaper articles and memoirs. His finest achievement in this mode is *The Rough Field* (1972), which is about Montague's home in Co. Tyrone, the village of Garvaghey (from the Irish 'garbh' meaning 'rough' and 'achadh' meaning 'field'; it is also used in the phrase 'Achadh Airt' to mean Ireland). The book-length poem considers the colonial legacy of Ireland along with the rapid industrialisation that the country underwent in the 1960s. The result of the first was the sectarian strife in contemporary Northern Ireland; this impinges on the poem in the section entitled 'A New Siege', which is about the violence in Derry in 1969. The result of the second is the loss of what can loosely be called the mythopoetic imagination. The Irish, like many peoples of the Western world, view their land and culture in purely utilitarian terms. In one section the construction of a dance hall is figured vaguely as the betrayal of the Irish cultural tradition. The new monoculture, because blind, cannot comprehend the land it finds itself in. It violently appropriates that land and is, for Montague, a more formidable coloniser than the British. Steven Matthews remarks that the modernity of the poem's form is in tension with the outright nostalgia of its content. He continues: 'The thought of community, and of the achievement of some kind of harmony with it which might become attainable through poetry, is more a part of the *history* which the poem seeks both to dramatize and to criticize rather than to rest in.'[30] Montague is aware of this paradox, as evidenced by the last section of the poem. He acknowledges the good things that modernisation brings, and he is scathing about agrarian nostalgia ('Only a sentimentalist would wish / to see such degradation again'[31]). But he himself remains tightly in its grip, for all his resistance. *The Rough Field* describes what is receding from both the poet and Irish people, so that they can experience their abjectness more completely. It is a thoroughly didactic poetry, and like good didacticism it is varied in its arrangements – by times humorous, satirical and solemn.

The ideas of community and harmony mentioned by Matthews would, in Montague's later work, become atrophied in diametric opposites: anything new and industrial is described in negative terms, while images of nature require an almost devotional tone because they are associated with the mythical past. 'Bog Royal' compares the glorious heroic figures who once who walked the Bog of Allen in the east-centre of Ireland with the degenerate industrialism of the present in which the turf is stripped to fuel power stations. There is, no doubt, much to be lamented in the consumption of the Irish bogs to provide electricity, but the contrast between the present and the past is crude, and the reductiveness of the intellect at work creates images no more inventive than those to be found in guide-books.

Another book-length sequence followed in 1978, *The Great Cloak*, which retreats from the earlier panorama of public history to that of the poet's love life, or as he puts it in the introductory poem, 'As my Province burns / I sing of love.'[32] He charts the break-up of one relationship and the beginning of another, with much self-accusation about the first and expressions of delight in the second. Occasionally the sweetness of the latter is cloying: 'Honeycomb of reconciliation: / thigh melting into thigh / mouth into mouth, breast / turning against ribcage'.[33] But even at such moments, Montague is intent on the wider panorama and the poem ends with the remark that the couple make love as if 'this small house were / a paradigm of the universe'.[34] Much has been made of Montague's grand ambitions in *The Rough Field*, *The Great Cloak* and another book-length poem, *The Dead Kingdom* (1984), but none of these equals the achievement of earlier lyrics such as 'The Trout' and 'The Water Carrier'. On occasion, in his recent work he comes close to this, as, for instance, in 'Landing' from *Smashing the Piano* (2001). It could be argued that if Montague's Modernist collages fail, then they are no different from the Modernist collages of Williams and Hart Crane, who set themselves unrealisable aims. However, it is dismaying to see their failures rehearsed again, over forty years later. Rather than such repetition, there might have been development, of the kind, say, to be found in the work of several subsequent American poets such as A. R. Ammons and Jorie Graham.

The line in American poetry that leads from Williams and Ezra Pound, through Objectivism, is the most important influence on a younger generation of Irish experimental poets, among them Randolph Healy (b. 1956), Trevor Joyce (b. 1947), Maurice Scully (b. 1952) and Catherine Walsh (b. 1964). Williams's grand dictum was 'No ideas but in things', and in practice this entailed the abandonment of traditional verse-forms in order to find an organic poetic form that would let the thing, the object, come forth most clearly. Those things and objects were deliberately unromantic and unsymbolic, such as a wheelbarrow or a power plant. The presumption behind this poetry was, and is, that to employ rhyme and regular metre would somehow distort the representation of the object. For later generations, such distortion is complicit with imperial domination: by mastering his materials into tradition forms the poet replicates the imperial mastery of subject peoples. A further important aspect of this is the avoidance of totalising narratives, or privileged authorial viewpoints, as these, in the opinion of such poets and their critics, suppress the phenomenal abundance of the world in the name of ideology. The result is a poetics of chaos and conflict, texts which aim to reproduce the randomness of the world within their confines. In America, this poetics has been represented most strongly by Language writing, and in some of its manifestations is associated with oppositional Marxist politics (Williams had earlier used it to create a feisty patriotic poetry).

In the Irish context, poets such as Healy and Joyce use these strategies most frequently to subvert Irish nationalist ideology. However, this has not led to a cosmopolitan abandonment of native materials, rather, they often return to issues of Irish language and literature in an attempt to find alternative meanings there. Thus, the first section of Joyce's selected poems, *With the First Dream of Fire They Hunt the Cold: A Body of Work 1966–2000* (2001), is comprised of *The Poems of Sweeney Peregrine*, a reworking of the mediæval Irish text of *Buile Suibhne*. These poets will often turn to stock themes of Irish nationalist poetry, such as the landscape, and deliberately employ a factual, scientific tone; this is done with the aim of resisting the distortions of nationalist narratives and attending more acutely to the lie of the land.

Healy's work, especially, is often mordantly satirical in his treatment of nationalism. 'Anthem' renders the Irish text of the national anthem, 'Amhrán na bhFiann', phonetically into hilarious, surreal English ('Sheen a fin with oil / A tall failed owl egg roaring', etc.[35]); the effect is similar to Jimi Hendrix's version of 'The Star-Spangled Banner'. '(The) Republic of Ireland' is comprised of lines which are anagrams of the title itself:

> her lie-lined tub of crap
> her pallid beef in court
>
> her pro-life bit unlaced
> her fluid celibate porn
> price trouble in fleadh
> fertile blue chip radon
>
> belief in carrot upheld
> birth pill feared on cue
>
> faith libel prurience
> able filth in procedure[36]

The second line refers to the scandals of the Beef Tribunals in the 1990s; the third refers to the anti-abortion campaigners who are designated 'pro-life'; a *fleadh* is a festival of traditional Irish dancing and singing; 'blue chip' might glancingly refer to the massive investment by large multinationals in Ireland, which reached its climax in the 1990s. What began as a word-game becomes revelatory of some of the most important social and cultural shifts in the country, as profound in its implications as Montague's explorations of mythology. Healy compares the mechanism of language with reality, and in this case finds that they correspond quite snugly, although in a way unlikely to satisfy the chauvinist.

Healy uses this method of comparison to broach other related themes. In 'Envelopes' he compares the neural mechanisms of the brain with its immediate environment in order to demonstrate how impossible the former's job is. The human subject, the mind, the soul is often considered the bedrock of systems of ethics and law; however, Healy shows it to be unsubstantial and certainly unable to bear the weight of such large systems. In this, he harmonises with Language writing along with philosophers such as Jacques Lacan and Michel Foucault, who are also suspicious of grand claims made for the ego.

What is striking, however, is that many of Healy's poems are straightforwardly and sweetly familial: his real imaginative base is not phenomenological exploration of the above variety, but songs of love and sadness evoked by domestic experiences. The dedication to his selected poems goes as follows: 'To my wife, Louise, and our children, Margaret, Florence, Genevieve, Beatrice and Theodore', and these same names are repeatedly mentioned in the poems. The bourgeois subject, in one of its more engaging manifestations, proves to be alive and well in these poems, despite the deconstructive strategies deployed against it elsewhere. Of course, one should not expect the same consistency from a poet as one does from, say, a scientist or philosopher: some of the glories of literature emerge from the writer's blithe disregard for this particular quality. But Healy's inconsistency is indicative of an imaginative failure to find the images and rhetorical resources to link the preoccupations of family, nation, language and phenomenology. Even his long poem, 'Arbor Vitæ', which ranges from his daughter's deafness to the development of sign language in Ireland to national politics, fails in this way, and ultimately is just a collection of essayistic fragments.

The same fascination with language and its rhetorical structures is to be found in the work of Maurice Scully, but what was fissiparous in Healy is more coherent in Scully. However, such a statement needs to be qualified immediately. Coherence implies structure, order and plan, and these are what Scully programmatically avoids. (The back cover of one of his books has this instruction: 'Be prepared: don't take a map.'[37]) Although he works in large orchestral structures (his most recent project, *Things that Happen*, might possibly run to 1,000 pages and was begun in 1982), he is ever anxious not to distort the raw material of his experience in the making of his poetry. He has referred to this as the artist's necessary humility,[38] and he often defines it in contrast to what he calls the 'Gem School' of Irish poetry – brief, beautifully structured poems which take as their subject rural and family life ('Mumsy and Popsy down on the farm show my Roots are Real & deck me out with Colourful Relatives I can't wait to write about. A really strange hand-me-down Identikit'[39]). The animus here is clearly against poets such as Patrick Kavanagh, John Montague and Seamus Heaney, and it demonstrates Scully's distance from mainstream Irish poetry. His influences are Charles Olson, not Patrick Kavanagh; Louis Zukofsky, not Padraic Colum.

Such oppositions lead us to think that Scully is an internationalist to Heaney's 'rooted man', and this is misleading. Just as Trevor Joyce engages with *Buile Suibhne* and Catherine Walsh introduces Irish words in her work, Scully was educated for the most part through the Irish language and this has left a profound mark on his writing. Phrases in Irish recur throughout his poetry (especially from the poems of Seán Ó Ríordáin) and he attends to them as part of the acoustic environment of his life in Ireland. Whereas some poets of the 'Gem School' have no scruples about translating Irish poetry without any knowledge of the language, Scully's involvement is more serious. He refuses to literalise and convey meaning mechanically, but rather explores how Irish resonates in the English language, how it rubs shoulders with English words and linguistic structures, how it has affected his own life: 'Bits stay in place. / Bits recombine. Bits underpin then vanish in the argument, / *fite fuaite* . . . *An tosach, ar deireadh.*'[40] Here Scully attends to the way the Irish words persist: like all language they are *fite fuaite* (firmly interwoven) – both *ina chéile* (with each other) and with the lives of Irish people to varying degrees.[41]

The second part of *Things that Happen* is *Livelihood* (2004), and the very title hints at the autobiographical nature of Scully's work. The locales range from Ireland to Lesotho and the only thing connecting them is the fact that Scully has lived in both places. One gets to know certain facts about Scully's life from the poetry (that he has often been in debt, the names of his family, an accident that occurred to his son when he was five, etc.), but he is not a Confessional poet. These circumstances are presented so that Scully can ground his explorations of the human mind at work amidst the weather, the sunlight, the vegetation, the buildings. 'Point', from *Livelihood*, brings together some of these concerns:

> Love plants peace. Not a catalogue of manipulative
> fairytales. The sky gives back. Gable-shape, tree-lines.
> The way the sunlight is, the way it comes down
> through leaves, and spider-silk gleams and
> doesn't suddenly, between lightly moving branches
> in the morning to be still. The order of the stones

in the wall beside the yellow dust-track magnified,
the insect ready, then away over and through a light
dustfall in a sideways breeze gone but, very small,
is noted. *Gósta garbh-Bhéarla*: brief spillage of
birdsong. The first second. The others are different.
The others are written down. *Ah whoom* goes the
orchestra, *spang* goes the Giant's buckle, *wisha-wisha*
go the trees in the grove. Hope, it is hope, and a glow
without a name, Mary, envelops all the places we've
ever lived in, been to, but never – *let the cloning
begin!* – presumed to own.[42]

The abstraction of the first lines are grounded immediately in notes about what the light is like at that particular time, in that particular place. '*Gósta garbh-Bhéarla*' is a stock phrase meaning 'an uncouth smattering of English', and this might be a self-deprecating description of Scully's poetry *in toto*, or the noise of the birds (raising the comic idea that although the Irish themselves no longer speak Irish, the birds might). Then he concentrates on certain sound effects (with the persistence of Irish in '*wisha-wisha*', a Hiberno-English murmur of consolation). And then we are back with abstraction again at the end, as a couple try to perceive some meaning in the life they've shared together. Scully is uneasy, however, about the way that the closure of the poem is pushing him towards emotional grandiloquence. It is not that he dislikes the consolations of the latter – he is clearly drawn to them – but that he must cross-hatch them with something humorous; hence the sound bite about cloning which suggests that we abjure emotional authenticity at such moments and become the clones of others. As he has commented in interview, 'Underneath it all I'm trying to work out how in this truly terrible contemporary world, one can be lyrical, without being trivial.'[43] It is a comment that resonates through Irish poetry, inviting realignments and reconsiderations; we will look at some of these in the final two chapters of this book.

Chapter 7

Ireland's Empire

Richard Murphy, Derek Mahon, Michael Longley

In 1889, the British South Africa Company received its charter from Queen Victoria. Its aim was to secure control over most of south-central Africa, and its especial interest was gold and copper mining rights in the area. In order to make these resources profitable, the company had to put in place the infrastructures of the modern state, such as a police force, a banking system and a government. It was one of Britain's last significant colonial efforts, organised for the most part by Cecil Rhodes, an English-born adventurer who had risen from poverty to become one of the most important men in the British Empire. However, within three decades the Empire was falling apart, and the African states that it left in its wake were transferred from the control of white minorities to black governments by the 1960s and 1970s. It was a brief episode in the history of the continent.

One small part of that episode was played by Richard Murphy's father, Sir William Lindsay Murphy. He had spent a distinguished career in the colonial service, having been Mayor of Colombo in Sri Lanka and ending as Governor of the Bahamas. As Murphy tells us in a note to the poem 'The God Who Eats Corn', which is about his father's experience in Africa, when his father retired he settled in Southern Rhodesia, and with his wife and Murphy's aunts, he established a school for farm workers, in a situation where the general tendency was to keep the natives illiterate.[1] The poem generates itself out of several conflicting impulses: admiration for his father's strength of character and idealism, disdain for the rapacious colonisers and awe at the natural beauty of the African continent. Of his parents and aunt who worked in the school, he remarks in the note that they tried to mitigate a bad situation, but he also is aware that they were complicit with the Empire's coercive practices, and in general adhered to Kipling's idea that the white man's burden is to civilise the lesser races of the world.

There is a further complexity here, one that is emblematic not just for the three poets I am concerned with in this chapter but for the hybrid nature of Irish poetry in English throughout the last two centuries of the previous millennium. In the same note to 'The God Who Eats Corn', Murphy remarks that his 'father's paternal grandfather had emerged from ignorance and poverty in Ireland through the Carlow village school of which he became master in 1840', and the last quatrain of the poem also reaches back into the family past, as the imperial colonised echoes two generations behind the imperial coloniser

In his memoir, *The Kick* (2002), Murphy comments on the way family history inspires heroism and sacrifice in the service of the Empire in strange ways, and here the memory of Murphy's grandfather makes Murphy's father stalwart in the face of adversity. But it takes the poet-son to reach back a further generation to that 'ignorance and poverty', which also most likely marks the conversion of the Murphy family from Roman Catholicism to Protestantism, from imperial victim to imperial agent. (The name Murphy itself is the Anglicisation of the old Irish name, Ó Murchadha, which means 'sea battler'.) The British Empire, like all empires before it, could never have been ruled only by Englishmen raised in the shires: it had to create imperial subjects in its colonies who would then take up positions of authority. Another example, one that outstrips Murphy's father, though not of Irish stock, was Horatio Herbert Kitchener (1850–1916), who was born in Listowel in Co. Kerry and went on to conquer Sudan, command the British forces in the South African War and mobilise Britain in response to World War I.

The Protestant experience in Ireland was polarised in the twentieth century by the foundation of the Irish state in 1922, which left the Protestant Ascendancy in southern Ireland in a minority, but still with large holdings of land and a residual respect not unlike the English respect for aristocracy. In the North, however, Protestants were in a majority and, in class terms, were on a lower rung than the southern Protestants, for the most part involved in industry and trades. Though these people had been on the island for more than three centuries, Irish nationalist history continued to view them as somehow alien to the country, and to view families of Murphy's kind as traitors. This has engendered complex responses from poets from Protestant backgrounds such as Murphy, Michael Longley and Derek Mahon. They insist on their identity as Irish poets, while resisting the idea that literature is conditioned by the nationalist agenda. As we will see in the next chapter, Seamus Heaney searches for originary myths of Irishness in order to stake an imaginative claim on the land in opposition to British occupation. This nationalist slant is in contrast to the approaches of the three poets here. To describe the different ways that these poets do not fit the nationalist agenda is to go a long way to understanding their importance in Irish poetry; furthermore, by acknowledging these poets' place in English poetry and their engagement with the theme of the British Empire and its decline, a richer and more complex idea of Irish poetry reveals itself, one that has been marginalised by nineteenth-century criticism to the more recent phenomenon of Field Day, the cultural co-operative set up by Heaney, Seamus Deane, Brian Friel and others. The usual way of viewing work by poets of Protestant background is to admit it a place, somewhat patronisingly, within the poetry of the Irish nation. These poets do something of greater magnitude: they offer ways for the poetry of Ireland to become cathected by the wider issues (poetic and historical) of Europe and the world.

Richard Murphy was born in 1927 in Co. Galway, and six weeks after his birth moved with his family to Sri Lanka (then Ceylon), where he remained for five years. He was educated in Wellington College and Oxford University, where he was taught by Belfastman C. S. Lewis, and lived for many years in the west of Ireland. There he renovated an old Galway fishing vessel, the *Ave Maria*, and took tourists out sailing on her. His first collection, *The Archæology of Love* (1955), was published in a small print run by the Dolmen Press in Ireland. His next book, *Sailing to an Island* (1963), reprinted many of the poems of the first book and can be considered his first principal publication. The title poem narrates the difficulties encountered on a brief voyage to Clare Island in Clew Bay in Co. Mayo. As in the passage from 'The God Who Eats Corn', there is an enraptured description of the natural world, and there is also a subtle negotiation underway between Murphy, the speaker of the poem, and the Mayo boatmen. Murphy's position in their world is unclear: he is vaguely aristocratic, English, seemingly not of the native soil; and yet, of course, he is just as native as themselves. They are brought together by the shared danger of the storm and the poem concludes with all safely in a pub: 'Later, I reach a room, where the moon stares / Through a cobwebbed window. The tide has ebbed, / Boats are careened in the harbour. Here is a bed.'[2] The last sentence is at once both comic (one imagines him falling down a little drunkenly on the bed after the full-stop) and comforting (the bed is his first foothold in the community of the island). The ordeal and its conclusion perhaps vouchsafe the long poem 'The Cleggan Disaster' from the same collection about a fishing accident that occurred in 1927 in which twenty-five men were lost at sea (in that poem, Murphy takes the voice of one of the fishermen to narrate the story). Several of the poems of *Sailing to an Island* are about outsiders coming to the west of Ireland (Ludwig Wittgenstein, Theodore Roethke), and this is indicative of Murphy's continuing tentative relationship with the place and its traditions.

Bernard O'Donoghue has argued that 'it was [Murphy's] poetic language that connected Yeats to the major school of Irish poetry in the last third of the twentieth century', and states how it employs the Irish vernacular along with varieties of a direct classical style that has a long provenance in English poetry;[3]

this mixture makes the poetry answerable to its Irish material and yet also able to exploit all the registers available to an Anglophone poet. Such hybridity was developed in Murphy's next book, *The Battle of Aughrim* (1968), with its long title poem about the battle of 1691 which decided the fate of Ireland for over two centuries. As Murphy has stated, his own ancestors fought on both sides of the battle.[4] Terence Brown characterises Murphy's particular approach to these historical events with exactitude:

> the disturbing question with which the poem opens, 'Who owns the land where musket-balls are buried?', reverberates through it towards a doubtful present. That's not a question a dispossessed native would ask; nor is it one that a planted occupant dare ask as he validates possession by work and improvement. But it is the sort of question a poet perplexed about his contemporary social position can, particularly when he knows that in attempting an answer he will summon up an impressive array of ancestors to help authenticate his own identity.[5]

The poem is a sequence of short lyrics that begins in the present, with the question 'Who owns the land?', and in its course shows the complexity of any possible answer. With acuity and tenderness it registers the twentieth-century divisions in Ireland that can still be traced back to the Battle of Aughrim, from the War of Independence in the second decade to the Orange marches and sectarian violence of the poem's present. It then moves to episodes within the battle itself and concludes with accounts of the fall-out of the battle on Irish history. But for all its historical accuracy and colour, the poem is, as Murphy makes clear at the outset, a kind of autobiography writ large. In one section, he sketches out a large range of events and images and then funnels them beautifully in the last line into his very veins, saying all this begins in his blood.[6]

Yet it would be wrong to say that Murphy uses Irish history for autobiography; rather the complexity of an individual resonates with the complexity of his country's history. Murphy's own bisexuality is thus explored on a national canvas: it is of note that of all the heroes of the uprising in 1916, he dwells on Roger Casement, whose homosexuality was used to discredit the nationalist cause. Murphy also depicts episodes within the battle itself that display the close connection between war's awful violence and untrammelled sexual desire. In 'Prisoner', a young boy is caught by the victorious Protestant army, stripped naked and made to kneel before the soldiers:

> 'Pretty boy.' 'Castrate the fucker!'
> 'Let the papist kiss my flute.'
> 'Toss a coin for the privilege to bugger . . .'

> He cries like a girl. 'Finish him off.'
> 'No, keep him alive to be our slave.'
> 'Shove a sword up his hole.' They laugh.[7]

As the boy loses his masculinity in the passage, we are reminded of Murphy's account of his own christening at the beginning of 'The Battle of Aughrim', where he is baptised by two clergymen, one of whom is deaf and has not heard the given name properly: 'He thinks I'm a girl. / The other bellows: "It's a boy, you fool!"'[8] The sexual confusion that the poem draws out in its account of Irish history is deeply subversive of nationalist accounts of the struggle for Irish freedom in which strongly masculine heroes fight bravely against the oppressor in order to protect the honour of their homeland, which is often figured as a beautiful young woman.

Murphy's work, then, was prophetic of much of the historical revisionism of the last couple of decades of the twentieth century which drew attention to the ellipses and gaps in nationalist history. Yet his poetry displays such historical fragmentation not in a purely critical or negative way, but in order to show what must be confronted before a reconciliation is reached. In 'Little Hunger' Murphy tells how he went to a dilapidated famine village in order to get stones for his new house:

> Once mine, I'd work on their dismemberment,
>   Threshold, lintel, wall;
> And pick a hearthstone from a rubble fragment
>   To make it integral.[9]

Murphy relishes the torsion of destructive and creative forces in the act of house-building. The poet both mourns the victims of the Famine in the 1840s and remains optimistic (witness the beautiful force he gives to the word 'integral' here at the end of the poem).

'Little Hunger' is from the collection *High Island* (1974), which begins with 'Seals at High Island', a poem whose splendour cannot be conveyed in quotation, and which has little to do with Murphy's themes of Empire and autobiography. In two other poems we see how his parents' didactic impulse was passed on to him. 'The Writing Lesson' is about his mother or aunt's attempt to teach a young Sri Lankan literacy and Christianity combined; and 'The Reading Lesson' is about Murphy's own attempts to teach a fourteen-year-old Connemara boy how to read. The benign imperialism of both transactions is not lost on Murphy, and it draws his attention to the English language itself as a transformative instrument of empire. He asks the boy whether he wants to read or not and the boy replies: 'I'll be the same man whatever I do.'[10] Murphy, who is so acutely aware of the way that empires make their subjects out of language, knows this to be wrong, and the knowledge possibly retards his own teaching. The boy, in the end, does not become literate, and he disappears out of the poem, just as one element of Murphy's own identity was lost to him when his family on his father's side switched from Irish-speaking Roman Catholicism in the nineteenth century.

The last important book of Murphy's career to date is *The Price of Stone* (1985), comprised of fifty sonnets which, with the exception of the final sonnet, take the voice of buildings that were important in some way to Murphy's life. The buildings address him directly – they guffaw, cajole, remind and assuage by turns – and in this way the book continues Murphy's poetic autobiography. To accommodate oblique references to his upbringing, his experience as husband and father, as homosexual, as son of colonisers, and to Irish history, his main device is the pun. In the passage below, he throws his voice and lets the men's public toilet in Piccadilly Circus talk:

> The public servant of men's private parts,
> Plain clothed in the underground below Eros,
> With white glazed stalls, and see-through mirror arts,
> I plumb our language empire's omphalos.[11]

It would take much comment to unpack the contrapuntal nuances that Murphy keeps suspended in the air in the first quatrain of this sonnet. A public servant is more usually a civil servant, and the slight shift suggests that the odd civil servant might visit the toilet for a homosexual dalliance. They are also servants of the British Empire, or what is left of it, and that imperial resonance is picked up in the final line. 'Plain clothed' suggests the danger of plain-clothed detectives out to catch those committing the crime of sodomy. Elsewhere, Murphy takes the voice of the gate lodge of his family estate:

> Two Irish yews, prickly green, poisonous,
> Divide my entrance, tapering in trim gloom.
> Old rookery buildings, pitch-pine resinous,
> Wake up shell-shocked, welcoming you back home.
>
>   . . .
>
> I face my forebear's relic, a neat sty
> That hovelled with his brogue some grateful clod
> Unearthed by famine; and I hear go by
> Your souper choir school voice defrauding God.[12]

The addressee is Murphy, and this suggests the homonym of 'yew' – Murphy's Irishness is divided: born and bred in that country, yet not of its Catholic majority. The soupers offered food during the Famine in return for conversion to Protestantism. The 'shell-shocked' of the fourth line glancingly refers to those members of Murphy's family who fought for Britain in the Great War. Pun and catachresis are then Murphy's methods in this book for orchestrating, not resolving, the confusions of his self and nation. The last poem in the sequence is entitled 'Natural Son' and recounts the birth of Murphy's child. That he speaks in his own voice in the poem marks the end of his own story and the beginning of another, as Murphy himself becomes something of an edifice in the subsequent life of his child. The poem is also noteworthy for the way that it drops his favoured devices of pun and catachresis, and opts for a mode of address that is more direct: 'This day you crave so little, we so much / For you to live, who need our merest touch.'[13] But there is a denotational uncertainty in the very title of the poem: a 'natural son' can be both a child that is actually born of one in wedlock (as opposed to children who are adopted), and a child born to you out of wedlock (illegitimate, in an older usage). So even at such a moment of physical and emotional intensity, when lineage is extended, there is ambiguity.

Derek Mahon was born in Belfast in 1941, where he attended the Royal Belfast Academical Institution, then went on to study French, English and Philosophy at Trinity College, Dublin. There he met Michael Longley, and later Eavan Boland. His first collection was *Night-Crossing* (1968), which was followed by *Lives* (1972) and *The Snow Party* (1975). Many of his poems were gathered in *Poems 1962–1978* (1979), and *The Hunt by Night* (1982) brings Mahon's first phase to a close. The poems of these books balance finely wrought structures of rhyme and metre against an ironic despair of cosmic proportions. The tone is elegant and detached, and yet at the same time there is an undertow of mourning for the world's lost possibilities. In particular, Mahon deplores the way Western technology has alienated humans from their environment; this sentiment often concludes poems, as though the realisation chokes all his witty ironies into silence. For instance, the subjects of 'The Banished Gods' 'sit out the centuries / In stone, water, / And the hearts of trees, / Lost in a reverie of their own natures'.[14] In such a passage, Mahon clearly relishes the opportunity of rural lyricism, but in the stanza that immediately follows, this is contrasted with humanity, whose wisdom has now degenerated to 'a five-minute silence at moonrise'.[15] These are the last mournful and appalled words of the poem.

Another important feature of this phase is the idea of the poet as a homeless wanderer through the world. Much Irish poetry stresses the historical and emotional attachments of place: here a significant battle might have occurred, there a family homestead might have stood. The implication of Mahon's work is that such attachments are at best problematic, at worst sentimentalisations that prevent us from perceiving the radical homelessness of humanity. Peter Denman has remarked that in successive revisions of some of his poems, Mahon has changed the place names, as if to say that such names are 'equivalents in the gazetteer of anywheres'.[16] Mahon himself has worked in Britain, the USA and Ireland, in a variety of jobs ranging from *Vogue* journalist to scriptwriter to professor of creative writing, and has eschewed any longstanding institutional affiliation. It is hard then not to see that restlessness as an expression of restlessness expressed in his poetry.

The lines of his poems seem to echo in a global rather than a provincial or national arena. Thus in 'Sunday Morning', the poet finds himself in the former centre of the British Empire, London, observing the last phase of its decay:

> Black diplomats with gorgeous wives,
> Promenading, notice the natives
> Dozing beside the palace gates –
> Old ladies under wide straw-hats
> Who can remember *Chu Chin Chow*
> And Kitchener. Exhausted now
> By decades of retrenchment, they
> Wait for the rain at close of play.[17]

This is an elegy for the end of the British Empire with its powerful figures such as Cecil Rhodes and Horatio Kitchener, an elegy of the same kind as Murphy's 'The God Who Eats Corn' (*Chu Chin Chow* (1923) was a silent movie based on a story from the Arabian Nights, a classic piece of imperial orientalism). The voice is neither that of disappointed coloniser nor embittered colonised, but is equable and, in parts, amused (namely, the comedy of the black diplomats viewing the English much in the same way they themselves were viewed by the English a century or so earlier).

Mahon's poetry works hard to figure the speaker as a cosmopolitan *poète maudit*, more a European poet than an Irish one. But there is a contradictory impulse at work, which proclaims Northern Ireland, where he grew up, as a place which might perhaps be of more importance than others. Fran Brearton suggests that Mahon 'regards English pieties with a perspective informed by his experience of Ulster' as his Ulster Protestant upbringing makes him remember episodes in British history that the British themselves have forgotten, with the exception of the old ladies of this passage.[18] Also, one of Mahon's first important poems was written in memory of Louis MacNeice, 'In Carrowdore Churchyard', and in it Mahon claims a Northern Irish poetic precursor. Of course, in his turn MacNeice was a cosmopolitan poet whose themes, as we saw, embraced the historical fate of Europe, and was not intent on making a profound connection with the 'blood-music' of the province. In a review of the selected prose of the Ulster poet John Hewitt, Mahon remarks:

> The Ulster writer, says Hewitt, 'must be a *rooted* man. He must carry the native tang of his idiom like the native dust on his sleeve; otherwise he is an airy internationalist, thistledown, a twig in a stream . . . He must know where he comes from and where he is; otherwise how can he tell where he wishes to go?' This is a bit tough on thistledown; and, speaking as a twig in a stream, I feel there's a certain harshness, a dogmatism, at work there.[19]

Hewitt's description fits the aspiration of Heaney much better, whereas Mahon will agree to be an Ulster writer only if Ulster can comprehend the world. Clearly, 'Sunday Morning' presents London as the world in small laid out before 'the mild theoptic eye', as Mahon has it in another poem.[20]

'Tractatus' provides another good example of the delicacy and complexity of that comprehension. Mahon begins by quoting Ludwig Wittgenstein's dictum that 'The world is everything that is the case', or in other words, the world is everything that can be expressed logically in language. Mahon concludes the brief poem with an image of the sun sinking into the sea at nightfall and ends with the question: 'who would question that titanic roar, / The steam rising wherever the edge may be?'[21] That Mahon can set up beautiful harmonies in a few lines of poetry is amply demonstrated by this. The edge of his poetic world is uncertain, and might never even be reached. But a 'titanic roar' with steam rising from it also strongly evokes the RMS *Titanic*, which sank in 1912, and was built in the Protestant shipyard of Harland and Wolff in Belfast (where Mahon's grandfather worked as a foreman). Brearton notes how that event 'has acquired a significance out of all proportion either to the scale of the disaster, or to its economic and political effect on the British Empire',[22] and more locally how the shipbuilding 'was (for the Protestant worker employed there), a tangible manifestation of the virtues of the union'.[23] (In an earlier poem, 'After the Titanic', Mahon takes the voice of an officer or engineer of the ship who is a *maudit*, haunted for the rest of his life because of the poor part he played in the event.) Mahon does not bring in this Belfast resonance purely for autobiographical purposes – the *Titanic* was an example of the overreaching nature of modern technology. The concluding image is paradoxical: it is at once a statement of extensive poetic range and a warning to civilisation not to exceed itself. The poem is not about Belfast, instead it makes an important event in its history ramify with wider concerns.

After *The Hunt by Night*, Mahon did not publish another full collection of poems for thirteen years. His loss of nerve as a writer then became one of the main themes of *The Hudson Letter* (1995), the other being his concern for the homeless people of the world. The themes come together in section II, which has Mahon sitting at night in his New York apartment waiting for something to happen. He has just made his coffee and listened to the news when interrupted by the voice of 'some psycho / [who] sends up a stream of picturesque abuse' from the street below.[24] As the poem progresses from this point, Mahon and his readers realise that this interruption is fortuitous, that the poet, by letting the voices of the marginalised into the poem, will recover his lost nerve. This growing awareness that the psycho's voice is, in fact, his own, that he too is homeless, a 'resident alien' in New York or anywhere, then becomes the poem's driving force, taking us to Chinatown, Key West and back in time to New York as seen by W. H. Auden, a young Irish immigrant girl and W. B. Yeats's father, John B. Yeats. What also emerges is that there are two senses to the poet's homelessness: on the personal level, he is separated from his family, and, on the artistic level, he is the poet working on the margins of society, a scion of the *maudits*, who hectors the modern 'world of internet and fax, / a still-thriving military-industrial complex, / situational ethics, exonerative 12-step programs, / health fascism, critical theory and "smart" bombs'.[25] The idiom of these poems is very different from Mahon's earlier style: it is written in loosely rhymed pentameter couplets that allow him to be more discursive than the earlier complex stanzaic forms did. They resemble diaries and include a lot of information about Mahon's day-to-day life and indeed of the consequences of his break with his wife.

Mahon's next volume is entitled *The Yellow Book* (1997) and is written in the same mode. It takes as its theme *fin de siècle* decadence, rhyming the end of the twentieth century with the end of the nineteenth (the title of the collection is the same as that of a quarterly magazine edited by Aubrey Beardsley from 1894 to 1897, famed for its dandyism). Mahon despairs of the contemporary world and turns his irony on it mercilessly. Essentially, the book picks up the note of disgust at Western civilisation first sounded in a poem like 'The Banished Gods' and makes it resound in a larger, more discursive structure. But whereas in the earlier poem, Mahon mentioned the reverie of the gods and concluded with disgusted irony, *The Yellow Book* inverts this order. After the jeremiad has spent itself, Mahon turns away from the contemporary world to view a different prospect. These are the book's concluding lines: 'I dreamed last night of a blue Cycladic dawn, / a lone figure pointing to the horizon, / again the white islands shouting, "Come on; come on!"'[26] (The second line here was omitted from the text of the *Collected Poems*.) The danger for Mahon is to keep rehearsing this farewell ('Resistance Days', which is the opening poem of *Harbour Lights* (2005), approaches its conclusion with a similar gesture); in other poems of this period, such as 'New Wave' and 'A Swim in Co. Wicklow', he is finding ways to write poems of that 'blue Cycladic dawn'. Certainly, these two poems rank among his finest and they notably omit strong auto-biographical elements and complaints about contemporary civilisation. The beautiful exhilaration of the opening of 'A Swim' announces a completely new and convincing note, freshened by the natural world, sharp in its observations.

Mahon's work as a translator of the francophone poets Philippe Jaccottet and Paul Valéry has indubitably helped him in this direction. I will discuss his work as translator in chapter 8, but here I wish to remark that in both these francophone poets Mahon has found a particular luminescence. Valéry's poem, 'Le Cimetière marin', which Mahon translated, takes its motive impulse from the play of light on the surrounding landscape, and Mahon's gravitation towards the same zone draws out his finest poetic gifts. Terence Brown describes this world 'as essentially calm, ahistorical, touched mysteriously by the numinous in the natural order of things' and says that for Mahon '[n]o place, however invested with luminous intensity or emotional depth . . . is bulwark against pain and loss which in Mahon's sense of things, is a given of the European and global inheritance'.[27] That said, the splendours of *Harbour Lights* are those poems where Mahon registers the shoddiness of contemporary culture only in passing, and reserves his imaginative energies, not for lament or complaint, but to concentrate on the transformations of the natural world.

Michael Longley was born in Belfast in 1939 to English parents and has lived in that city since. Like Derek Mahon, he was raised a Protestant and attended the Royal Belfast Academical Institution. His father was a veteran of two world wars and he has said in interview that 'Sometimes I feel Irish, sometimes I feel British, often neither.'[28] He read Classics at Trinity College Dublin, where he met Derek Mahon, and also Edna Broderick, who would later become his wife and one of the outstanding critics of Irish literature. He has remarked that as a child he would walk out of an English home on to Irish streets,[29] and this juxtaposition of cultures has informed much of his poetry. He is deeply indebted to the English poetic tradition, especially the line which stretches from Edward Thomas (1878–1917), Keith Douglas (1920–44) to Philip Larkin (1922–85); at the same time, his poetry has engaged with the Troubles in Northern Ireland in a profound way, and his response to them has been wide-ranging and acute. It should, however, be noted that Longley rarely writes directly about the violence that Northern Ireland has experienced over the last three decades of the twentieth century. As we will see, in this matter he goes by indirection. Fran Brearton has remarked that 'Longley's work, like MacNeice's, disrupts both the stereotypes of an "Irish poet" and a "Poet from Northern Ireland".'[30] Paradoxically, disruption is what generates literary tradition, and the paradoxes of Michael Longley's poetry – like that of Yeats, Heaney, Kinsella and Muldoon – place him at the heart of the English poetic tradition as well as the Irish poetic tradition; more fundamentally, in a similar way to Mahon and Murphy, his work clearly shows that those two traditions are one.

But for all this talk of disruption, Longley, like many poets of his generation, is traditional in the matter of poetic technique. With only the slightest overstatement, he has remarked that every line in his first collection, *No Continuing City* (1969), is rhymed and many of its poems employ the intricate stanzaic structures of the seventeenth-century English Metaphysical poets, especially George Herbert. The book also announces many of the themes that Longley would amplify and explore further in his subsequent career: there are love poems (Longley has joked at readings that he is probably the only poet to write love poems to a critic); there are also precise descriptions of the metamorphoses of the natural world; there is Greek legend, as well as poems about his father's involvement in World War I and the West of Ireland. Above all, there is in evidence Longley's sinuous ability to combine these elements in startling ways; this ability developed in tandem with his poetry, and might even be called its main generating force, so that by the 1990s a poem about the West of Ireland could spill amazingly through ancient Greece, World War I and the Troubles, without any sense of dislocation.

The publication of the book came after Heaney's first publication, *Death of a Naturalist* (1966), and Derek Mahon's *Night-Crossing* (1968), and together these three publications constitute the beginning of what has been called the Northern Irish Renaissance, when three spectacular talents emerged at the same time as the Troubles broke out in Northern Ireland (soon after, Paul Muldoon followed with the publication of *New Weather* in 1973). All three poets were conservative in their use of rhyme and metre, and were drawn especially to the New Critical ideal of the poem as ironic, detached and elegant in its technique. In interview Longley has commented on how this poetic model gave them a means to deal with the explosive material of the Troubles.[31] In the next chapter I will discuss the political pressure on Heaney to write a more partisan poetry, and in this Heaney was no exception. Longley also refused to write poems that celebrated Unionism or the Orangemen, but instead chose an ideal of æsthetic balance and nuance. This might seem escapist to some, but it is underwritten by the moral conviction that the poet cannot align himself with paramilitary movements, that to do so would be to betray the art itself.

One effect of this was to create a kind of non-sectarian coterie between poets from both the Catholic and Protestant sides, or at least the desire to create it.[32] This coterie joined together poets who would otherwise be separated by the religious affiliations they grew up with. Thus Longley's second book, *An Exploded View* (1972), is dedicated to Derek Mahon, Seamus Heaney and James Simmons (1933–2001), referred to familiarly as 'Derek, Seamus & Jimmy'. (Heaney's collection of 1972, *Wintering Out*, is dedicated in turn to Longley, and the singer David Hammond, and Mahon's collection *Night-Crossing* is dedicated to the Longleys.) The use of first names, and even a familiar form, is noteworthy for the way that it creates a sense of intimacy between the four poets. This intimacy is born out of the men's shared vocation as poets at the very moment when they are confronted with awful sectarian violence. This is particularly clear in the letter-poems of the collection. One addressed to Derek Mahon begins thus:

> And did we come into our own
> When, minus muse and lexicon,
> We traced in August sixty-nine
> Our imaginary Peace Line
> Around the burnt-out houses of
> The Catholics we'd scarcely loved,
> Two Sisyphuses come to budge
> The sticks and stones of an old grudge . . .[33]

1969 saw many fierce riots between Protestants, Catholics and the security forces. The Peace Line is paradoxically the name for a wall that divided Catholics and Protestants living in proximity to one another to limit the opportunities of violent confrontation. 'Line' also has a poetic resonance, and here Longley intimates that their ambition as poets was somehow to create a new peace line that would move the 'sticks and stones' of eight hundred years of sectarian hatred. This is a poem from one poet from a Protestant background to another, and it registers Longley's allegiance to those who might tentatively be called his people (namely, 'The Catholics we scarcely loved'). He will never abandon that allegiance, but neither will he allow it to distort a more important allegiance to his art and its pacific moral imperative, with attendant values of craftsmanship, balance and solidarity with other poets, regardless of their backgrounds.

The book also contains one of Longley's anthology pieces, 'Wounds', which begins by telling us of Longley's father's memories of World War I. The soldiers cries of defiance ('Fuck the Pope!' . . . 'Give 'em one for the Shankill!'[34]) are cries that might still be heard in Northern Ireland today, but here they are less an expression of sectarian hatred than a fearful shout of desperation as many of the soldiers go to their deaths at the hands of Germans. Indeed, many of the Germans soldiers might not have disagreed with this opinion of the Pope. In this way Longley deflects sectarian hatred into another context, and his eirenic tendency is strengthened at the end of the first section as Longley touches the head and hand of his dying father.

In the second part of the poem, Longley brings us back to the contemporary situation in Northern Ireland as he mourns the deaths of three teenage British soldiers and a bus-conductor. Mention of the soldiers alone might suggest that Longley is being partisan but by including the murder of the bus-conductor (another uniformed servant of the state and yet not necessarily Protestant or Catholic), he shows us the full absurd horror of the Troubles. The conductor was

> shot through the head
> By a shivering boy who wandered in
> Before they could turn the television down
> Or tidy away the supper dishes.
> To the children, to a bewildered wife,
> I think 'Sorry Missus' was what he said.[35]

As Brearton points out this is an elegy not just for Longley's father, the soldiers and the bus-conductor, but for the young assassin also.[36] The poem also opens out in two directions from the Troubles: on the one hand it places the conflict against the larger context of the wars which marked the decline of the British Empire in the twentieth century, and at the same time it zooms in on the domestic scene of the latest assassination.

Man Lying on a Wall (1976) and *The Echo Gate* (1979) followed, and then Longley did not publish his next full collection, *Gorse Fires*, until 1991. The book was large and expansive, moving easily between familiar themes, but with a new-found ease and mastery. The tones were by times languid, acerbic, comical and tragic; and yet the same voice spoke in all the poems. And if a greater sense of elemental airiness was now present, this was not because Longley's forms had expanded: on the contrary, the poems had become even more minimalist than before. For instance, one of the finest poems in the book, 'Terezín', is only two lines long. On the page facing it there is a longer poem of four lines, 'Geisha', which explains this minimalist method: it describes how a geisha makes a pinhole in her paper screen, and this enables her to view people outside. They are watching a large bomber which, we are told, 'Journeys to her mirror and jar of rouge'.[37] Thus in Longley's poetry huge events such as world wars are refracted through a minimalist art of domesticity.

The book also makes widespread use of Greek myth. As Longley remarks in the notes to *Gorse Fires*, 'In differing proportions and with varying degrees of high-handedness but always, I hope, with reverence, I have in seven of these poems combined free translation from Homer's *Odyssey* with original lines.'[38] In 'The Butchers', Longley writes about how Odysseus returns home after his long journeying to find his house filled with suitors who are importuning his wife, Penelope, and devastating all his property. The violence which he brings down on them echoes with the Shankill Butchers who terrorised the Catholic community, and at times their own, in the 1970s and early 1980s. He has explained this in interview:

> [W]e were in Mayo, in this very remote cottage which we go to in Co. Mayo, and the insight I had was that Ithaca must have looked very like this little secret part of Mayo, which is sandy and remote. And the little smallholdings and outhouses . . . And that was my feeling – and at that time one of the things people were talking about was the Shankill Road murders. There'd been some dreadful killings and torturings in outhouses, very remote places like that. My physical circumstances brought to the surface, or brought to my attention, perhaps, that passage in the *Odyssey* . . . where Odysseus, with the help of Telemachus and the swineherd and somebody else, wipes out the suitors. And I had in the back of my mind the Shankill Butchers – I had in the back of my mind the sort of outhouses and smallholdings that would have been on Ithaca and which were reflected in the landscape of Ireland.[39]

There is no straightforward parallel here, rather the violent energy of the Greek episode is harnessed for different ends in the Northern Irish context. In his next collection, *The Ghost Orchid* (1995), he relates an episode from the Iliad where Priam, the King of Troy, forgives Achilles, who has killed his son Hector in battle. The poem was entitled 'Ceasefire' and appeared in the *Irish Times* the week that the IRA declared a ceasefire on 31 August 1994. The final couplet of the sonnet emphasises the necessity of forgiveness, no matter how horrific the crime. Priam talks: 'I get down on my knees and do what must be done / And kiss Achilles' hand, the killer of my son.'[40] Longley's use of Greek myth does not permit easy parallels between the murderer and victim in the *Iliad* and the murderers and victims of Northern Ireland. The poem commends forgiveness, but does not say that it is the Protestants who have to forgive any more than the Catholics: Longley carefully seeks out non-sectarian ground in order to address a political situation that is divided by sectarian hatred.

The book, like *Gorse Fires* before it and *The Weather in Japan* (2000) and *Snow Water* (2004) which have followed, includes many nature poems of mesmerising beauty. Longley also adds further homages to the English and Irish poets who died in both world wars, Edward Thomas, Keith Douglas and Charles Donnelly among others. Brearton has shown how Longley's preoccupation with this tradition has tempered his response to the Troubles in Northern Ireland, and indeed has informed the work of Heaney and Mahon also. As an index of the way these two preoccupations involve each other, I give the final couplet of 'Edward Thomas's Poem' from *Snow Water*: 'The nature poet turned into a war poet as if / He could cure death with the rub of a dock leaf.'[41] A poem like 'The Ice-Cream Man' works on this supposition. It is about the victim of a sectarian killing in Belfast and Longley begins by listing the flavours of ice-cream that he sold. Then, without explanation and in an address to a child, he names 'all the wild flowers of the Burren', many of which are endangered, and the last four lines of the poem provide that catalogue, as if he could cure death with their fragrance or the fragrance of their names.[42] Longley knows this is impossible, but still provides the consolation.

As mentioned earlier, Longley is married to the critic Edna Longley, who has argued against sophisticated nationalist readings of Irish literature. Like his wife's critical work, Longley's poetry does not fit into the prevailing paradigm of what is considered to be quintessentially Irish poetry. Similarly, his deep preoccupation with the poets of the two world wars is mirrored in her critical essays, especially those of *Poetry in the Wars* (1986). As the dedicatory poem to Edna Longley in *No Continuing City* has it: 'My children and my dead / Coming of age / In the turn of your head / As you turn a page'.[43] This marks the shared concerns of family and literary tradition, and the critical engagement between Michael and Edna Longley has lasted his entire writing career and informed his finest work.

Mahon and Longley have especially proved hugely influential on the succeeding generation of Irish poets, with Murphy's work somewhat sidelined by the fact that he was not part of the Northern Irish Renaissance. Their influence will be especially apparent in chapter 12, where I deal with the generation of poets born after 1960 who have no interest in nationalist narratives of Irish history and literature. Longley is first and foremost a poet of love and nature who, by force of circumstance, has become a war poet also. His war was the Troubles in Northern Ireland, but his approach to it has been to place it against the European backdrop of the British Empire's decline in the twentieth century. In this way his poetry exceeds the geographic borders of Ulster and takes on many other themes. He refuses to take the Troubles on their own terms, insisting on seeing them against this wider context, and this goes against the British interpretation of the violence in Northern Ireland as a problem among the

Irish, as well as prevailing Irish ideas of what an Irish poet should be (for a start, he or she should not write with imaginative sympathy about the British Empire). Although the character of his work is very different from that of Murphy and Mahon, like them he opens up the ground to new interpretations purely by the force of his scrupulous art.

Chapter 8

Seamus Heaney

One of the remarkable aspects of imperial expansion is the way that it makes diverse languages engage with one another. Loan words and syntactical constructions go flying back and forth, changing the nature of not only the language of the colonised people, but also of the colonisers themselves. Thus, Hindi is transformed by the British Empire's presence in India, but that language in its turn transforms English. One index of that are the 426 words in the English language that the *OED* lists as being of Hindi origin; not to mention the 210 from Urdu and the 82 from Tamil, to give but two further examples of India's many languages. Because of the success of the Empire, the English language appears to be outstandingly impure; also, it never suffered attempts to purge it of foreign elements, as, say, did Hungarian in the nineteenth century. Of course, no language is really 'pure' or 'impure' – that is just a trick of chronological perspective. English seems 'impure' in this respect only because it was invaded by so many foreign words as recently as the last few centuries.

Restricting our perspective to what has been called the Britannic Isles, we witness the interaction of several languages in the imperial pressure-cooker – among them, Irish, English, Scots, Scots Gaelic, Welsh and Cornish. English is undoubtedly triumphant among them as the first language of Britain and Ireland, as most of the others are to varying degrees struggling to survive, and Cornish is extinct. To read a contemporary novel in Irish is to feel the oppressive force a major language can exert on a minor language (loan words abound for situations and things that have traditional Irish expressions, grammar is gradually buckled into English shapes); but likewise English has been a native language of Ireland for under a millennium, and those who used it did not ask permission from the Plantagenets or the Windsors to change it. These linguistic transactions offer a record of the changing historical fates of lands and nations, so that to attend to the sound of words, to the eddies of their denotations and connotations, is a kind of archæology, or historical inquiry. Seamus Heaney's poem, 'Sruth' from *Electric Light* (2001), begins like this:

> The bilingual race
> And truth of that water
> Spilling down Errigal,
>
> The *sruth* like the rush
> Of its downpour translated
> Into your accent . . .[1]

Errigal is the highest mountain in the county of Donegal, which is one of the remaining areas of Ireland where the Irish language is still spoken. The Irish word 'sruth' means 'stream', 'river', 'current' or 'flow'. Heaney does not give the literal meaning of the word, but tries to explain it acoustically ('race' and 'truth', 'rush'). He drops the foreign word into English and watches the detailed ramifications. By punning on the word 'race' (at once the speed of the water and the people of Ireland), he suggests at the outset the grand issues involved when one small word crosses between languages. The poet is aware that it is only he who brings the word over ('sruth' never became an English word), and so self-consciousness about his own methods is an integral part of the poem. The theme of the poem, as indeed is the theme of so much of Heaney's work as poet, critic and translator, is to attend to such moments of linguistic crossing, and their implications for the fate of literatures and peoples of the Isles.

Seamus Heaney was born into a farming family in Mossbawn, Co. Derry, in 1939. As a beneficiary of the Butler Education Act which came into force in Northern Ireland in 1947, he was able to attend Queen's University, Belfast, where he studied English. One of the teachers at the School of English at that time was Philip Hobsbaum, who set up regular informal meetings for poets and critics. Among those who visited these sessions were the poets Michael Longley, Derek Mahon and Heaney himself, along with the critics Edna Longley and Michael Allen. These poets would loosely be called the Group, and constitute what has been called the Northern Irish Renaissance. It was an outstanding convergence of talent, both poetically and critically. Hobsbaum had been influenced by the poetry of the Movement in England, and its emphases on traditional poetic forms and casual descriptions of mundane events were absorbed by the Northern Irish poets. Most of the poems in Heaney's first collection, *Death of a Naturalist* (1966), are in this mode. The same year that book was published, Heaney took up a position at the School of English at Queen's, where he remained until 1972.

At the end of the 1960s, the Troubles had broken out; terror and violence would become part of everyday life in Ulster for almost three decades. The religious divide of Catholic and Protestant organised everything in its wake, and made Northern Ireland arguably one of the last places in Europe where the Thirty Years War was still being fought. The early 1970s was a particularly violent period, and Heaney and his family took up the offer of a house in Co. Wicklow in the Irish Republic. In 1981 he joined the English Department at Harvard University, and most of the following fifteen years he spent between Boston and Dublin. In 1989 he was elected the Oxford Professor of Poetry; in 1995 he was awarded the Nobel Prize for Literature; and in 2003 Queen's University established the Seamus Heaney Centre for Poetry. He is also perhaps the only living poet, Irish or otherwise, to be quoted in a U2 lyric. These institutional positions and international awards are an indication of Heaney's status as the most celebrated Irish poet in the second half of the twentieth century. There is already a large body of secondary material that deals with his work, and his opinions on the political situation in Ireland are regularly sought by the Irish and international media. This public status has had important implications for his poetry. Heaney writes in the knowledge that the poems must resonate responsibly within the public arena, much like a newspaper editorial would. In a violent and volatile zone, Heaney's poems try to achieve balance and reconciliation. What is marvellous about his work is that it does these things without ever reneging on the prerogatives of art, much like Michael Longley's 'Ceasefire'. A poem will never become a political tract, but it will harness the concern and subtlety of such a document for its own purposes. In what follows I will discuss the phases of Heaney's poetry as it finds its way through the binaries of Catholic and Protestant, politics and art, Irish and English.

Heaney was not the first Irish writer to exploit the interface between the Irish and English languages. The strongest example in the twentieth century is the drama of J. M. Synge, in which vernacular Irish is given an English voice, and in the process violently and profitably twists the target language in its own image. Perhaps it was because Heaney grew up in Northern Ireland, where the Catholic minority experienced systematic discrimination – in matters such as the allocation of public housing and gerrymandering – that he felt that his imaginative force should be expended in redressing the balance. Thus in *Wintering Out* (1972), poems like 'Anahorish', 'Toome' and 'Broagh' draw attention to the Irish etymology of Ulster place-names, and stake a cultural claim to territory that de facto belonged, and still belongs, to the United Kingdom.[2] Much in the same way as he does in 'Sruth' above, he attends to the valency of these words in English and observes the way they ruckle the coloniser's title deeds to the province. This is the kind of linguistic archæology I referred to earlier, and it is analogous to another kind of archæology which announces itself in this book. 'The Tollund Man' is about the sacrificial victims from the Early Iron Age whose bodies were preserved in the bog and exhumed in the twentieth century. For Heaney, the bodies are a kind of consolation when confronting the sectarian murders of his own era, as they provide a wider context for their understanding. Several critics have identified this as a mythologising of contemporary violence, and think that such consolations merely elide political complexity and grievance. In other words, Heaney's solutions are a little too easy.

And yet, in their turn, those critics elide much of the complexity of Heaney's work in this period. It is true that *North* (1975) continued the mythologising of *Wintering Out*. (There is another poem, 'The Grauballe Man', about a preserved Iron Age victim; and 'Funeral Rites' expresses the pining for 'ceremony / customary rhythms'[3] in the face of sectarian violence and then imagines an all-Ireland cortège that would wind its way to the Neolithic passage grave at Newgrange in Co. Meath.) But it also plays havoc with traditional identifications and in the process demonstrates the deep cultural value of insouciant imaginative play. The title of 'Ocean's Love to Ireland' from *North* adapts the title of Sir Walter Ralegh's poem 'Ocean's Love to Cynthia', thus immediately evoking an intricate nexus of politics, literature and sexuality. How close is Heaney, a poet from a Catholic and nationalist background, to this English conqueror and poet? Do the conquests of courtly love have anything to do with the conquest of England by Ireland?

In Heaney's poem, Ireland is figured as a woman who is seduced and ruined by 'Sweet Sir Walter'. Here the double life of Ralegh both as writer and man-of-action is reflected in the way that Ireland is overrun not just by English occupying forces but also by iambic pentameters. It would seem that Heaney is merely recycling the antiquated opposition of Ireland as woman ruined by England as rapacious male. Political conquest is figured as sexual congress, and in this context the Irish poets of the time are dismissed as effete. The tradition of *aisling* poems, which emerged most forcefully a century later after the conquests of Ralegh, constantly presents Ireland as woman who has been defiled by the English and implores the poet to effect a change. With its injunction to poetry to make incursions in the political sphere, the *aisling* tradition had obvious attractions for Heaney. And yet, there is little of this here.

In fact, the poem is something of a sleeper. Its effect isn't felt until we read the next two poems that follow it in *North*, and then a number of complex issues unfold. The poem 'Aisling' serves only to bolster the tired political and gender identifications of 'Ocean's Love', but this only makes the shock of 'Act of Union' all the more forceful. The latter poem conflates two narratives: the first is of a husband talking to his wife, who is about to give birth to their child, and the second is of England invading Ireland. The poem is narrated by the husband/England. This change of voice is crucial, for it forces Heaney, the supposed 'slightly aggravated young Catholic male',[4] as he once spoke of an aspect of himself in interview, to take the voice of the oppressor. Thomas C. Foster has remarked how Heaney has always had problems with representing the other side in his poetry, and gives 'Act of Union' as one example of this. Extensively revised after it first appeared in the *Listener* in 1973 under the title 'A New Life', 'Act of Union' is a model of the well-made poem, a poem that achieves an æsthetic poise and unity, but in this case without foreclosing the complex political events unfolding at that time in Northern Ireland.[5] Indeed those events are the very life-blood of the conceit. What is remarkable is the way in which it refuses to adhere to the racial and religious polarities informing those events. The man/coloniser remarks to the woman/colonised that 'I am the tall kingdom over your shoulder / That you would neither cajole nor ignore', but goes on to admit that their relationship is more one of his concessions rather than his conquests.

> And I am still imperially
> Male, leaving you with the pain,
> The rending process in the colony,
> The battering ram, the boom burst from within.
> The act sprouted an obstinate fifth column
> Whose stance is growing unilateral.
> His heart beneath your heart is a wardrum
> Mustering force.[6]

By rhyming the narratives of lover and conqueror, the poem answers up to the difficult political situation in Northern Ireland in the early 1970s, but on its own terms, by which I mean that it is difficult to say whether that 'obstinate fifth column' is Ulster Protestant or Catholic Nationalist.[7] It is exactly this kind of uncertainty that has unsettled some critics of the poem.

Moreover, one hesitates to use the word 'rape' since the tone seems more that of the repentant seducer than unscrupulous defiler. There is an understanding of the seduced/vanquished which is not utterly self-regarding. Some critics have protested that the whole conceit renders the poem unfaithful both to the historical situation and to the realities of married love; Ciaran Carson in a review of *North*, remarked that in Heaney 'Ireland's relationship with England is sentimentalised into something as natural as a good fuck'.[8] And yet how many husbands have tried to dominate their wives and ended up making concessions, and how many fathers have felt resentment towards their children at one time or another? As for its being untrue to history, it is by virtue of the absence of exact allegorical equations for the different groups in Northern Ireland – the loyalists and nationalists are equally the offspring of the union – that the poem is able to search out areas of commonalty between the opposed factions that journalese and polemic usually refuse.

Patricia Coughlan, in a feminist critique of the poem, sees this figuration of the landscape as woman as culpably androcentric, a 'reification of traditional modes of perceiving feminine identity'.[9] Her reading is persuasive in many respects but she shows no awareness of how Heaney's use of these traditional modes of representing feminine identity is subversive of the traditional modes of Irish social identity. Coughlan discusses 'Act of Union' and 'Bone Dreams' as merely more instances of Heaney transforming the land into a woman to play out the drama of male sexual fulfilment at her expense. Whereas in the first he takes the voice of the English invader, imaginatively throwing his voice beyond the bounds of his Northern Irish Catholic identity; and in the second he regains his Irish male identity, but then looks to England and figures her as a woman, thus turning on its head the usual identification of England as male rapacious coloniser, and Ireland as ruined maiden.

Edna Longley and Seamus Deane bring different agendas when they come to read the poem. Deane fixes Heaney firmly down on one side of the sectarian demarcation:

> His guilt is that of the victim, not of the victimizer. In this he is characteristic of his Northern Irish Catholic community. His attitude to paternity and authority is apologetic – for having undermined them . . . That which in political or sectarian terms could be called nationalist or Catholic, belongs to maternity, the earth itself; that which is unionist or Protestant, belongs to paternity, the earth cultivated . . . Thus his central trope is marriage, male power and female tenderness conjoined in ceremony, a ritual appeasement of their opposition.[10]

Deane's description of the significant polarities at work in Heaney's poetry is precise only up to a point. He becomes uneasy when Heaney steps beyond these bounds, for instance in 'Act of Union' where, as I have remarked, Heaney takes on the voice of the victimiser, the English man, the dastardly Sir Walter of 'Ocean's Love'. This is a type of cross-dressing that Deane does not countenance and goes on to dismiss 'Act of Union', saying that this poem and 'Ocean's Love' 'go too far in their extension of the subtle sexual and political tensions of the others, turning into a rather crude allegory what had been a finely struck implication'.[11] Deane refuses to see the finesse of the poem because it crosses into no man's land and makes free with Northern Irish political identities. It raises the troubling idea that a member of the 'Northern Irish Catholic community', as Deane designates Heaney as both man and artist in this passage, can deftly and sympathetically adopt the voice of the vilified victimiser.

It is interesting then to see a critic like Longley similarly rebuking Heaney for this poem. She says the speaker's role in the poem 'fits uneasily'. And then adds that 'the allegory could apply to begetting Loyalism as much as "obstinate" Republicanism'.[12] As I have tried to show, this is the poem's strength rather than its weakness. Commenting on the book as a whole, Longley says that '*North* does not give the impression of the urgent "matter of Ireland" bursting through the confines of "the well-made poem". Heaney's most "artful" book, it stylises and distances what was immediate and painful in *Wintering Out*.' But pain and immediacy are not the prerequisites of good poetry; occasionally the poet must step back and stylise instead of pursuing experience head on, as Longley is aware elsewhere in her criticism. The distance here might also be the distance between Belfast and Wicklow, to where Heaney moved in 1972. It is true that events in Ireland do not 'burst through' in 'Act of Union' – the conceit is too well-wrought for such a description, especially when we know how much Heaney reworked the poem after its first publication. Nevertheless it is a successful attempt to find an idiom that is capable of giving on to current events without giving in to them. With the responsible insouciance it displays towards inherited archetypes and racial and religious identifications, it is an idiom that might not be 'an independent long-term agent of change', to use Longley's phrase,[13] but which can exert imaginative force against the pressure of political reality.

Heaney's next collection, *Field Work* (1979), contains an elegy for the American poet Robert Lowell, one of the protagonists of the Confessional school of poetry, who died in 1977. The two poets had become friends towards the end of the American's life, and Lowell's example confirmed Heaney in his use of poetic autobiography. From his first collection, Heaney's stories of family life and childhood freighted large issues, such as the growth of the spirit and even the fate of Ireland. For example, this is obvious in the first poem of *Death of a Naturalist* (1966), 'Digging', and also in its last, 'A Personal Helicon', which refers to the mountain in Greece, sacred to the Muses, and which is more generally used to refer to poetic inspiration. The title itself, then, announces the importance of autobiography, and the poem ends with the statement: 'I rhyme / To see myself, to set the darkness echoing.'[14] But there are important differences between the poetic autobiographies of Lowell and Heaney.

In *Life Studies* (1959), Lowell is deliberately revelatory about the details of his family life; because he was one of the scions of a long-respected New England family, Lowell could relate a straightforward scene from his own marriage and it became a comment on the state of America. The more lurid the story, the more condemnatory the social comment. As Heaney put it in his elegy: 'what was not within your empery? / You drank America / like the heart's / iron vodka.'[15] Heaney is more restrained in what he tells of his family life, and autobiography in his poetry is for the most part subordinated to the story of the growth of a poet in Ireland. Particular episodes in Heaney's life become the occasion of poems about the tension between the artist's responsibility to his art and to his people.

This is what the title sequence of the collection *Station Island* (1984) tries to resolve. It is set on Lough Derg in Co. Donegal, an island where Catholic pilgrims undergo a three-day retreat; however, it is only the coulisse of the poem that is religious. Heaney uses the setting to confront the ghosts of his past – both people he has known personally and literary precursors – in order to grasp the sense of his own vocation as a poet. James Joyce comes forward in the last encounter: ' "Your obligation / is not discharged by any common rite. / What you must do must be done on your own . . ." '[16] Although the sequence ends with a massive sense of release, the issue is not finally resolved. One of its echoes can be heard twelve years later, in 'The Flight Path' from *The Spirit Level* (1996), where we witness Heaney going over the same argument again. A childhood acquaintance approaches him on the Dublin–Belfast train and says: 'When, for fuck's sake, are you going to write / Something for us?' and Heaney's reply is 'If I do write something, / Whatever it is, I'll be writing for myself.'[17] Issues such as this are never finally resolved – not for Heaney, not for anyone. Their significance ebbs and flows in relation to historical events.

Arguably, 'The Flight Path' is something of a nostalgia trip. The narrated event occurred in 1979, as Heaney tells us in the poem, and his later collection *Seeing Things* (1991) registers such political debates only from a distance, much like 'newsreel bomb-hits, as harmless as dust-puffs'.[18] Of all Heaney's books, this collection is perhaps least concerned with the matter of the nation, but explores instead themes of mortality, family and spiritual growth. The phrase 'seeing things' indicates the way the book attends to the solid particulars of experience, but also to visionary moments, and the title poem balances precariously between the losses and dangers of life and an assertion of continuity. It is worth remarking on Heaney's use of the tripartite structure: the first section has a group of people in a small boat in choppy seas; he observes 'How riskily we fared into the morning, / And loved in vain our bare, bowed, numbered heads.'[19] After this personal anecdote, the second part is about the way that art can handle such feelings of danger and offer consolation. But for Heaney the danger is not dispelled thus, rather it exists thrillingly alongside the fixity offered by art. Heaney tells us how art stylises the traumas of our lives and consoles us, and the Western canon has a chorus of poems that remind us of just this fact. Heaney's theme then is not new, but the way he orchestrates solace and danger in the poem is. The third and final part of the poem returns to childhood experience and casually relates an event when the poet's father was nearly drowned. The anecdote comes close to fairy-tale stylisation, especially in its opening, and its close, which I give here:

> That afternoon
> I saw him face to face, he came to me
> With his damp footprints out of the river,
> And there was nothing between us there
> That might not still be happily ever after.[20]

The enjambment of the final lines is masterful: the penultimate line shows the absence that is often at the centre of even the most intimate human relations, and the final line carefully places an optative statement against that very emptiness. The lines stay poised there, and the poet silently moves away.

The collection also contains a long sequence, 'Squarings', of forty-eight parts, each twelve lines long. The sections have no titles, only numbers, and this contributes to the fluent articulation from one part to the next. 'Squarings' is one long continuous meditation in which many of the ideas of 'Seeing Things' are amplified. The sequence is playful and improvisatory in a way that is new for Heaney. The structure itself alleviates the pressure to provide a clinching final cadence to each poem (and Heaney, like most lyric poets, systematically increases the intensity at the poem's close); rather, it is important as one part ends that it throw forth several vectors to be picked up later on. In this way 'Squarings' catches something of the drift of what it calls 'the soul-free cloud-life'.[21]

For the most part, *Electric Light* and *District and Circle* (2006) have not extended Heaney's range in the same way that *Seeing Things* did; one index of this is the high number of poems in which he revisits his childhood. Such occasions have become almost routine in his poetry now. However, the second book contains two sequences which are markedly different from this mode – the first is the title poem, and the second 'The Tollund Man in Springtime'. In these poems he figures himself moving through the grids and codes of urban space, but he does not reach for the usual consolation of his farming background. Rather, he keeps his focus steadily on the difficult colours, patterns, sounds and encounters of this strange zone:

> So deeper into it, crowd-swept, strap-hanging,
> My lofted arm a-swivel like a flail,
> My father's glazed face in my own waning
> And craning . . .
>   Again the growl
> Of shutting doors, the jolt and one-off treble

Of iron on iron, then a long centrifugal
Haulage of speed through every dragging socket.

And so by night and day to be transported
Through galleried earth with them, the only relict
Of all that I belonged to, hurtled forward,
Reflecting in a window mirror-backed
By blasted weeping rock-walls.
                    Flicker-lit.[22]

This is the conclusion of the poem, and although Heaney gestures towards his childhood, he is 'hurtled forward' away from that. A phrase like 'galleried earth' suggests Hades, but Heaney's poem does not amount to a hackneyed comparison between the London Underground and the Underworld. He is more intent on catching the quality of a life lived among urban crowds, and the large machines and buildings they move through, hence the concentration on describing the experience ('Haulage of speed through every dragging socket'). Heaney has become unhitched from his usual narratives, and there is an edginess and risk to the poem that is exhilarating.

Heaney has been influential as a critic and translator also. His practice was formed under the ægis of the New Criticism, which stressed detailed attention to the texts of poems, and many of his essays have, at their centre, a close reading of one or two poems. He is for the most part an advocate rather than a critic: he uses the occasions of lectures and reviews to generate enthusiasm in his listeners and readers for the work in question. He does not bring new historical contexts to bear on the poetry and he does not use the poetry to theorise about the larger relations between art and society, in the manner of some recent academic criticism. He is deeply suspicious of the claims that multiculturalism and identity politics make on poetry, always emphasising the poem's ability to exert its own imaginative pressure back against the forces of the world. Above all, his criticism demands to be read as a kind of autobiography, as an account of the growth of one particular reader's, and poet's, mind. In Heaney's case, the criticism is clearly subordinated to the development of his own poetry. He will occasionally quote the entire text of one of his own poems and then elucidate it by reference to his reading at the time, the technical difficulties involved and the wider meaning of the stance taken up. In most other poets, such a manœuvre would be purely self-serving; undoubtedly, Heaney does serve himself on such occasions, but his generosity and intelligence as a reader of poetry ensure that his autobiography never distorts or obscures the poets he discusses. He may stress some aspects of their work at the expense of others (which I will come to soon), but that is the job of interpretation. To read his criticism chronologically, then, is to understand the motivations behind many of the important stylistic and thematic shifts in his poetry.

His first book of criticism, *Preoccupations: Selected Prose 1968–1978* (1980), set the tone for much that follows, beginning as it does with a cluster of brief memoirs of his childhood in Derry and early adulthood in Belfast. The book contains an important essay on Patrick Kavanagh that establishes a rural precursor poet for Heaney himself. When he says of the earlier poet that 'Much of his authority and oddity derive from the fact that he wrested his idiom barehanded out of a literary nowhere',[23] Heaney is referring to the fact that before Kavanagh's advent Irish poetry had not ingested the experience of farming life. The Revival, as I remarked in chapter 5, presented many portraits of the Irish peasant, but for the most part these were the idealisations of the middle classes. Kavanagh elevated mundane farming life – accounts of borrowing an ass to go to the fair or spraying potatoes – to the status of poetic material, and Heaney's essay is a mark of his gratitude. The book also contains an essay on W. B. Yeats, which stresses the eirenic aspects of the late poetry. This is a surprising take on a poet who in the poems of his last two decades frequently relished the prospect of Armageddon and supported Fascism. Yet Heaney's conclusion – he quotes 'Cuchulainn Comforted' in its entirety – drives the argument forcefully home. The question-mark in the title 'Yeats as an Example?' obviously refers to the violent aspects of the late poetry, but the end of the essay leaves us in no doubt that the question-mark should be dispensed with. The example that Heaney finds in Yeats is more suited to the Ireland of the 1970s, especially the Northern Ireland of the 1970s, where qualities of restraint and reconciliation were required. This recuperation of Yeats is important because otherwise Heaney would only have two options: either to write poems for his paramilitary acquaintance on the Dublin–Belfast train, or to reject Yeats as an example. His response to the dilemma is, then, decidedly not the advocacy I mentioned early: it is a critical choice – in both senses of the word critical – that has profound implications for Heaney's own poetry.

An important aspect of his next book of essays, *The Government of the Tongue* (1988), is advocacy of poets from Central and Eastern Europe, above all the Russian poet Osip Mandelstam (1891–1938) and the Polish poet Czesław Miłosz (1911–2004). As Heaney can neither speak nor read either Russian or Polish, his criticism has only a tenuous purchase on the poetry itself. He is more interested in the examples of their lives as poets who resisted both the blandishments and terrific dangers of repressive political regimes. Mandelstam is a particularly potent figure in this respect, as he died unrepentant as a prisoner in one of Stalin's labour camps. For Heaney, who is so preoccupied with the relations between poetry and politics, the fascination exerted by Mandelstam needs no explanation. Another aspect of note in this book is the scarcity of reference to Irish poets, as well as his continuing interest in American poets, in this case Sylvia Plath and Robert Lowell; his next book of criticism, *The Redress of Poetry: Oxford Lectures* (1995), contains an essay on Elizabeth Bishop. These choices helped to create the canon of American poetry for British and Irish readers for two decades – all the poets Heaney discusses remained in print in the UK during the 1970s and 1980s, and major American poets such as A. R. Ammons and James Merrill, whom he does not discuss, were only sporadically in print, or not at all, during the same period. Similarly, his advocacy of Paul Muldoon established his place in the canon for an American audience.

I remarked on the autobiographical nature of much of Heaney's criticism; the same holds for some of his translation work also. His important publication in this respect is *Sweeney Astray* (1984), which was a translation of *Buile Suibhne*, the mediæval Irish poem that relates how the seventh-century Irish king, Sweeney, was changed into a bird as punishment for his violent treatment of a Christian cleric. (Trevor Joyce had done a version of *Buile Suibhne* a few years previously.) First, and not negligibly, there is the rhyme between Heaney and Sweeney; also, the name Heaney comes from the Irish for bird, *éan*. His affinity with the king is also manifest in the third part of *Station Island*, entitled 'Sweeney Redivivus', where Heaney takes the voice of Sweeney for twenty poems. There is a further important aspect. As we saw before, Heaney implicates his autobiography within national history, and in an essay on the translation, he remarks:

> The translation of a text from the Irish language into English by an
> English-speaking Irish writer usually involves considerations other than
> the strictly literary. The additional contexts are historical, cultural and
> political, as when a Native American author turns to material in one of
> the original languages of the North American continent. In each case, a
> canonical literature in English creates the acoustic within which the
> translation is going to be heard; an overarching old colonial roof
> inscribed 'The land was ours before we were the land's' is made to echo
> with some such retort as 'You don't say!'[24]

Heaney is first and foremost an English poet, by which I mean that he is a poet of the English language and not the Irish language. His primary concern then is with the ripples of implication that are created in his own language by such a translation. The same can be said of his translation of the Anglo-Saxon epic, *Beowulf* (1999). Here is a poet who was born as a British subject and now is an Irish citizen translating a classic of English literature from Old English into contemporary English. In the preface he remarks that it was a long time before he realised that he was an English poet in the sense above: 'to persuade myself that I was born into its language and that its language was born into me took a while: for somebody who grew up in the political and cultural conditions of Lord Brookeborough's Northern Ireland, it could hardly have been otherwise'.[25] Around the same period he was asked in interview what makes him distinctly an Irish poet and not a British poet, and he responded thus:

> Well, the issue probably wouldn't arise at all were there not the political situation in the North. All of those remarks about Irish versus British are actually intended as irritants rather than definitions. The adjectives have nothing essential to do with the noun. They have to do with the aggravation of the political and current situation. They're a form of game-playing.[26]

This is a long way from his description of his own poetry in 1977 as 'a kind of slow, obstinate, papish burn, emanating from the ground I was brought up on'.[27] The juxtaposition of these remarks spanning twenty years shows how Heaney's ideas about the relations between poetry and politics have changed. Perhaps the IRA ceasefire in 1994 and the subsequent developments in the political situation in Northern Ireland contributed to this loosening up. Whether or no, it is worth recalling Edna Longley's *Poetry in the Wars* (1986), where she discusses the poets of the Northern Irish Renaissance within the context of the English lyric tradition from Thomas Hardy through Edward Thomas to Philip Larkin; Heaney's remarks and practice as a translator flow out as one brilliant consequence of this.

They are also an index of the wider change taking place in Irish culture. The nationalist framework that was imposed upon literature in both English and Irish is gradually being lifted away, and it is becoming easier to see that Heaney writes in a native language of Ireland just as much as, say, Louis de Paor does. In previous chapters, I have discussed the anxious desire of poets and translators to convey from Irish into English some native essence that would guarantee the difference of Irish literature from that produced in Britain. Even as that anxiety fades, the translation work continues, in both directions, as is proper for an island that contains two languages. And thus there is a different border from the one that separates Northern Ireland from the Irish Republic, a border that is more fundamental for the study of literature and arguably also for political identity on the island, that between Irish and English. In this chapter, we have looked at one of the finest Anglophone poets in Ireland; in the next we have a look over the border.

Chapter 9

Irsko po Polsku: poetry and translation

Seán Ó Ríordáin, Máirtín Ó Direáin, Nuala Ní Dhomhnaill,
Gearóid Mac Lochlainn, Michael Hartnett, Michael Longley,
Derek Mahon, Peter Fallon, Aidan Rooney, Samuel Beckett

On 10 August 2006, the *Irish Times* reported that there were now 147,659 Poles registered to work in Ireland, 40,237 Lithuanians, 20,312 Slovaks, 20,301 Latvians and 10,302 Czechs; along with the numbers from other nations, the total registered migrant workers was 251,032. It is a long time since so many languages have been spoken by large groups on the island. One would have to look back to the late Middle Ages when Irish, English and to a lesser extent French all flourished at the same time, along with a widespread scholarly knowledge of Latin. It is not the first time then that the island has been so polyglot, but it is the first time that Eastern European languages have established themselves. A further difference is that in the Middle Ages there was much overlap between linguistic communities (for Irish speakers could often translate into French or Latin), whereas now it is unlikely that many Irish citizens speak Polish or Lithuanian. If these immigrants remain in the country then most of their children, like those of immigrants to the United States, will only have a passive understanding of their parents' language, and their children's children will know nothing but a few phrases or the correct pronunciation of a name. So while there is much media noise about the recent linguistic and cultural diversity, the phenomenon is unlikely to endure.

Meanwhile the language that offers Ireland the greatest chance of multicultural diversity is still in difficulty. The census of 2002 states that 1.57 million people in the Republic speak Irish and 10.4 per cent of the people in Northern Ireland have some knowledge of the language, but realistic figures range between 20,000 and 70,000, and Irish, along with languages such as Rusyn, Eastern Mari, Udmurt and Permyak, is on UNESCO's list of endangered languages. Despite massive investment in TG4, the Irish-language television channel, as well as innovative webzines such as *Beo!*, a major political party in 2006 could still seriously debate the idea of making the language an optional subject for the state school-leaving examinations; it is impossible to imagine a similar situation in any other European country. Even a principality as small as Monaco insists that its children learn Monégasque, a language which can be employed in far fewer circumstances than Irish. There is also now An Coimisinéir Teanga (The Language Commissioner) whose job it is to ensure that no citizen encounters discrimination if he wishes to conduct his business with the State in Irish. This is encouraging, but it also serves to draw attention to the embarrassing fact that Irish laws are still not available in their entirety in the first official language of the State. One thinks again of the remark in Tomás Ó Duinnshléibhe's novel, which I quoted in chapter one: 'Ní thig le tír ar bith a teanga a chailleadh gan a hanam a chailleadh agus nuair a bhíonn an t-anam caillte tá deireadh léi mar náisiún.'[1] But Ó Duinnshléibhe should not have the final say on the matter. Only from the nineteenth century has Irish been connected with the fate of Ireland as a nation, and a recent study has shown that the language is again becoming unhitched from nationalist ideology.[2] Now, competence in Irish is perceived as an expression of individuality rather than of nationalist feeling.[3] Whether this will be enough to sustain the language will be seen in the following decades.

The job of this book is to give an account of Irish poetry in English over the last two centuries (a separate study would be required for Gaelic poetry). Nevertheless, it is impossible to do this without taking into account the complex negotiations between Anglophone poetry in Ireland and the Irish language, and to a lesser extent, French and Latin. The chapters which dealt with nineteenth-century poetry up to and including the Revival were dominated by questions of translation from Irish (James Henry and William Allingham were the exceptions to this). The later part of the twentieth century had a different dynamic, as the debates about the connections between translation and cultural nationalism were no longer definitive for the work of most, if not all, Irish poets. Perhaps the most important cause for this is Yeats, who established the modern Irish poetic tradition and yet had no knowledge of Gaelic. This is not to say that cultural nationalism per se waned in importance in the twentieth century (it arguably reached its zenith in 1991 with the publication of the first three volumes of *The Field Day Anthology*), but that Gaelic was marginal to it, as indeed it was marginal to both the social and political life of the Free State and the Republic of Ireland. For this reason, a separate chapter is required for the question of translation in the later part of the twentieth century. The issues here are particularly complex as the Irish language and the act of translation itself become themes in both Gaelic and Anglophone poetry, and this at the very moment when these poems are moving from Irish into English, and as English literary and linguistic influences make themselves felt in Irish.

Translation has always been fraught with political and cultural consequences: that Islam forbids its believers to read the Koran in translation reminds us of the tight controls which Christianity placed on translation of the Bible for many centuries. In the beginning may have been λόγοϛ, but that is not the same as the 'Word' we translate it as. This anxiety echoes also in the translation of poetry to the present day, and one often hears the platitude that poetry cannot be translated, or that much is lost in the process. Admitting some of these difficulties, cultural nationalists in the nineteenth century nevertheless were insistent that the national spirit could indeed be brought over from Gaelic into English. They did so despite the lack of consensus on the criteria for judging the quality of a translation in the same period. Michael Cronin offers a more profitable way of thinking about these issues:

> Translation is always unsettling for essentialism. One of the recurrent fictions of certain kinds of history-making is the Fall from Linguistic Grace. In other words, once upon a time there was a Gaelic Ireland untainted by predatory ambitions of barbarian tongues, a 'pristine' state that would eventually give way to the corruption of the longboats and late Latin rhetoric. The opposite is the case. Literature and culture in Irish would never be stronger than when engaged in constant exchange with Latin and English in medieval Ireland.[4]

Thus when twentieth-century Irish poets brush with Gaelic poetry they are not somehow replenishing their Irishness (though several would like to believe that); and if poets turn to European languages such as French, Latin and Greek, that does not somehow make them rootless cosmopolitans. To think in such terms is to assume an extremely limited nationalism. Padraic Colum's line echoes again: 'As in wild earth a Grecian vase'.[5] The native poetry of Ireland can come through Greece as easily as through the west of Ireland.

The Irish language itself has become one of the great themes of poetry in both languages. The overriding tone is elegiac, but there are importance nuances of difference between the way the language is elegised; certain challenges are laid down by the Irish poets, and for the most part these remain unanswered by Anglophone poets who do not speak or read Irish. The terms of the Anglophone elegies are similar to those of William Cullen Bryant in elegies for the native peoples of America, written at the very time when those peoples were being wiped out. There has been no genocide of Irish speakers in the twentieth century, but Irish speakers together with the language are clearly a richer theme if they are imagined to be completely lost. Eavan Boland does not speak or read Irish and she elegises the language in exactly this way in 'My Country in Darkness'. She imagines a Gaelic poet drifting off to sleep, and possibly death:

> The Gaelic world stretches out under a hawthorn tree
> and burns in the rain. This is its home,
> its last frail shelter. All of it –
> Limerick, the Wild Geese and what went before –
> falters into cadence before he sleeps.
>
> He shuts his eyes. Darkness falls on it.[6]

Of this passage David Wheatley asks who exactly this poet is and '[b]y what piece of bardic hyperbole has he become consubstantial with the entire "Gaelic world"?'. For its effect, Boland steamrollers towards that last poignant half line quoted here. Wheatley continues: 'The effect Boland creates thrives on such generalisation, to the point where specific details may be more of a hindrance than a help.'[7] Michael Longley is more circumspect in 'On Hearing Irish Spoken'. He finds himself in the west of Ireland listening to fishermen talk and he catches a word he knows 'Repeating itself at desperate intervals / Like the stepping stones across a river in spate'.[8] The word 'desperate' suggests the fate of the language, but it might also be the desperation of Longley, who cannot understand what he is hearing. The language is 'in spate' and thus full of energy and life, but on the other hand, Longley seems to imply that if it sweeps him off the stepping stones then the language will decline. Yet Longley, it is clear, is not going to go so far as to learn it, even though he has summered for decades near a Gaeltacht area.

Longley's lines unwittingly echo lines by Seán Ó Ríordáin (1917–77), from his first collection, *Eireaball Spideoige* (1952). 'Cuireadh' is about an invitation (the title's meaning) to a lover, and it ends thus: 'Is ní labhrann an abhainn thíos ach gramadach, / Is bímse chomh dall le dlíodóir.'[9] This is the time-honoured dismissal by lovers of mundane matters, such as laws, whether they be of language or the state: they fly beyond all that in their ecstasy. Here the river speaks 'grammar', and the lovers wish to ignore that; they also wish to be as 'blind as a lawyer'. The implication here is that they will overlook the state and its laws in the same way that that state and its laws have overlooked the two people in the past. The originality of Ó Ríordáin's image is in the association of a natural object with the scientific categorisation of language. It is also of note that the lines seem to be prescient of the reception of *Eireaball Spideoige*, when Ó Ríordáin was attacked in reviews for his unIrish handling of language.[10]

I am interested in these lines and their connection with Longley as a kind of failed allusion: in both poems the river is associated with the Irish language, or an aspect of it. In making this point, I do not wish to rake over the idea of the untranslatability of poetry. Rather the coincidence and independence of imagery between Ó Ríordáin's and Longley's poems are an index of how the Irish and Anglophone traditions miss each other on the island. (Thomas Kinsella remarks on 'the situation in the early eighteenth century, with Aogán Ó Rathaille and Jonathan Swift – contemporaries dealing with the same forces, major poets – neither aware of the other's existence'.[11]) It is as though they exist in different worlds, while resting on the same land. Despite his slight œuvre, Ó Ríordáin occupies the same position in twentieth-century Gaelic literature that James Joyce does in English literature. If Longley and Ó Ríordáin wrote in the same language, then it would be very difficult for 'On Hearing Irish Spoken' not be changed by the existence of 'Cuireadh'. Although Irish-language poetry has influenced Anglophone poetry in several respects, the balance of trade lies on the other side. For instance, one can see Ó Ríordáin throughout *Eireaball Spideoige* finding himself as a poet through intense debate with English literature.

Kinsella has argued that neither Gaelic nor Anglophone literature in Ireland can be understood without the other:

> Irish literature exists as a dual entity. It was composed in two languages. The changing emphases between one language and the other reflect changing circumstances through the centuries. The Irish language is a difficult language to learn, and has little contemporary relevance, so that it is convenient to confine one's attention to Anglo-Irish literature – defining this, roughly, as Irish literature composed in the English language since the seventeenth century, and having certain relationships with English literature. But this is not an accurate or a sufficient view.[12]

The critical writing of poets is always an oblique apologia for their own poems and this is evident from the passage quoted here. I would argue that one of the reasons that Kinsella's poetry has not received the same attention as Yeats and Heaney is because his interpretation of Irish literary history – which cannot of course be separated from his own creative work – is so plainly wrong. One of the proofs he gives of the dual tradition is that of Swift and Ó Rathaille quoted above, and this seriously weakens rather than strengthens his argument. He has persuaded few critics, which may be due to their ignorance of Irish. But it also implies that the distance between the two languages and their worlds is greater than Kinsella will admit: you can only have a 'dual tradition' if there are enough readers and writers who are bilingual.

But to misinterpret so strongly is not to be in error. Kinsella's misprision resulted in one of the finest bilingual anthologies of Irish poetry, *An Duanaire:1600–1900, Poems of the Dispossessed* (1981), edited by Seán Ó Tuama and with translations by Thomas Kinsella. The anthology changed the perception of Gaelic poetry, alerting readers to unexpected continuities as well as registers that Revival translators, and others before them, had suppressed. But once again, the excited reception of the book indicates the absence rather than presence of a dual tradition in Kinsella's sense of it; a century of outstanding poetry had been produced in Ireland without *An Duanaire.*

Ó Ríordáin published his second poetry collection, *Brosna*, in 1964. He was part of a generation of major talents that emerged in the mid century, which included Máirtín Ó Direáin (1910–88), Máire Mhac an tSaoi (b. 1922) and Liam S. Gogán (1891–1979). The title of the book means 'decayed twigs' and it is clear that this refers to the remnants of the Irish language. The short poem 'Reo' (frost) is about the poet's search for a metaphor for what he experienced on a frosty day. It ends with the stunning lines:

> Lá dar phógas bean dem mhuintir
> Is í ina cónra reoite, sínte.[13]

The first line means 'the day I kissed a woman of my people', and indeed the book is dedicated 'Do mhuintir Dhún Chaoin' (to the people of Dunquin, a Gaeltacht area in the south-west of Ireland). The word 'people' here is not used in any national sense, rather what he means is that the woman is either from Ó Ríordáin's extended family or from his locality. If the latter, then to kiss a woman of one's people promises the continuation of that people, and by implication, the continuation of its language. Here it seems that linguistic abstractions are all present in the physical meeting of lips. The next line however wipes this away: 'And she laid out frozen cold.' This grim closure resonates with many other moments in *Brosna* and in Ó Ríordáin's poetry more generally. The death of the woman is part of the larger death of the Irish language, which Ó Ríordáin sees occurring in his lifetime. The purpose of eight lines which precede the closing couplet is clearly to lead the attention away from matters of the Irish language, so the shock will be all the greater at the end. The metaphor's vehicle turns out to be the true subject of the poem.

Ó Direáin has a similarly doomed sense of the community of Irish speakers, and thus of the language. 'Stoite' (uprooted) was on the Irish national school curriculum for many years and thus helped create a very powerful image of the fate of the language in the twentieth century; it is overwhelmingly moribund:

> Beidh cuimhne orainn go fóill:
> Beidh carnán trodán
> Faoi ualach deannaigh
> Inár ndiaidh in Oifig Stáit.[14]

The first line defiantly states: 'We will be remembered yet', but this is immediately undercut in the next three lines, in a manner very similar to Ó Ríordáin's poem above: 'A stack of files / Weighed down with dust / Will survive in a government office.'[15] While this is elegiac, it also snarls with bitterness towards the Irish state, whose bureaucracy merely records the demise of the language and does not actively promote it. But complaint in Ó Direáin's poetry is balanced by an intense vision of the life of Irish speakers in the West, specifically on the Aran Islands, where he was born:

> Ár n-aithreacha bhíodh,
> Is a n-aithreacha siúd,
> In achrann leis an saol
> Ag coraíocht leis an gcarraig loim.[16]

These are the first lines of the poem: 'Our fathers / And their fathers before them / Were at grips with life / And wrestled with the naked rock.'[17] Despite the expertise of the translators, the English lacks the lapidary precision of the original. In part this has to do with the regularity of the line lengths in the Irish and the way that the main verb appears in the very first line, so that it reads more literally: 'Our fathers were'. Before we find out what they were, the second line makes the reader wait with a qualification about the preceding generation. The spare diction and controlled delivery echo with the landscape description. If you have seen the bare Aran rocks surrounded by the Atlantic you will understand this immediately; and if you haven't, you are probably not a part of Ó Direáin's intended audience.

As well as being the year that *Eireaball Spideoige* was published, 1952 also saw the birth of Nuala Ní Dhomhnaill. More than any other Irish-language poet in the twentieth century, she has brought attention and interest to Gaelic literature. She gives readings, plenaries and holds visiting professorships around the world; her work is translated into English by some of Ireland's finest Anglophone poets. There are several reasons for this, among them that Ní Dhomhnaill is a marvellous performer of her own poetry, and an excellent raconteur, wittily and economically sketching out the dilemmas and problems of being an Irish-language poet at the present time. Another reason is that her take on Irish mythology is consonant with magic realism, especially that of writers like Angela Carter and Marina Warner; this is revisionist folklore of a particularly rich strain. A further reason is that her work does not employ the complex bardic forms of the Irish tradition, but for the most part uses the loose free-verse forms which spread from the USA in the 1950s. Thus, arguably, when Ní Dhomhnaill is translated into English it is a type of homecoming.

In 'Ceist na Teangan' ('The Language Issue'), she is cautiously optimistic about Irish: 'Cuirim mo dhóchas ar snámh / i mbáidín teangan . . .'[18] ('*I place my hope on the water / in this little boat . . .*'[19]). This is from Paul Muldoon's translation and more than any other of her translators he has brought a sense of play to his work: for him, to translate entails more than the rendering of literal meaning, or trying to find an equivalent voice in the target language; rather, he makes his translations of Ní Dhomhnaill an extension of his own poetry. For instance, a line in Ní Dhomhnaill's 'Loch a'Dúin' reads 'is an capall coille', and Muldoon renders this 'the acrostical capercaillie'.[20] The addition is the superfluous word 'acrostical', which refers to Muldoon's own acrostic entitled 'Capercaillie', which is discreet enough, but the liberties he takes elsewhere, for instance in his translation of 'An Traein Dubh', display an impatience and lack of interest in the original. This is hardly surprising as Muldoon is a far superior poet, and ultimately his translations amount to a criticism of her limitations.

In the poetry of Gearóid Mac Lochlainn (b. 1967), the Irish language itself is also the main theme. His poem 'Aistriúcháin' ('Translations') is set in a poetry reading where Mac Lochlainn is the Irish-language poet who performs before the Anglophone one. It ends with him sitting depressed and drunk in a corner, while the evening drifts off into English. He is frustrated because the audience, like the Irish bureaucracy of 'Stoite', pays only lip service to the language, saying how great the poetry sounds, without any idea of what it means (is any language, on a purely phonetic level, beautiful?).

Amanna, éiríonn tú tuirseach
de chluasa falsa Éireannacha.

. . .

Iad sásta go bhfuil sé thart,
sásta go bhfuil an file Béarla ag teacht in mo dhiaidh
le cúpla scéal grinn
a chuirfidh réiteach ar an snag seo san oíche.

Agus seo é anois againn
lena chuid cainte ar '*café culture*' is ar 'Seamus'.[21]

Here it is noteworthy that Seamus Heaney is invoked. As we saw in the last chapter, Heaney throughout his whole career has tried to connect his poetry with the Irish tradition (he speaks Irish and translates from the language; many of his poems are about the intertwining of Gaelic with the landscape), yet Mac Lochlainn gives his name as a sign of the country's hypocrisy. This is not a criticism of Heaney, but rather of a culture which would like its Gaelic elements only in English (Mac Lochlainn is asked by one of the audience: 'Don't you do translations?'). The sign 'Seamus' reassures the audience that it is possible to possess Irish identity, even though one is an Anglophone monoglot, and thus not be mistaken for an English person.

In the late twentieth century, the poet who embodies so many of these debates both in his life and work is Michael Hartnett (1941–99; Mícheál Ó hAirtnéide, his name in Irish). Hartnett emerged in the late 1960s as an Anglophone poet of great promise but then switched to writing poetry in Irish in the late 1970s. He spoke Irish as a child, but English was his first language. Like Pádraic Ó Conaire before him, it was not until he was living in London in the period 1965–8 that he realised the full significance of his bilingual heritage. There have been and are other bilingual poets, such as Eoghan Ó Tuairisc (1919–82), Frank Sewell (b. 1968), but it is in Hartnett's career that the dilemmas of such poets take the most dramatic form. When he returned to Ireland from London in 1968, he met regularly with Irish speakers, and by 1970 he was, as he said, 'enmeshed in a bilingual chaos – poems abruptly changing languages in mid-verse, words from one tongue insinuating themselves into poems written in the other'.[22] He was particularly out of sympathy with the pro-EEC stance of the Irish government of the day, which stressed industrialisation and had little respect for Gaelic culture:

> And it was alleged that a child had died in Galway hospital asking for *deoch uisce* and no-one understood it. True or not, it rang in my head and sometime after that my brain succumbed to the flood of Gaelic I was pouring on it and I found myself able to think and write whole poems in it, however bad.[23]

The same year, he declared his intention in the title poem of the collection, *A Farewell to English* (1975):

> I have made my choice
> and leave with little weeping:
> I have come with meagre voice
> to court the language of my people.[24]

Here the echo with Ó Ríordáin is no failed allusion. But the question remained for Hartnett who his people were: were they the remaining Irish speakers in the country or were they the Anglophone monoglots who must be reminded that their language is not native to them? He never resolved the question, but the uncertainty, while obviously a source of pain for the poet himself, prompted some of his best work. Nuala Ní Dhomhnaill was one of those native Irish speakers, who was also a poet and knew Hartnett at that time. In a memoir written after his death, she describes his difficult situation during the period:

> [H]e wrote in Irish only for about ten years. He got little thanks from the established writers of either language for this enormous sacrifice. The English-language literati, perhaps threatened at some deep level by this

action, turned snide, muttering about his farewell to English that 'nothing so became him as his leaving it'. He also found the welcome of the Gaeilgeoirí somewhat less forthcoming than he might have expected.[25]

While it catches something of the general consternation on both sides, the critical reception of *Adharca Broic* (1978), the first book that emerged from this period, was not so negative.[26] There followed *An Phurgóid* (1983), *Do Nuala: Foidhne Chrainn* (1984) and finally *An Lia Nocht* (1985).

But it did not last and in the early 1980s he returned to the English language, and for the remainder of his career he remained with it. Or as he put it in *Inchicore Haiku* (1985): 'My English dam bursts / and out stroll all my bastards. / Irish shakes its head.'[27] It is the bastards rather than the thoroughbreds that have always been better for literature, and this collection of haiku set in an old working-class district of Dublin is among his finest. During his Irish period he had ensconced himself in Templeglantine in West Limerick. Hartnett's return from the countryside to the capital city is consonant with his move from Irish to English (the English language has been native in Dublin perhaps longer than in any other part of the island). Hartnett also encounters modernity in its rawest form in the city and he is disgusted by it: 'In local chippers / sad cod dream in fresh batter. / The Atlantic cries.'[28] The natural world laments its loss, but without that loss we wouldn't have the beautiful image of the second line here. Although he might despise what modernity has done to Ireland, his imagination draws on it marvellously. This is the recognition that the book of eighty-seven haiku moves towards:

> 82
> Dying in exile.
> To die without a people
> is the real death.

> 86
> All divided up,
> all taught to hate each other.
> Are these my people?

> 87
> My dead father shouts
> from his eternal Labour:
> 'These are your people!'[29]

The pun on the word 'labour' wittily mixes creation myths with social welfare (Ní Dhomhnaill remarks that he was known as 'the fastest pun in the West'[30]).

The exile of the first haiku is the exile of the Irish poet among the Irish people. He comes around to his patrimony in the end, however, and acknowledges the complexity of his relations with his people.

In *A Farewell to English* Hartnett is angry not just about the status of Irish but also about the modern world. Particularly vituperative is the poem entitled 'USA', which concludes (the land is referred to as a woman): 'She does not love this race. / She will not open her legs to enclose / the scum of Europe, jockeying for grace.'[31] This strain in his poetry would strengthen with the years; when mixed with the self-pity of the middle-aged man, the result was not good. The problem with these lines, as with most of his poems in this mode, is that they violently reduce a complex situation in order to sing the jeremiad. For instance, what will the USA do with the 'scum' of Africa? They do not appear in the poem. Another anti-modern poet like Yeats would never have written these lines as he would have recognised their central untruth: the land of America of course can and has accepted the white settlers, just as it has accepted the children's children's children of slaves: they are now native also. On the other hand, Hartnett wrote some excellent 'curse poems' in the old Irish bardic tradition. Outstanding in this mode is 'On Those who Stole Our Cat, a Curse', one verse of which goes:

> May all their kids come down with mange,
> their eldest daughter start acting strange,
> and the wife start riding the range
>   (and I don't mean the Aga);
> when she begins to go through the change
>   may she go gaga.[32]

This is a better poem than 'USA' because the rant is laced with humour; that mixture of mood brings with it a greater flexibility of address (namely, the dramatic gesture of the parenthesis here – one can almost see the downturned mouth and slowly nodding head of the speaker). However, Hartnett was unable to marry the bardic and jeremiad modes, so that the first remained light verse and the second lugubrious protest.

Four years after *Inchicore Haiku*, Hartnett published a collection entitled *Poems to Younger Women*, and the book delivered exactly what its beguiling title promised. It includes many poems of praise and some of invective. On the dust cover and when introducing the poems in readings, Hartnett was almost apologetic about the simplicity of their style, but that is their great strength, as for instance in the unforgettable 'Water Baby', which I leave without comment as pure example of Hartnett at his joyful best:

> Already the chestnuts, each a small green mace,
> fall in the rusted chainmail leaves. The swifts,
> like black harpoons, fail against the whaleskin sky.
> Wasps in this skyless summer have no place,
> small quarrels swell to great and flooded rifts;
> lime trees, prematurely old, decide to die.
> The heavy steel-wool curtain never lifts.
> Many cling to rafts of music but I,
> I am not happy with the human race
> aching for its sun-god – *he* kills as well –
> I skip dripping in the shining rain
> and feel the minute fingers tap my face
> and breathing in St Bartholomew's bell
> I look up to the sky and kiss the rain.[33]

Earlier I said that Hartnett remained with English for the remainder of his career; he also immersed himself in the translation of Irish poets such as Dáibhí Ó Bruadair, Aogán Ó Rathaille and Pádraigín Haicéad, as well as translations of Catullus, Federico García Lorca and Heinrich Heine. He knew Latin, Spanish and German, and so these are different from his rendering of the *Tao Te Ching* (which he declared in a prefatory note not to be a translation as he knew no Chinese, but is included in the posthumous *Translations* (2003)). Hartnett belonged to the second-last generation of Irish people who were taught Latin in secondary school as a compulsory subject. The consequence of this for poetry is that we are soon likely to see the end of Latin translations by poets (although 'versions' may still abound). Older ideas of creative activity did not differentiate between a writer's original work and his translations. Having lost that apprehension, we thus have difficulty acknowledging that John Dryden's masterwork is his translation of the *Æneid*, and not his satires. It would somehow feel like a derogation of a great writer to place his translations above his own poems. Translation has worked for Irish poets in the second half of the twentieth century in a different way. Many have indulged in 'versioning' from languages they do not know, and this is a relatively quick and easy job, mainly carried out as a courtesy to Gaelic poets, as well as poets from Eastern European countries. But the work of translation is more time-consuming, if one includes the time spent learning the language.[34] The poet spends more time breathing foreign airs, and so the imagination must adapt itself accordingly to the new atmosphere.

Two good examples of this distinction are Michael Longley and Derek Mahon. Both have done some versions of Nuala Ní Dhomhnaill's poetry, and neither speaks nor reads Irish; consequently, the versions have had no impact on their own work. However, when we turn to their translations and versions from languages they know, the situation is radically different. Michael Longley studied Classics at Trinity College, Dublin, and motifs from Latin and Greek literature are present in his work from the very beginning.[35] In the poems of *Gorse Fires* (1991) it became impossible to draw a dividing line between his own poems and his translations and versions of Homer. It is as though Longley and Homer become a composite poet. This arrogance is justified only by the excellence of the resulting work. In his next collection, *The Ghost Orchid*, the influence of Ovid is particularly strong. 'Spiderwoman' recounts the Arachne episode from the *Metamorphoses*, but before the story begins there is a one-line preface: 'Arachne starts with Ovid and finishes with me.'[36] Fran Brearton comments on the richness of this: 'In its simplest interpretation, it means that Arachne's story was first told by Ovid, and has then finished up, much later, in the hands of "me", being the poet Michael Longley. But equally, it may be read the other way around as Arachne starting with "Ovid" after having finished with "me", and the implications of that are very different.'[37] In addition, the line carries predatory overtones ('finish off' as well as 'finish with'). For Longley, translation becomes a way of thinking about the world, as well as about literary tradition.

These relationships with poets such as Homer and Ovid create certain patterns of thought and poetic practice that spill over into Longley's approach to Anglophone poets also. He has always been drawn to the English poet, Edward Thomas (1878–1917), and indeed his wife, the literary critic Edna Longley, has written excellently on Thomas's work. In *Snow Water* (2004), Longley has a poem entitled 'Edward Thomas's Poem' which is about reading the notebook that Thomas had on him when he was killed in World War I. He sees that Thomas has drafted a poem, but cannot make out his small writing; this prompts Longley to imagine what Thomas heard and saw in the days before his death, and here Longley passes over military matters (which hardly need mentioning in any case) in favour of the birds that would have been singing at the time. Then he concludes with a couplet: 'The nature poet turned into a war poet as if / He could cure death with the rub of a dock leaf.'[38] On the first level, this refers to Thomas's own transformation in the years 1915–17, but it also reflects upon Longley's imaginative work in the poem, as he uses the old pun of 'leaf' as both foliage and page. Longley wishes that his own poem, his translation, or restoration, of a lost original, could assuage Thomas's trouble, could become a kind of dock leaf. Indeed, given Longley's imaginative preoccupation with Thomas over the preceding decades it is difficult to say if 'Edward Thomas's Poem' (a form of title which Longley often uses for translations or versions) is a poem, a translation or a restoration.

John Kerrigan has written brilliantly on the importance of Ovid for Northern Irish poets, and especially for Derek Mahon. Famously out of tune with the technological aspirations of modern civilisation, Mahon criticises them by describing junk: 'Mahon finds an aura around rubbish not only because it shows things reverting to nature but because it represents æsthetic value in the making.'[39] That 'reversion' to Nature is Ovidian, since decay is a metamorphosis as well as birth. In 'A Garage in Co. Cork' Mahon re-works the story of Philemon and Baucis from the *Metamorphoses* (which episode has also been translated by Longley), in order to describe a filling station that has been abandoned, its owners emigrated to England or America. Here the virgin escapes the lust of Zeus and ends up as in a shrine as the Virgin Mary, still intact. From this new position, she primly 'sanctions' the country, and is both as native and as alien as the Greek god in Co. Cork.[40] In 1994, James Lasdun and Michael Hofmann edited an anthology entitled *After Ovid: New Metamorphoses*, and while Longley contributed seven translations, Mahon contributed only one (he has translated some sections of the *Amores*). Nevertheless, a passage like this is also translation, although in a looser, more mediæval sense.

Like Austin Clarke in *Tiresias* (discussed in chapter 5), Mahon adapts Ovid to an Irish setting (and, in its turn, Ovid's own poem was an adaptation of Greek stories). In his translation of Virgil's *Georgics* (2004), Peter Fallon also adapts a Latin poet to the landscape and husbandry of Ireland. The technique is not like that of a production of a Renaissance play in modern dress, but rather in such instances the poet-translator finds a tone and a diction that allows him to move fluidly between two different places and times. Fallon retains all the Latin place-names, and the names of flora and fauna, but ghosting Virgil's translated instructions about farming and the seasons is the knowledge that Fallon himself is a farmer in Co. Meath. The poem itself is a combination of farming manual and ecstatic celebration of nature, delighting in the mixture of majestic declamations about the Roman Empire and matters of the earth. The business of farming becomes charged with imperial mission. Farmers and empire builders have to work hard against nature because the 'world forces all things to the bad, to founder and to fall'.[41] Fallon's translation also becomes a way to meditate on latter-day issues of Empire and war.

Integral to the translator's art is choice of the original. As he implies in his Afterword, Fallon, a farmer and poet, was drawn to the *Georgics* for their combination of farming and poetry. When Derek Mahon translated 'Le Cimetière marin' in his sixtieth year, he made Paul Valéry's meditation on death his own. Mahon designates his work as a 'version', but that is not an accurate description.

It is true that he does not replicate Valéry's rhyme scheme, but at key points Mahon is determinedly literal. For the most part he renders the French poet's cries of self-pity more detached and neutral.

> Comme le fruit se fond en jouissance,
> Comme en délice il change son absence
> Dans une bouche où sa forme se meurt,
> Je hume ici ma future fumée,
> Et le ciel chante à l'âme consumée
> Le changement des rives en rumeur.

> *But even as fruit consumes itself in taste,*
> *even as it translates its own demise*
> *deliciously in the mouth where its form dies,*
> *I sniff already my own future smoke*
> *while light sings to the ashen soul the quick*
> *change starting now on the murmuring coast.*[42]

Mahon loses much in the first line here, but in the second, he translates Valéry's 'il change' to 'it translates': the smallest turn of nuance makes the line resonate with Mahon as translator facing death with Valéry. The remaining lines are almost exactly literal, with the added felicity of the enjambment 'the quick / change', which puns brilliantly on the matter of life and death. As in previous cases, the question of authorship remains unanswered. It is perhaps most confusing at the poem's conclusion:

> Le vent se lève! . . . Il faut tenter de vivre!
> L'air immense ouvre et referme mon livre,
> La vague en poudre ose jaillir des rocs!
> Envolez-vous, pages tout éblouies!
> Rompez, vagues! Rompez d'eaux réjouies
> Ce toit tranquille où picoraient des focs!

> *the wind rises; it's time to start. A vast breeze*
> *opens and shuts the notebook on my knees*
> *and powdery waves explode among the rocks*
> *flashing; fly off, then, my sun-dazzled pages*
> *and break, waves, break up with ecstatic surges*
> *this shifting surface where the spinnaker flocks!*[43]

Mahon quietly beards five of the six exclamation marks in the original, but engagingly risks one at the very end. One wonders if Mahon visited Valéry's cemetery in Sète before or during the translation of the poem; by turning

Valéry's 'livre' into a 'notebook', Mahon wants us to think so. It is the tiniest change in what is an almost literal rendition of the original, and it serves to foreground the translator, or at least let us view Mahon contemplating his imminent ghosthood, after Valéry has passed into his.

Wallace Stevens once remarked that 'French and English constitute a single language',[44] and that is the premise of Aidan Rooney's poem 'Magic Antennae', which tells the story of an Irish boy who goes to Paris the summer after his Leaving Certificate, only to get arrested as a terrorist suspect. The police eventually realise their mistake, but send him packing anyway to ensure that there are no awkward complaints:

> 'Vaut mieux vous éclipser un peu, young man.
> Décamper. We'll drop you off in the van
> à la Gare du Nord and give you the price
> d'un aller simple. If another bomb
>
> s'explose ici, we go looking for you.'
> Raisonnable enough, you have to admit.
> D'ailleurs, mon père, who wants me in Maynooth,
> exige que j'ai mon BA to pursue;
> et alors, je rentre, to quell what hitherto's been hapless youth.
>   (L'Ami Butte, rue André Barsacq, '82, l'été après le bac)[45]

Rooney capitalises on the habit of pretentious English speakers to pepper their speech with French phrases. But he stretches beyond that, through the use of proper slang ('décamper') and more difficult constructions. Also, when bilingual speakers are in the company of others who speak the same two languages they tend to switch between the languages – for a word, a phrase or a whole sentence. Having been immersed in Paris for a summer, Rooney has caught this habit also. This allows him to refer jauntily to career pressures in Ireland and his anxious father who is turned into 'mon père'. One cannot emphasise enough the effect of this last *ostranenie*: in the given context, the metamorphosis of 'my father' to 'mon père' is worthy of Ovid. The world-weary sigh of 'et alors' continues in the flamboyant archaism of the last half-line. The affectation is humorous, and indeed there is a winsome Byronic swagger to the entire poem.

Rooney balanced beautifully between the two languages; as is well known, Samuel Beckett (1906–89) went further and wrote a lot of his mature work in French. Besides the more famous dramas, there were the 'Mirlitonnades' (a 'mirliton' is a reed pipe). Beckett translated his French plays into English and it is possible to think of them as originals. He made the switch in 1938–9, writing some poems in French, and after the war he began to write prose and drama in that language. He did not translate 'Mirlitonnades', and because they are rhymed poems with very short lines (sometimes of just a word or two) they are virtually untranslatable. When the left margin comes in so close against the rhymes on the right the result is a mixture of struggle and love affair with the language. The embrace is too tight to be broken. Here is the first one:

> en face
> le pire
> jusqu'à ce
> qu'il fasse rire[46]

And here is a draft translation:

> *to face*
> *the worst*
> *of the case*
> *till laugh you must*[47]

This is not adequate for several reasons. First, in order to get the rhyme, the sense of the first two lines has to be qualified in the third. This is bad because it upsets the symmetry of the poem and also because it limits the sense of 'le pire' to a particular case: in the original, the 'worst' seems limitless. Second, the anapæst in the third line sounds wrong. Third, in order to get the B-rhyme an egregious 'you' has to be introduced. Here is another translation, this time by David Wheatley:

> *Facing*
> *the worst*
> *laugh*
> *till you burst*[48]

The problem here is the word 'burst' which Wheatley needs for the rhyme, but unfortunately brings in a type of music-hall jollity that is completely at odds with the austere subjunctive; also it introduces a 'you', whereas the original has just a statement of general, detached necessity. When a poem's lines are longer there is more room for the translator to manœuvre. Losses in some places can be compensated elsewhere. But the 'Mirlitonnades' offer no such room.

The manuscripts of the 'Mirlitonnades' went on sale in Sotheby's on 13 July 2006 and, as the *TLS* reported, they proved to be written on Craven 'A' cigarette packets: 'The poems are scrawled on the buff innards and – proof of Beckett's attachment – are signed and dated.'[49] They range widely: quiet contemplation, fleeting notes, recommendations for the traveller, epigrams and, quite frequently, breath-taking glimpses of being and nothingness, and they are always sinewed with Beckett's wry humour:

fin fond du néant
au bout de quelle guette
l'œil crut entrevoir
remuer faiblement
la tête le calma disant
ce ne fut que dans ta tête[50]

far end of void
beyond what blind
night watch eye spied
head dimly swaying
soothed it saying
all in the mind[51]

The first four lines present us with a typical scene of existential angst as the eye looks into the void imagining that it makes out some weak movement; the implication is that this would bring an end to a terrible solipsism. However, in the last two lines, the head, which encases the eye, dismisses such a hope, remarking that it's 'all in your head'. The humorous play of contact and solipsism, the grotesque idea that the eye has a head inside itself, are kept brilliantly for the last two lines here (Derek Mahon's translation, otherwise compelling, strangely omits the possessive pronoun).

Beckett, rather than translating French poetry, translated himself into French. In this way he escaped the question for Irish writers in English that is by times troubling and by times profitable: what makes them Irish if they write in English? The binary of Ireland versus England could also become an imaginative bind. (When asked once if he was an Englishman, he replied: 'Au contraire'.) We are left with the conundrum of the 'Mirlitonnades' in their original French glory. In their midst, one of them remarks on a woman buried in a graveyard in Tangier who had fled Ireland for the heavens and had remained true to her beliefs. It is little wonder that Beckett was fascinated, for the space of a Craven 'A', with her particular fate.

Chapter 10

Feminism and Irish poetry

Eavan Boland, Paula Meehan, Catherine Walsh,
Medbh McGuckian, Eiléan Ní Chuilleanáin

In December 1992, a conversation between Medbh McGuckian and Nuala Ní Dhomhnaill was facilitated by Laura O'Connor in the suburbs of Dublin; it was recorded and later published in 1995. In several important ways, the text bears witness to the extraordinary upheavals that took place in Irish society since the 1970s as a result of feminism. The first important events were the formation of the Ad Hoc Committee of Women's Organisations in 1968, and then, two years, later the formation of the Irish Women's Liberation Movement (one member of which was the future President of the Irish Republic, Mary Robinson). Among the immediate issues were pay discrimination and contraception, but to restrict the feminists' impact to those areas would be to underestimate the force of their critique of Irish society in general. Ailbhe Smith argues that:

> Feminism has not been the only movement for social change, but has launched the most enduring, widespread and resonant challenge to the ideology and politics of our nation-state. I don't mean that feminist challenges to the institutions and practices of the state are necessarily explicitly articulated as challenges to nationalism, but their effect is to undermine the ideological bases of the 'nationness' on which the state was founded.[1]

Because certain ideas of gender are enshrined in nationalist ideology and Irish Roman Catholicism, arguments about contraception and pay necessarily pre-cipitated revaluations of the political and religious roles of women.

In literary studies, and more particularly poetry, this has brought about reconsiderations of gender representation in the work of established Irish writers such as W. B. Yeats and Seamus Heaney. In chapter 8, I referred to Patricia Coughlan's essay on gender in the poetry of Heaney and John Montague; fifteen years later she would publish an essay charting Heaney's changing reaction to it and to the challenge of feminism in general, from which it is clear that it has had a profound effect on his thinking and his writing.[2] Another consequence is the revaluation of female poets such as Emily Lawless, Eva Gore-Booth and Blanaid Salkeld. If a classic work such as Zora Neale Hurston's *Their Eyes Were Watching*

God has not been discovered, then at least our ideas of certain literary periods, such as the Revival, have been brought into sharper focus. A third consequence of this activity is that greater attention is now paid to contemporary poetry by Irish women, and to the ways that these poets reflect the critical debates surrounding gender and nation. Indeed, more women than before are finding their way to publication. A fourth consequence is apparent in the poetry of Irish men. There is a signal shift from the neo-nationalism of the senior generation of poets: gone are the representations of the Irish landscape as female, no matter how nuanced, and along with this ebbs a general preoccupation with the Irish nation.

McGuckian and Ní Dhomhnaill's conversation reflects many of these themes, and also marks an important fault line between their own generation and that of the senior Irish poets of the time:

MMcG: . . . You see, what annoys me is that there is no way that you and I, Nuala, and John Montague and Thomas Kinsella could all sit in a room and without any embarrassment go over these things, because they have so much to lose. Or at least they feel that we are trespassers.

NNíD: They want to corral us off as 'women poets', as if that were a form of inferior being.[3]

Ní Dhomhnaill's comment here challenges the very organisation of this chapter, and I should immediately state that the subject demands a separate chapter precisely because of its significance, and in what follows I will show how the work of poets like McGuckian, Eiléan Ní Chuilleanáin and Eavan Boland has become central to ideas of Irish poetry in the last three decades.

There is a further important strand in their conversation: the Irish language:

MMcG: . . . . Because [English is] an imposed language, you see, and although it's my mother tongue and my only way of communicating, I'm fighting with it all the time. I mean even the words 'Shakespeare' and 'Wordsworth' – at some level I'm rejecting them, at some level I'm saying get out of my country, or get out of my . . .

NNíD: . . . soul.

MMcG: Get out of me. Get away, and give me these Ó Rathailles and all these people that I've no immediate intercourse with. And yet I do feel that there's a psychic hunger – what Nuala called it – and that all I've had in my education has been shoved onto me, and I'm lying like a corpse under it all. And so every time I use a word I'm shovelling off, and maybe at the end of my life I'll begin writing in Irish. Myself. But, no . . . no, no, that would never happen, but . . .

NNíD: But in an English that would be in Irish, a recreation of something.

MMcG: Yes, to reach an English that would be so purified of English that it would be Irish.

NNíD: Maybe purified of the whole male thing as well?

MMcG: And that too, yes.[4]

An Irish-language poet herself, Ní Dhomhnaill is extremely sympathetic to the hurt and confusion that McGuckian expresses here. Attempts at the recreation of Irish within English, as we have seen, have been going on at least since the late nineteenth century, but it is apparent here that they have failed, since McGuckian remains dissatisfied with her poetic idiom. The strong nationalist viewpoint expressed here by McGuckian is largely untypical of her generation and the following one; but what is indeed typical is McGuckian's uncertainty about her status as an Irish poet writing in English. The same uncertainty was visible in Vona Groarke's comment quoted in the introduction to this book. In chapter 4, I proposed that one reason that Yeats was an important forebear for twentieth-century Irish poets was that he established a tradition in the English language, with minimum reliance on Gaelic. No Irish poet since Yeats, not even Thomas Kinsella, displayed the same degree of troubled uncertainty that McGuckian does here.

Along with Mary Robinson, Eavan Boland joined the Irish Women's Liberation Movement in 1970, and her engagement in feminism deeply affected the development of her career. She had attended Trinity College, Dublin, at the same time as Michael Longley and Derek Mahon, and her apprentice work of the period very much resembled theirs: stanza forms with regular rhymes and meters in which the speaker is detached, ironic and values above all elegance of expression. Her talent was recognised at an early stage and she published her first collection at the age of twenty-three. She married and moved with her husband to the suburbs of Dublin; children followed. Boland found herself living the life of a suburban housewife, a life that was very different from her student years at Trinity. As her prose memoirs of the period attest, she began to feel that there was no place in poetry, and especially in Irish poetry, to accommodate the domestic experience of a wife and mother living in suburbia. Her subsequent career can be seen as a concerted attempt to change this situation.

Many of her poems foreground the figure of a woman, and most often it is an autobiographical persona. Boland writes of her own difficulties in transforming the lyric poem so that it can accommodate women's experience. In this matter, she was greatly influenced by the American poet Adrienne Rich (b. 1929). Also, like Rich, she explored the connections between gender and nation, leading her to a strong revision of Irish nationalist ideology. This was something of a turnaround for Boland, as in the 1960s she had written admiringly about Patrick Pearse, the leader of the Easter Rising of 1916.[5] However, while she has come to view such figures more critically, she has not moved beyond their terms of reference: Ireland, as a nation now revised by feminist ideology, remains her greatest theme, and she has not registered the changes which Ailbhe Smith outlined above. There are perhaps many factors at work, but the most important is the fact that Boland's attention has for many decades been turned towards America (she is now the Director of the Creative Writing Program at Stanford University). The same is true of other poets such as Seamus Heaney, Thomas Kinsella and John Montague who have spent many years teaching in the USA: it is as though the American audience will not let the Irish poet forget his or her nation. (In the next chapter, I discuss Boland's treatment of the theme of emigration, especially to the USA.)

Boland's 'Anna Liffey', from *In a Time of Violence* (1994), is a meditation on the river that runs through Dublin. Boland mixes autobiography with Irish history in an effort to see how they cohere and where they are pointing to:

> Maker of
> Places, remembrances,
> Narrate such fragments for me:
>
> One body. One spirit.
> One place. One name.
> The city where I was born.
> The river that runs through it.
> The nation which eludes me.
>
> Fractions of a life
> It has taken me a lifetime
> To claim.[6]

On a superficial level, this might seem to question the idea of the nation, but in fact it is the nation, and no other political arrangement, that eludes the grasp: that is what she is searching for and that is what conditions her poetic. In any case, the object (or significant parts of it) is finally claimed with liturgical solemnity. Boland is insistent that her reclamation of the nation does not repeat the violent nationalism of her forebears ('I won't go back to it', she declares in 'Mise Eire' – meaning the patterns of nationalist poetry that led to the blood sacrifices of the likes of Pearse[7]), and in 'Anna Liffey' the speaker drifts deathwards and out of the old murderous patterns. She also asserts a new pattern:

And I make this mark:
>   A woman in the doorway of her house.
>   A river in the city of her birth.
> The truth of a suffered life.
>   The mouth of it.[8]

Here Boland is punning 'life' with '*An Life*' (life), the Irish name of the river (with the subsequent pun on human mouth and river mouth). As in Kinsella's Peppercanisters discussed in chapter 6, suffering is marked as the social adhesive of the nation, and a foundation is sought in the distant past. Much of her work subsequent to *In a Time of Violence* has merely repeated the gesture of 'Anna Liffey', and there has been a consequent repetition of technique and methods of structuring material. She has tried various means of escape, none of which have succeeded, and so seven years later in *Code*, a poem like 'Suburban Woman: Another Detail' is hardly distinguishable – stylistically and atmospherically – from 'Anna Liffey'. What was once an act of imaginative liberation has hardened into a monotonous authority that intones staccato half-sentences. It is of note that one of the best poems she has written in the last two decades is extremely different from the majority of her late work. This is perhaps because it abjures authority (and thus gains more). In 'The Necessity for Irony' Boland tells how she used to visit antique fairs with her young daughter, who eventually grew up and was no longer there beside her. As the final stanza progresses, it focuses ever more closely on the speaker and her self-reproaches, only to turn brilliantly in the final line to sudden praise of the daughter, her beauty and the awfulness of her absence.

As Paula Meehan (b. 1955) makes clear in a poem dedicated to Boland, she owes several debts of style and content to the older poet, but Meehan is not as preoccupied in nationalism. Her imaginative hinterland is the inner city of Dublin, where she grew up, and she frequently confronts issues of poverty and violence. The tone is often occasionally moralistic as she rails against greed and injustice. Her most effective poems harness the demotic voice of working-class Dublin, for example in 'History Lesson' from *Dharmakaya* (2000):

> Spelt out in brick and mortar,
> a history lesson for every mother's daughter.
>
> Who owns which and who owns what?
> The devil owns the bleeding lot![9]

The idiom of the first three lines here is bland enough, but this is changed in the final line. 'Bleeding' is an intensifier particular to Dublin, and Meehan effectively holds back its slangy force for the punchline of the poem. Meehan shares this anger at social injustice with Rita Ann Higgins (b. 1955); and Catherine Walsh (b. 1964) also registers some of the threats and dangers of city life. The following passage is set in the city, when the woman has settled her children to bed for the night, only to have them woken up by events out on the street.

> night accommodates all
> cries   children   swinging
>   trees   street shattering
> glass   glass the vein pricks
> stand naked with their
> clothes on uniformly faceless
>   advertising their
> skill motionless flickering
> eyes   then the yahoo
> the dart   wrestling
>
>   thudding feet
> hammering down the road
>   by   shouts or screams
> stop it stop it fuck off you
>
> putting the children
>   back to sleep   closing
> a window or 2 despite
> heat
>   are the jeans still
> on the clothesline   who's
> had the trainers pulled off
> their[10]

The technique here owes much to some of the poets discussed in chapter 6, especially Maurice Scully. As the words float over the page in irregular patterns, so Walsh tries to imitate the chaos of life. She does not comment or condemn, she merely records and tries not to indulge in 'the analysis / afterward'.[11] She deliberately forgoes mastery over the scene in an attempt to capture the contours of experience more accurately. Nevertheless, by exercising some degree of choice over her materials, Walsh, like any writer, structures the reader's experience, and here there can be no doubt that she is registering class tension. The evening scene with the children is extremely close to many of Boland's poems, but it is clear that we are a step or two closer to the breadline when we move from Boland's to Walsh's neighbourhood. Like Meehan, but in a very different style, Walsh quietly but firmly introduces urban material, conscious that the Irish tradition has been predominantly pastoral. Several academic critics have argued for the importance of Walsh's work, connecting it to poets such as Lyn Hejinian in the USA and Denise Riley in the UK, but she is not as formally interesting or adventurous as those poets.

The critic Moynagh Sullivan argues that because Medbh McGuckian writes about the female body and its sexual and reproductive experience, her work is frequently marginalised, while male experience is designated as somehow universal.[12] Certainly, two generations of critics have been baffled by her poetry and are uncertain of its subject on a simple denotative level. McGuckian has further complicated the situation by stating in interviews and cover notes that her poems are often about nationalist politics, even while those same poems make no direct reference to such issues. Even Clair Wills, as she tries to give a political meaning to a particular poem, admits that 'there is nothing within the poem itself which would determine such a reading'.[13] As such arguments continue, McGuckian, a particularly prolific poet, has continued to dazzle readers with lyric beauty. One frequently might not know what her poems are about, but one cannot fail to be mesmerised by them.

McGuckian was born in Belfast in 1950 and attended Queen's University in Belfast, where Michael Allen, Edna Longley and Seamus Heaney were teaching at the time, and where Paul Muldoon and Ciaran Carson were students; the other important poet closely associated with the group was Michael Longley. McGuckian had a strong sense of being surrounded by brilliant male poets, but her given subject matter was different from theirs. Her early books – *The Flower Master and Other Poems* (1982), *Venus and the Rain* (1984) and *On Ballycastle Beach* (1988) – suggest that she is conducting a conversation with many of these figures, or at least a composite version of them. Her voice is by times challenging, seductive, matter-of-fact, apathetic, impassioned and precise. Michael Allen remarks that:

> McGuckian's gamut of forms, from the 'well-made' and lucid poem, through the gnomic and baroque symbolist modes into the free symbolism of much of *Venus and the Rain*, can be seen as presenting various ways of enacting, transmitting and making accessible this 'wild' experience. She has said that the audience of poets 'is made up mainly of men': 'I write to please a male audience and also to make them aware of how a woman thinks.'[14]

Readers of her work are shown an economy of desire – its slipstreams, eddies, debouchures – they never suspected of existing, or if they did could never have expressed. The poems are a continual conversation with a silent man in the midst of metamorphosing landscapes and house interiors. And what landscapes, so extensive and lavishly deployed. For instance:

The scented flames of the sun throw me,
Telling me how to move – I tell them
How to bend the light of shifting stars:
I order their curved wash so the moon
Will not escape, so rocks and seas
Will stretch their elbows under her.[15]

There is no sense whatsoever that these rocks and seas might be the same ones abutting on to the tract of land in which Union Jacks and Tricolours hang from telegraph poles, in which peace-walls are constructed and armed helicopters fly overhead. Speaking in interview about her work, she admits its difficulty and by way of explanation comments: 'My life has been – well living here [in Northern Ireland] has been – pretty unliveable. So you wouldn't expect the poetry to be anything else but awkward.' She continues:

> I don't care so much about being understood now, but I want to give pleasure. I know I am dealing with very ugly material, and a very ugly world, but I am always concerned with trying to take out of that what is most uplifting . . . I got a letter the other day which said, 'I read the first verse of that poem over and over again – I didn't understand it at all, but I thought it was beautiful,' and that seems like a wonderful response to me.[16]

McGuckian's poetry has often been dismissed as merely decorative, but here she insists on the connection between it and the political reality of Northern Ireland. It would be too easy to dismiss such poetry as escapist, and McGuckian clearly has deeper designs on the reader. This will become apparent especially in her work of the 1990s.

'Aviary' from *Venus and the Rain* follows a trajectory of negotiation with a person we presume to be the speaker's lover towards a spectacular image of 'flourishing', or sexual ecstasy. The addressee is a painter. But unlike Boland, who indicts male painters for misrepresenting females, McGuckian negotiates and converses with the painter:

> Well may you question the degree of falsehood
> In my round-the-house men's clothes, when I seem
> Cloaked for a journey, after just relearning to walk,
> Or turning a swarthy aspect like a cache-
> Enfant against all men. Some patterns have
> A very long repeat, and this includes a rose
> Which has much in common with the rose
> In your drawing, where you somehow put the garden
> To rights.[17]

While there are local difficulties of meaning here, the rhythms and contours of the engagement with the other person are immediately recognisable as belonging to a familial or lovers' relationship. The addressee puts 'the garden / To rights' in his painting, which is the kind of thing that Boland would take umbrage at, but here, while those 'rights' might be slightly ironic, the even tone of address rules out the possibility of accusation and recrimination. The patterns with a long repeat might refer to the pattern of convalescence and falsehood in the first sentence, but more importantly they set up a continuum between the floriage, the painting and the textile designs. Whereas the first sentence marks a small fracas between the couple, the second flows forth in rapprochement. Representing this type of nuanced ebb and flow in a relationship is McGuckian's forte.

The poem continues in what has been taken as a gloss on McGuckian's poetry in general:

> You call me aspen, tree of the woman's
> Tongue, but if my longer and longer sentences
> Prove me wholly female, I'd be persimmon,
> And good kindling, to us both.
>   . . .
> I can hear already in my chambered pith
> The hammers of pianos, their fastigiate notes
> Arranging a fine sightscreen for my nectary,
> My trustful mop. And if you feel uncertain
> Whether pendent foliage mitigates the damage
> Done by snow, yet any wild bird would envy you
> This aviary, whenever you free all the birds in me.[18]

Edna Longley remarks that the harder persimmon is chosen over 'the womanly, tremulously garrulous aspen' and 'persimmon's "chambered pith" also promises new kinds of shape: "good kindling" for poem-making and love-making';[19] she also draws attention to the fact that persimmon is very astringent until softened by frost, and this is picked up in the last sentence of the poem. The last verse of the poem, which I quote above, rises to the sexual climax of the last explosive image. But as well as being a stunning figure for orgasm, it encapsulates the bizarre mixture of freedom and confinement (in both senses, namely, 'the difficult daughter' earlier in the poem) at the heart of any relationship. The birds inside the female speaker are indeed freed, but they are freed into a cage. Nevertheless, this cage is described by the female speaker as something any wild bird would envy, so that its trammelled freedom is preferable to the untrammelled variety.

With the publication of *Captain Lavender* (1994), McGuckian began to refer more overtly to politics and history. On the book's cover is Jack B. Yeats's painting 'Communicating with the Prisoners' (1924), the prisoners being those of anti-Treatyites from the Civil War. The cover note to *Shelmalier* (1998) clearly announces that the book is concerned with the rebellion of the United Irishmen in 1798. Similarly, collections such as *Drawing Ballerinas* (2001), *The Face of the Earth* (2002) and *Had I a Thousand Lives* (2003) meditate on various aspects of nationalism and violence in Irish history and the contemporary situation; while *The Book of the Angel* (2004) and *The Currach Requires No Harbours* (2006) are concerned with more spiritual matters. In the last decade, McGuckian has published 458 pages of poetry, as much as some poets publish in a lifetime. By times it is obscure only then to become richly suggestive and resonant; occasionally it startles with plain speech. It will take some years yet for readers to absorb and respond properly to such profusion. In what follows, I will look at her treatment of nationalist iconography in three poems from *Had I a Thousand Lives*, and then discuss the theme of spirit in *The Book of the Angel*.

Many of the poems of *Had I a Thousand Lives* are preoccupied with the idea of voice as it moves through 'honest and usable Englishings'[20] all the while remembering the 'native silence'[21] of the Irish language. The last phrase is from 'Cathal's Voice', in which the Irish language is figured as interleaved with the Irish landscape, and these two elements are associated with the idea of 'home'.[22] She expresses repulsion towards English here, as she did in the conversation with Ní Dhomhnaill, but she also sees the possibility of détente between the languages in Ireland. Nevertheless it must be noted that the 'embrace' of the final line is only attempted.

The next poem in the book goes even further into the physical mechanisms of voice and tongues. 'The Mirror Game' begins by describing a sound moving up through someone's body until it reaches the mouth:

> You make the most space possible in your mouth,
> tightening the supple organ of your tongue,
> and the muscles hidden in your unpeaceful neck,
> though your anchored ribs are free to move.[23]

Language is often thought of as abstraction added to phonemes, but here McGuckian literally anchors it in the body. The question of 'Irishings' and 'Englishings' is thus played out on the most basic anatomical level, and is not a mere political issue. It becomes clear that the poem's speaker is in conversation with the addressee, on the most intimate level. As the poem progresses, we see that they are possibly making love, but this is kept unclear. The book celebrates the bicentenary of the uprising organised by Robert Emmet, and this nationalist hero takes on Orphic dimensions in the last stunning poem of the book, 'Forcing Music to Speak'. The poem has Emmet standing to be beheaded in 1803, and it is nationalist hagiography of a completely new type, one that is startlingly sensuous and which expresses its awe of its subject in a new way. At the moment when Emmet becomes literally disembodied at the age of twenty-five and his breath is taken away from him, a larger song rises up, which McGuckian tells us at the end of the poem is not a requiem but the 'Gaudeamus' (the students' song, 'Gaudeamus igitur, juvenes dum sumus', 'Then let us be merry while we are young').

Perhaps the most surprising aspect of McGuckian's poetry is the way she energises themes and topoi that are generally considered passé: domesticity was for Katharine Tynan and the other poetesses of previous ages; nationalism had been rendered unfashionable by revisionist readings of Irish history; Catholic iconography had been left behind by the secularisation of Ireland. Yet these are the central preoccupations of one of the most original of contemporary Irish poets. As Sullivan implies in another essay on McGuckian, it would be wrong to consider these preoccupations as separate, as her poetry brings them together and takes on 'Irish literary cultures and traditions, which are fixed in subject–object positions which designate the woman primarily as an iconic mother and as an unchanging structure from which a historical body of male poets may negotiate their relationship to the nation, or the island'.[24] McGuckian is not ironic about the iconic status of women in nationalist ideology and the Catholic religion, rather, she goes back to the very roots of these discourses, seriously and sympathetically. A different poet, frustrated, say, by the representation of women within revolutionary nationalism would ironise or dismiss the likes of Robert Emmet; McGuckian, as we have seen, writes a stunningly erotic love poem for him.

At the centre of *The Book of the Angel* is a sequence entitled 'Studies for a Running Angel'. In several of its poems, a woman is in conversation, or communion, with an angel. Despite the angel's ethereality, there is an intense sensuality to the encounter. We are told that 'The angel, from the behaviour of the cloth / in his waistband, seems to have no body / beneath his drapery';[25] and this suggests that the woman is looking with sexual curiosity at the apparition. Elsewhere, when they talk, they touch:

> She lay clothed, indefinite as the room,
> or the green stair carpet woven
> with yellow globes of the world;
> and by the guidance of sunlight,
> some blur in the misleading chandelier,

> they conversed directly in bright daylight,
> her hand overlapping his draped elbow,
> as though a garden flowered foolishly
> above the town houses, and the future
> who left them in our keeping.[26]

The touch here is chaste – after all, we are told that she is 'clothed' and he is 'draped' – but balanced against that is the fact that the woman is lying down, and the strong emphasis on clothing and drapery also suggests the flesh and air that they gird. The 'stair carpet' brings to mind a line from earlier in the sequence: 'The stairs begin with Jacob's Ladder.'[27] Reference to 'town houses' indicates the modern world (one of the leitmotivs of the book is suburbia – gardens 'surrounded by other gardens, / housing the seasons'[28]). Whereas angels suggest first things and the beginning of time, the houses suggest the present; and so we get a glimpse of the course of human history. It is also important to note that the conversation with the angel has a national resonance, as the book's cover note remarks that the book takes 'its title from the Old Irish eighth-century Latin document, *Liber Angeli*, in which Saint Patrick is granted the ecclesiastical see of Armagh through colloquy with an angel'. We are perhaps catching a glimpse then not of the course of human history, but that of Irish history. It is an index of both her ambition and achievement.

Language and translation is one of the most important themes of the poetry of Eiléan Ní Chuilleanáin (b. 1942). She knows Irish, Italian, French and Latin; when asked to produce English versions from cribs of poems by a Romanian poet, instead she learned Romanian. Such a depth of courtesy and imaginative involvement is singular in Anglophone culture, where translations by monoglot poets are routinely tolerated. The gesture is also iconic for Ní Chuilleanáin's poetry, which listens hard at the silences of history and other people's lives. It refuses received wisdom, and it refuses to make quick characterisations and conclusions. One result of this is that 'her poems are marked by restraint and indirection', as Guinn Batten and Dillon Johnston remark. [29]

In 'Gloss/Clós/Glas' we witness a scholar hunting through his books to find the correct translation of two terms, 'as opposite as *his* and *hers*'.[30] Conveyance of thought from one language to another entails such difficult searches, and the worst aspect of such work is that failed attempts usually produce silence in the target language, leaving no mark of the things, emotions or issues they left behind. Ní Chuilleanáin attends to the tiny, subtle traces of silence and translation, such as the breath at the end of the poem. Because grammars of different languages configure gender in different ways across sentence structures, one of the most difficult tasks for a translator is the transfer of gender relations from one language to another (English, in this respect, is much less 'gendered' than many other European languages). Ní Chuilleanáin's poem turns upon this sexuality at the base of language. Though the door remains locked in the poem, there is a sensuous verdure in the last line (*glas* in Irish means both 'green' and 'lock').

The poem appears in *The Girl who Married a Reindeer* (2001), and in the same book, 'Translation' listens closely to a silence of another kind. Its sub-title tells us that the poem is written on the occasion of the reburial of the Magdalens, inmates of Catholic-run institutions for 'fallen women'. The reburial itself is a kind of translation. But Ní Chuilleanáin is wary of another type of translation that would put words in the mouths of the dead women. The scruple is strong, but laid aside in the prayer of the poem's conclusion.

> Allow us now to hear it, sharp as an infant's cry
> While the grass takes root, while the steam rises:
>
>> Washed clean of idiom · the baked crust
>> Of words that made my temporary name ·
>> A parasite that grew in me · that spell
>> Lifted · I lie in earth sifted to dust ·
>> Let the bunched keys I bore slacken and fall ·
>> I rise and forget · a cloud over my time.[31]

(The asylums were often laundries in the twentieth century, hence the references to 'steam' and 'washed clean'.) At the moment when normal syntax and punctuation is abandoned, Ní Chuilleanáin paradoxically adopts a rhyme scheme reminiscent of a sonnet's sestet. Thus she registers the necessity to memorialise, and perhaps even distort the lives of the dead women (she admits that their voice is 'washed clean of idiom'). The poem makes apparent the connection between ethics and translation: there must be utter exactitude (for in that way one remains true to the dead), but there must also be stylisation (for in that way one remains true to one's art). Arguably, Ní Chuilleanáin, for most of her career, let the first consideration outbalance the second. Her scrupulousness about maintaining the silences of the past was often too successful, producing poems for an esoteric circle of one. In an early poem she concedes that she 'produce[s] paralysis in verse / Where anger would be more suitable'.[32] *The Girl Who Married a Reindeer* is a signally different book then, not because it is angry – it isn't – but because she has heightened the characterisation of the silences, the lost lives, even while retaining her scruples about the dangers of misrepresentation.

Many of the issues which preoccupy McGuckian and Ní Chuilleanáin significantly extend the matters discussed in chapter 9. (It is also worth noting that both poets have translated Ní Dhomhnaill into English.) Moreover, several younger poets such as Vona Groarke, Sinéad Morrissey and Caitríona O'Reilly might also be contained in this chapter. But already as feminism branches out into other issues, so too do these writers enlarge their purview, and they are not truly a part of the cultural debates that were opened up in the 1970s and 1980s. Indeed, in the editorial of a special issue of *Verse* devoted to the subject of Irish women's poetry in 1999 Groarke expressed the wish that 'all such issues will eventually be redundant'.[33]

Chapter 11

Out of Ireland: Muldoon and other émigrés

Paul Muldoon, Greg Delanty, Eavan Boland,
Peter Fallon, Eamon Grennan, Harry Clifton,
Peter McDonald, Tom Paulin, Bernard O'Donoghue,
Ian Duhig

Aleš Debeljak has written of the ways that America affects a poet from a country the size of his own Slovenia.[1] Its literary community is small, and its borders are maintained, more or less, by its language: the world is split into poetry which is Slovene and non-Slovene (but with some obvious overlaps with surrounding countries). The poet's place in this literary heritage will be designated to a large degree by his use of cultural signifiers to which his Slovene audience will respond immediately. However, when a Slovene poet travels to America he must introduce not only his own poetry but his country, as well as the particular pressures and freedoms of its poetic tradition, to a largely unknowledgeable audience. This might seem an onerous task, but for some poets it offers the opportunity of self-reinvention: the bulk of their imaginative energies is no longer expended in communicating *within* Slovene culture, but in presenting that culture in its totality to an outsider. For poets such as Tomaž Šalamun and Debeljak himself this has been an enabling experience which transformed their poetry.

The analogy with Irish poets in America holds up to a certain point. When Yeats was short of money, he would invariably consider a lucrative American lecture tour. (The financial lure of the USA for foreign writers remains fundamental to the cultural transaction.) On completing his lecture tour in 1903–4, he returned to Ireland with more than an expensive fur coat. R. F. Foster records the indignation of Dublin's *littérateurs* at the extent of Yeats's transformation through quoting George Moore: 'And we looked round asking each other with our eyes where on earth our Willie Yeats had picked up such extraordinary ideas.'[2] As Moore remarks, Yeats did not pick up the ideas themselves in the USA; rather, those ideas, his own ideas, had crystallised under the pressure of presenting himself and his country to American audiences.

But Irish-America is different from Slovene-America. Because of the large numbers of Irish emigrants to America over the last two centuries, the opportunities for self-reinvention are somewhat different for the Irish poet. The American audience will already have a strong idea of Ireland, which is colourful, detailed and occasionally inaccurate. This means that the Irish poet must live up to certain expectations, but also find skilful and imaginative ways to subvert those expectations.

In the academic world, that Irish-American audience has become more sophisticated, especially with the establishment of Irish Studies programs in universities such as Boston College and Notre Dame. Dennis O'Driscoll has gone as far as to remark that 'Irish Studies Programs in America increasingly influence the terms on which Irish poetry is read – maybe even written – at home'.[3] The remark is significant because it supposes a model of poetic production in Ireland that resembles the production of Aran sweaters: a small authentic cottage industry which exports to foreign markets. The demands of those markets, however, transform, even sully, the authentic product. O'Driscoll's remark is part of a brief essay that pleas for a more attentive approach to Irish poetry by American readers. They should be ready to recognise American poetic influences, and acknowledge that those influences render Irish poetry no less authentic. Purity is an illusion in such matters. The source *should* be sullied.

There is a further twist to this. Several Irish poets, foremost among them Paul Muldoon, have settled in the USA, and their poetry reflects their experiences in their adopted homeland, yet at the same time they remain an integral part of Irish poetry. The cottage-industry idea of Irish poetry becomes untenable under the force and significance of their example. Muldoon is a compelling poet for many reasons, and one of these is the way his hybridity spectacularly challenges the borders of national literature. In chapter 7, I pointed out how Richard Murphy's poetry of the British Empire is integral to the story of Irish poetry. Muldoon and some of these other poets find themselves living in the midst of a more recent empire, and their poetry at once folds these new experiences back into Ireland, but also unfolds Ireland further out into the world. They do so to such an extent that it becomes difficult to say whether ideas of Ireland and Irishness remain useful for understanding not only their poetry, but even that of the stay-at-homes also.

I have dwelled on the opposition of Ireland and America, but this represents only the most recent episode in a series which stretches back to the Middle Ages, when the languages of Ireland were Irish, English, Latin and French. This polyglot situation brought about important engagements between these literary traditions. In the last two centuries covered by this book, many Irish poets have been resident in England and indeed dependent on English audiences for an income. The negotiations between Ireland and England in the matter of poetry, as in much else, are infinitely more difficult to untangle; perhaps, finally, impossible. For instance, much of the poetry of the first half of Yeats's career can be read as the adaptation of Irish material for an English audience. Proximity and a shared history of colonial oppression and resistance (which led to a shared language) have irrevocably made Irish literature a part of Anglophone literature, which does not mean British literature. Also of importance are the careers of several poets who were born and raised in Ireland, and now live in England. Themes of autobiography and emigration flow through their work in different ways. Moreover, because they are more at home in Britain than in Ireland, they stand as good indices of that tangled situation I referred to above. I will also briefly consider here Irish poets resident in non-Anglophone countries.

There is also a further category of 'inner émigrés' – poets who were born and raised in one part of the island and have settled in another, among them Gerald Dawe, Seamus Heaney, Dennis O'Driscoll, Paul Durcan, Eiléan Ní Chuilleanáin and Vona Groarke. I note this category only in passing, but it demonstrates the useful flexibility of the idea of emigration. Dawe, for instance, was born in Belfast in 1952, and has now settled in south Dublin. Much of his best work depicts the unruffled calm of suburbia, but ghosting this are memories of his more explosive hometown: this is a memory of a different state as well as a different state of mind. The move from the country to the city, or between two cities as different as Dublin and Belfast, can be just as profound for a poet's imagination as an ocean-crossing.

Paul Muldoon was born in 1951 in Portadown, Co. Armagh. His mother was a schoolteacher and his father worked at many jobs including farm labourer. Even before he began studying English at Queen's University, Belfast, he was introduced to Seamus Heaney and Michael Longley at a reading they gave in Armagh, and Heaney soon began directing the attention of editors in London to Muldoon, who was anything but a tyro at this stage. At Queen's he was taught by Heaney, Edna Longley and Michael Allen, and his fellow students included Ciaran Carson and Medbh McGuckian. His first collection, *New Weather*, was published in 1973 by Faber and Faber. In 1974 he began working as a radio producer for the BBC in Belfast, where he remained for thirteen years. In 1987 he married the American novelist Jean Hanff Korelitz and moved to the USA, eventually settling at Princeton University in New Jersey.

New Weather established many of the themes and techniques that have occupied him during the rest of his career. There are poems that employ narrative extensively, in which he describes the farming life he witnessed in his childhood. For the most part he uses traditional verse forms – half-rhymed quatrains and longer stanzas. Perhaps most importantly of all, Muldoon established a tone that is a striking mixture of tenderness and mockery. It allows him to tell stories of shocking events while seeming detached and ironic, only to reveal compassion in the smallest of details. This shifting tone enables him, in Tim Kendall's words, 'to encompass the rival perspectives of innocence and experience in a single vision'.[4] He moves smoothly between a *faux naïveté* and real naivety, often leaving the reader unable to judge the import of what's being said. The poem 'Hedgehog' is a good example of this. The tone is childlike and innocent: 'We say, *Hedgehog, come out / Of yourself and we will love you.*'[5] The hedgehog, however, refuses these winsome entreaties and the speakers of the poem can't understand this. In the final stanza, the voice of the children continues but has subtly modulated into a mature vision: 'We forget the god / Under this crown of thorns. / We forget that never again / Will a god trust in the world.'[6] This has moved us to an adult domain of mourning for lost gods. The hedgehog has shut us out and will not communicate with us, and in this, and in the sharp points that guard him, he resembles Jesus Christ. The tone does not change here, but rather the floor drops from under us, and innocence is gone. Muldoon has spoken with admiration of Robert Frost, with his 'apparently simple, almost naïve, tone of voice and use of language, underneath which all kinds of complex things are happening'.[7]

The collections, *Mules* (1977) and *Why Brownlee Left* (1980), followed *New Weather*. In these books we find many short lyrics resembling 'Hedgehog' – the innocent tone undercut by Muldoon's elliptical mode of address. *Why Brownlee Left* also contains a long poem of three-hundred lines, 'Immram', which mixes a hard-boiled narrative mode reminiscent of Raymond Chandler with material from Native American and Celtic mythology. The title of the poem itself is taken from the eighth-century legend entitled 'Immram Mael Duin' – *iomramh* meaning voyage in Irish, and Mael Duin chiming obviously with Muldoon's own name. The poem is about a billiard-player who, in his search of his father, has to range across America, and while it is not autobiographical, it is prophetic of the importance which American material would come to play in his subsequent poetry.

Several other long poems followed. *Quoof* (1983) ends with 'The More a Man Has the More a Man Wants' which employs Native American Trickster cycles and shuttles between the USA and Northern Ireland. It is Muldoon's first extended consideration of the political violence of the Troubles. Whereas Heaney and Longley have both written moving elegies on victims of the violence in Northern Ireland, and Heaney has written many poems meditating on the relation between politics and poetry, Muldoon's approach is more oblique. He refuses to deal with the issue of paramilitary violence in the terms set by politics:

the violent scenes appear incidentally in more wide-ranging and surreal narratives. As Kendall remarks, 'the incomprehensions and irretrievabilities of "The More a Man Has" suggest a confused world of factions, splinter groups, follow-up searches, undercover agents, and at times, terrible brutality ... [C]haracters merge, come back to life, shift from continent to continent and timescale to timescale, even transform themselves into animals to avoid capture.'[8]

'Gathering Mushrooms', a shorter lyric, which opens *Quoof*, subtly negotiates between nationalist ideology and art, and was written at a time when Northern Ireland was going through a particularly violent period. The poem's first verse is located in a farmyard where Muldoon's parents are growing mushrooms commercially. The second verse changes all this. In the stanza break, we move without warning from the family scene to memories of drug hallucinations. What is also surprising is how matter-of-fact Muldoon is in making the transition: there is no sophisticated condescension towards the child's experience in the first verse; and neither is there an implication that the child's world was better than life fifteen years on with psilocybin. The mushroom farming of the first verse blends into the magic mushroom hunting of the second. The last two lines of the stanza are quoted from a humorous ballad also entitled 'Gathering Mushrooms'.

Apart from the drugs there is also the jarring, comic image of the two men 'like girls in long dresses'.[9] He goes on to tell us that rather than being concerned about the latest bombings and atrocities, the two men were more intent on looking for more magic mushrooms. The ones they'd already eaten were having a fine effect, however, as the friend has a vision. Here Muldoon draws on the tradition in Irish poetry of the *aisling*, or dream, when a woman embodying Ireland appears before the poet and exhorts him to inspire the nation to rise up against the British occupier. That Muldoon's partner meets the maid suggests that he is a fellow poet (the collection is dedicated to the Belfast poet Ciaran Carson). We are thus led back to nationalist ideology, this time however with large amounts of irony, as we see the *aisling* figure now through psychedelic spectacles. Mirroring this traduction is a rhyme, 'linen / psilocybin': the linen industry flourished in Northern Ireland and here Muldoon makes all the associations of that tradition collide with hallucinogenic experiences which do not have a codified position in that tradition as they do, say, in some of the Native American tribes.

The third verse describes his father farming mushrooms and the fourth returns to the tripping pair and their peregrinations (they trip both because they are on drugs and because they are, archaically, treading lightly). The gold-black dragon of the first verse reappears in the fourth with one colour changed, to make it all the more psychedelic perhaps, but also to joke at the expense of the nationalist tricolour of green, white and orange. What follows in the next verse, voiced through metamorphosis and ventriloquy, is a marvellous pastiche of the *aisling* episode: here one junky, turned into something like a 'rude mechanical', implores another to remain faithful to his people. But the tone here is not completely one of revisionist guffaw at bombastic patriotic literature. There is something touching about the effort to communicate and the entreaty to abandon the high-flown illusions of nationalism as well as the green-gold dragons seeded in his brain by psilocybin. The pastoral of childhood recollections and of 'tripping through Barnett's fair demesne' are also pushed forcefully aside by the lines 'Beyond this concrete wall is a wall of concrete / and barbed wire.'[10]

On the face of it, the straw and dung are the furnishings of the outbuildings the pair find themselves in. But the late 1970s and early 1980s were also the time of the Dirty Protests by IRA prisoners in Northern Irish jails, in which they wore nothing but blankets and smeared their fæces on the walls of their cells; protesting like this was called going 'on the blanket'. The barbed wire could well be that of a prison like the Maze where a lot of these protests took place, but could also be that of the peacelines dividing Catholic and Protestant communities in urban areas in the North. One of the slogans of militant nationalism is 'Tiocfaidh ár lá' ('Our day will come'), and Muldoon seems to be referring to this when he thinks, however negatively, of 'the day we leap / into our true domain'.[11] But by this stage 'our true domain' is unlikely to be a straightforward nationalist utopia. What it might be is impossible to say from the poem. Loyalists and republicans have little hesitation in identifying their 'true domains' (respectively, without Catholics and without Protestants), and Muldoon's refusal of those demarcations is richly subversive. It is also a refusal to confront the Troubles on their own terms. Irony and pastiche are deployed as ways of defusing polemical charges. Like all the best comedians, Muldoon is extremely serious.

Meeting the British (1987), like 'The More a Man Has', also deals with American experience and ends with a long poem entitled '7, Middagh Street'. This was the house in Brooklyn where, between 1940 and 1945, a variety of artists and writers stayed – W. H. Auden, Gypsy Rose Lee, Benjamin Britten, Richard Wright, Salvador Dalí, Carson McCullers and Louis MacNeice. The last is perhaps the most important figure for Muldoon, because he was a Northern Irish poet who refused to accept the borders of his province as the borders of his world, both in intellectual and geographical senses. The poem consists of the dramatic monologues of several of the inhabitants and there is a combination of racy anecdotes, in-jokes and serious meditation on the relations between politics and poetry. MacNeice is the last to speak and is given the most perspicacious lines. He disagrees with Auden's idea that 'poetry makes nothing happen', but it is clear that any such happenings involve a complex set of negotiations. After the cosmopolitanism of the Brooklyn boarding-house, MacNeice finds himself in the end in a pub called Muldoon's and then in the crowds of men streaming into Harland and Wolff in Belfast:

> The one-eyed foreman had strayed out of Homer;
> 'MacNeice? That's a Fenian name.'
> As if to say, 'None of your sort, none of you
>
> will as much as go for a rubber hammer
> never mind a chalk rivet, never mind caulk a seam
> on the quinquereme of Nineveh.'[12]

MacNeice was from a Protestant background, and the misrecognition indicates the persistence of religious division even for the writer who has flown the nets of Northern Ireland. These are also the last lines of the collection, and they serve to bring all the American *immrams* of its author back to his native country. In Muldoon's subsequent work, this mooring becomes ever looser. The boat of the last line refers to John Masefield's poem, 'Cargoes', which, paradoxically, denigrates British ships in favour of the more exotic vessels of Nineveh.

'Madoc – A Mystery' is the title poem of his next book (1990) and takes up most of its 250 pages. It is dedicated to his American wife and the long poem marks the deepening of Muldoon's engagement with American subject matter. The narrative is fragmented into short, obscure lyrics, which are titled with the names of philosophers, from the pre-Socratic Thales to Stephen Hawking. In a halting, louche way it imagines what would have happened if Robert Southey and Samuel Taylor Coleridge had in fact set up a Pantisocratic colony in America as they had once thought they might. The title of the poem refers to the Welsh prince who was supposed to have sailed to America and to have been the ultimate ancestor of the Native American tribes. It is something of a colonial story then in which Southey aggressively imposes his ideas on the land and peoples of the New World, resulting eventually in the megalomania of 'Southeyopolis'. Coleridge, on the other hand, displays more sympathy for the natives and gradually comes to know their ways. As Kendall remarks, Coleridge 'unlocks the mystery of Madoc by discovering that to locate what Muldoon has called the true "home" or "inheritance" requires not fidelity to a tribe or fixed identity, but escape from them'.[13] The poem conducts an argument, albeit oblique and circuitous, about the conflict over the question of how to act when you arrive in a new land, that is, do you try to conquer and colonise like Southey, or do you try to assimilate like Coleridge?

That Muldoon approves of the figure of Coleridge, who is able to step beyond himself, becoming 'the blossom in the bud / of peyote',[14] is clear from the gently humorous description of his accoutrements and mode of travel. Further evidence of which side Muldoon is on is provided by an earlier description of Coleridge. That Coleridge cannot impose large philosophical arguments on the material, remaining on the level of objects themselves and their names, aligns him with Muldoon, whose relish for recherché words and objects is obvious to even the most cursory reader of the poem, and this enriches the rhyming considerably. The connection between Coleridge's attitude and Muldoon's rhyming is far from trivial. In the section of the poem where Coleridge approaches Southey's city, the rhymes fan out from the centre of the poem, with 'coyote / peyote' in the centre, and then later such gems as 'sacred / ziggurats', 'laver-bread / Lava beds' and 'calumet / Klamath'.[15] Their great feature is that they are so surprising, as though in the interstice between them the consonants and vowels travel through a bizarre set of alembics and end up reconfigured and in another world altogether. There is an important contrast between the throwaway tone of most of Muldoon's poetry and the intricate dexterity of the rhymes. But more than just a sustained tour de force, the rhyming, as it reassembles the letters of words into new objects, insists in its oblique way on the extra-poetic values of wandering and surprise, on the rejection of grand narratives, be they of politics or poetry. Southey is the villain of the piece because he prosecutes his agenda so relentlessly and so blindly to the new land he lives in.

Hybridity – Coleridge's quality – has always been the prime value and theme for Muldoon, and this hybridity that has been argued over intensely by critics: for instance, Edna Longley holds that *Madoc*, for all its American subject matter, is more rooted in the cultural politics of Northern Ireland and Muldoon's relationship with Heaney, whereas other readings suggest the book is both retrospective in its concern with Ireland and at the same time seeks to escape that concern by absorbing or being absorbed by America.[16] Michael Allen says that the book shows 'Muldoon testing out ways to bring his Irish identity with him into the wider – not merely American – world he was now entering'.[17] *Madoc* then can be seen as a transitional book, Muldoon's ambitious attempt to find a poetic which spans the Atlantic and thus comprehends the two countries where he has spent his life.

It takes several readings of the poem to get a clear idea of its structure, and even then many readers have decided that it is not worth the candle. Despite some local felicities, the book itself founders; it is as though Muldoon's verbal invention has become an end in itself, disconnected from any emotional and intellectual resources. The organisation is tricksy and mechanical. (Michael

Hofmann, in a review of the book, remarked that he wanted 'to throw the whole thing at a computer and say: "Here, you do it"'.[18]) The poem increasingly resembles a hulking, rusting wreck grounded at the end of twentieth-century poetry. In contrast, when Muldoon harnessed his ludic verbal talents in several long works in the 1990s, the results were major achievements.

The Annals of Chile (1994) presents the first 'Incantata', an elegy for his former lover, the American artist, Mary Farl Powers. In lamenting Powers, Muldoon also recalls his own life during the 1980s in Ireland, making the poem also something of a *roman-à-clef*:

> I thought of the night Vladimir was explaining to all and sundry
> the difference between *geantraí* and *suantraí*
> and you remarked on how you used to have a crush
> on Burt Lancaster as Elmer Gantry, and Vladimir went to brush
> the ash off his sleeve with a legerdemain
> that meant only one thing – 'Why does he put up with this crap?' –
> and you weighed in with 'To live in a dustbin, eating scrap,
> seemed to Nagg and Nell a most eminent domain.'[19]

The near homophone of '*geantraí*' (a laughter-inducing music) and Gantry mirrors the macaronic rhyme of '*suantraí*' (a lullaby) and 'sundry' (it is not incidental that the rhyme-scheme is the same as Yeats's 'In Memory of Major Robert Gregory'). Powers mishears the word deliberately so that she can upset the somewhat didactic disquisition on the meanings of Irish words, and Muldoon clearly relishes the collision that occurs, both on the social and cultural levels (insofar as those levels are separate). The impish aside and the macaronic rhyme are indeed Muldoon's own method for disappointing certain expectations (for instance, of what Irish poetry is). The momentum that the poem builds up (mainly through the use of anaphora) is spectacular. By the time 'Incantata' reaches the home-stretch, it becomes almost pure catalogue, declaiming its grief for the world that was lost and the loved one above all.

The Annals of Chile also contains a long poem entitled 'Yarrow', which is written in a complex form that Muldoon calls an exploded sestina.[20] The intricacy and extent of the rhyme scheme are extraordinary; Muldoon is using what Joseph Conte calls procedural form, that is, 'predetermined and arbitrary constraints that are relied upon to generate the context and direction of the poem during composition'.[21] As unexpected harmonies and commonalities are discovered between words themselves, the reality which they refer to becomes ever more chaotic. 'Yarrow' begins in a conventional autobiographical mode somewhat like the beginning of 'Gathering Mushrooms', but then breaks loose (never to return, like the previous poem) 'into a channel surfing universe, a violent disorientation of the senses'.[22] In the third section of the poem, the barn is part of the Muldoon farm and here it is mixed in with fairy-tale elements in the imagination of the boy (and channel-surfing man). This mixture, in which quotidian life and fantastic stories are equally real, is all swept away by the passage of time. As the poem gathers momentum and Muldoon moves from childhood to early adulthood the references widen to include other concerns (so in places we find Muldoon 'crouch[ing] with Schwitters and Arp'[23]), but the structural device of channel-surfing between different contexts remains. For all the vaunted difficulty, 'Yarrow' reads quickly and easily. Much of its pleasure is due to the wandering and surprise generated by the procedural form of the exploded sestina; but beneath these changes, as the critics agree, is a deep hurt that the poem wants to confront but keeps evading.

The passage quoted above begins with a phrase that is repeated throughout the poem and which is possibly taken from an Emily Dickinson poem: 'All things swept sole away / This – is immensity – '.[24] This would be fitting for a work that is so concerned with various manifestations of the female principle. It is also fitting as the immensities of Muldoon's poem and Dickinson's work in general hardly ever give on the public world, and seem, for all their expansiveness, to be enclosed within the self. Granted, Muldoon continues to refer to violent scenes from Northern Ireland, but these are less a part of the continuing narrative of that province than the flashbacks of an erstwhile inhabitant. The mainstay is now recollections of family and amorous life in the Ireland he left behind and his marriage in New Jersey. In the light of his subsequent collections, *Madoc*, for all its engagement with American history, appears to be something of a red herring, as *The Annals of Chile* and *Hay* have little or no interest in the topic.

In *Hay*, the poem 'The Bangle (Slight Return)' has Muldoon imagining that his father, instead of dying, went on to live another life in Australia. He is led through the dream by Virgil, and is simultaneously eating an opulent meal in a Parisian restaurant; he cuts between these three contexts (the *Æneid*, Australia, the restaurant) in the same way as in 'Yarrow', and overall the poem carries a charge of elegiac feeling for his father. And yet its atmosphere, like that of the collection in general, is stifling. That it is clotted with self-parody is deliberate, but such an intention is not enough to forestall the feeling that Muldoon has reached a difficult juncture in his explorations of autobiography. No matter how far-flung the reference or the rhyme we are always landed back with Muldoon, his Irish mother and father, his American wife and children. No world seems to exist beyond the garden fence. One imagines Muldoon's house in New Jersey as an amazing repository of phantasmagorical animals, eclectic books and strange exotic objects, all of which are choreographed to the same show-tunes day after day.

Perhaps the biggest surprise, in *Moy Sand and Gravel* (2002), was one of its shortest poems, 'Cradle Song for Asher', a simple and profoundly moving lullaby for his newborn son. Certainly, the long poem that ended it, 'At the Sign of the Black Horse, September 1999', provided little surprise. It recounts the events of flooding near Muldoon's home in New Jersey, and intercuts these with his family history and that of his wife, some of whose forebears were killed in the Holocaust. The method is the same as before: a deeply felt hurt is laid down as ground-swell to counterpoint the verbal game-playing that takes place on the wavelengths above. The same pattern is to be found in *Horse Latitudes* (2006). Perhaps the strongest poem is 'Turkey Buzzards', in which Muldoon has pared back the line lengths to, roughly, trimeter and dimeter; while the long poem which concludes the collection, 'Sillyhow Stride', an elegy for Warren Zevon which also mourns the death of Muldoon's sister, employs the same method and register as a poem like 'At the Sign of the Black Horse'. *General Admission*, published the same year, collects the excellent lyrics written for the band he plays with, whose music, the cover-note has it, 'can only be described as three-car-garage rock'.

Muldoon clearly feels the limitations of his autobiographical subject matter by this stage, and it would seem that he is trying to get beyond them through his wife's family, which encompasses one of the central events of twentieth-century European history, and, given the amount of Jewish immigration to the USA, of American history also. But these preoccupations are merely processed by old methods, and haven't precipitated any formal innovation on Muldoon's part, and this is the crucial index. As Bono said, 'outside it's America', and the major achievements and major failures of Muldoon's poetry since the 1990s illustrate the difficulties and rewards of getting out there, of writing a poetry that itself is hybrid instead of merely talking about hybridity.

The period also witnesses several other Irish poets negotiating their resident alien status in America, among them Nuala Archer (b. 1955), Eavan Boland (b. 1944), James Liddy (b. 1934), Eamonn Wall (b. 1955), Greg Delanty (b. 1958) and Mary O'Donoghue (b. 1975). Delanty places his own experience against the long history of Irish–American encounters:

> We, a bunch of greencard Irish,
>   vamp it under the cathedral arches
>   of Brooklyn Bridge that's strung like a harp.
> But we'll not play
> the harp backward now, harping on
>   about those Micks who fashioned

> this American wind lyre
> and about the scores
>   who landed on Ellis Island
> or, like us, at Kennedy and dispersed
> through this open sesame land . . .[25]

To play the harp backwards, as Delanty notes, is to wax sentimental about the past, which is a frequent activity of emigrants. He registers the contribution of Irish labourers to American achievement, as well as the improved material status of the new Irish immigrants. However, he merely replaces one wadge of schmaltz with another, as he sentimentalises the possibilities which America offers the younger generation. Arguably, he retains the old schmaltz also. The poem ends with a reference to how the Irish are stricken 'with the plaintive notes / of the drawn-out tragedy / of the old country's sorry history', which lays it on fairly thick.[26]

In the 1990s, Irish emigration became a theme in the work of Eavan Boland (b. 1944), at the same time that her friend Mary Robinson, as President of Ireland was helping to promulgate a new attitude towards émigrés, both within and without the country. The Irish abroad had prospered and yet, even after several generations, Irish descendants, though thoroughly naturalised in their new countries, were reluctant to let go of the old. Robinson realised that this nostalgia (etymologically, the longing for the journey home) could increase the cultural capital of Ireland manifold. Little of this sense of optimism and prosperity is expressed in Boland's work, however, as she dwells on the émigrés' sense of loss rather than their prosperity. If there is any mention of success, it is attributed only to figures such as Boland and Robinson. The dedication of Boland's collection *The Lost Land* (1998) grandiloquently reads 'For Mary Robinson – who found it', and in general the poems of that book deal with the subject rather clumsily. Much more engaging is 'Emigrant Letters' from *Code* (2001) which imagines '[e]ach page six crisp inches of New England snow' sent back across the Atlantic to Ireland, to be gathered by the family left behind:

> all of which they stored side by side
> carefully in a cupboard drawer which never
> would close properly: informed as it was
> by those distant seasons. And warped by its own.[27]

While its punctuation is idiosyncratic to no real effect, 'Emigrant Letters' leaves us with a beguiling image for the way the old country can be changed by the new. Boland is not attuned to the particular ways in which foreign elements have 'warped' Ireland in the last few decades (many critics have commented that her Ireland is caught in a time-bubble[28]); that is the work of the poets I consider in the final chapter.

Peter Fallon has spent several periods in the United States and his imaginative engagement with the country is expressed in 'The Deerfield Series', an occasional poem set in and around Deerfield, Western Massachusetts. Fallon does not deal with American material as a foil for Irish issues, or in order to explore ideas of emigration: rather, he confronts it and responds to it on its own terms. The attentiveness to nature and landscape displayed throughout 'The Deerfield Series' harmonises with his translation of Virgil discussed in chapter 9 and his other poems. The poem celebrates the clever husbandry of the land, even while registering the terrible crimes committed against the indigenous population. It was written, a note tells us, 'to commemorate the Bicentennial of Deerfield Academy, 1797–1997'.[29] Like Virgil, Fallon has a strong didactic edge and the series ends with valedictory advice to students who will soon go forth into the world.

A compelling engagement between Ireland and America takes place in Eamon Grennan's poetry. Grennan was born in Dublin in 1941 and did not publish his first book until 1983, at the age of forty-two. After receiving his doctorate from Harvard he has lived for most of his professional life in the USA. His subject matter for the most part splits into two spheres: that of his early adulthood in Ireland and his middle-class American suburban life. On occasions when he writes about contemporary Ireland it is about the landscapes of the west of Ireland without reference to the historical changes that have taken place in the country over the last thirty years; in other words, as Jonathan Hufstader says, he writes mostly from the point of view of 'a man on holiday in his own country'.[30]

Grennan works in the mode of free-verse lyric autobiography. There is a formal impulse in the work to group lines into regular units of regular length, but it does not stretch to rhyme. His poetry provides an example of the verve and brilliance possible within this mode, from the bravura linguistic effects to the entranced apprehension of the immediate world of the senses and the larger configurations of love. Or, as Hufstader has it again:

> There is a page in 'Station Island' where Seamus Heaney imaginatively exchanges the fog-bound anxieties of the Irish religious atmosphere within which he grew up (and here he recalls his adolescent sexual initiation) for the sunny, secular and self-confident pleasures of Horace's oak tree, under which one may reasonably sit, make love and write poetry. That oak tree grows in Eamon Grennan's back yard.[31]

Grennan's poetry registers his continuous shock at the variety of the sensual world – everything from the precious stones to the body of his wife moving around his own. It can occasionally grade into sentimentality, but at its strongest it sponsors an imaginative agility that has the poet's gaze ranging beyond the usual confines of the autobiographical anecdote into an associative mode like Robert Pinsky's.

'Stone Flight' is an object poem that starts off fairly conventionally: 'A piece of broken stone, granular granite, a constellation / of mica through its grey sky'.[32] As the poem gathers momentum, it begins to range through different 'relations' (*Relations* is the title of his American selected poems, which appeared in 1998). The stone is like his father's kiss, but not like that of the grunt of a condemned man:

> Nor yet the small
> grunt of surprised satisfaction you've heard
> when you're as deep inside and around one another
> as you two can be, body bearing body away and
> you push, once, and flesh grunts with a right effort
> that seems outside, beyond the two of you, something
> old and liberated, a sort of joyous punctuation point
> in the ravelling sentence that leaves you both as one
> breathless wrap of skin and bone, your double weight
> hardly anything as you kiss your way down and back
> to your own selves, maybe rolling an inch or two
> and then lie still, alive, in matter again, the tick of it
> starting to fill the silence . . .[33]

The poem is a kind of effervescence, an expansive buoyancy of imagination that chases the object in unpredictable ways. The caprice and surprise of the trajectory are part of the poem's pleasure, the other being the luxuriance and invention of the metaphors. As with many of Grennan's poems, the focus goes voyaging out from a given scene or object to reveal the fecundity of possibilities and likenesses in the world before us, only to return by way of conclusion. There is didactic edge to this, a desire to demonstrate just what is being missed in everyday perception, but it is didacticism of the sweetest and most persuasive variety. The course of the poem is given in small in the stone's parabola at the beginning of the poem, but then the poem surges out again from this, employing a panoply of devices such as apostrophe, prosopopoeia as well as dense alliterative and assonantal effects. The contexts that suggest themselves through the negations carry various emotional charges, from the difficulty of the relationship with the father (dealt with at greater length in 'Walk, Night

Falling, Memory of My Father' and 'Common Theme') to the execution to the coupling of spouses; the suggestion being that to apprehend something as simple as a stone one has to know these other things also. When the lovers' 'right effort' of ecstasy is over he say they are 'in matter again, the tick of it', and the qualifying phrase evokes how they once again are smallest parts of something with its own huge rhythm. The first phrase suggests a closing down of possibilities, a loss; the second opens out the new state of awareness (while rhyming with the phrase 'in the thick of it'). The focus of the poem glances off into a panning shot, leaving the stone, once the hub of the whole world, it seemed, just the smallest element of the landscape scene.

Grennan has talked of 'pushing my own experience of myself and of the Irish landscape I was encountering through the filter of an "American" style'.[34] One consequence of this acquisition of America in his poetry is a general unconcern with matters of Ireland and in general the historical contexts so integral to the work of Seamus Heaney, Thomas Kinsella and Eavan Boland, to name just three. In interview he has remarked on this aspect of his work:

> I feel incapacitated and without authority when it comes to the public and, for want of a better word, the political. I don't feel as if something in me will say, 'You have no right here'. Obviously I have every right in the world. But I don't feel the right to talk about here, except in the most private of ways. But that seems a perfectly legitimate stance. As a poet, you say what you can, in every sense. And what I can say seems to be anchored very close to home.[35]

He goes on to comment that this is not necessarily because of his amphibian status in the USA and Ireland; the reason is simply that his particular poetic temperament is not attuned to the political. However, one cannot help but wonder how much that temperament has been shaped by his status as resident alien in America (the biographical note to his American *Selected Poems* says, he 'is an Irish citizen who has lived in the United States for thirty years') with the peculiar set of public responsibilities and irresponsiblities that such status entails. One inevitably occupies a role of spectator of, and not participant in, public life, and this must have an effect on the sensitive observer of the world that Grennan is. Like Muldoon's, his loss of a public world leaves him with the personal as his main theme, and like Muldoon he looks for different ways to push out the boundaries of the personal; Grennan rather attends to the tangs, vibrations, fragrances, solidities and coloraturas of mundane events.

Harry Clifton (b. 1952), in interview, has reflected on the meaning of foreign experience for the Irish writer:

> When I began to publish in the late seventies and early eighties, the kind
> of poetry I was writing, out of African or Asian experience, was
> completely off the agenda. Now both in poetry and in fiction it is entirely
> acceptable for writers to write out of Japanese, Argentinian or American
> experience and for all of that to be included in their Irishness; I think my
> work, perhaps coincidentally, has become more understandable as the
> society itself and the concept of Ireland have changed . . .[36]

The remarks were made in 1996 during a period when Ireland was undergoing
large social transformations such as an economic boom and an attendant rise
in immigration from Eastern Europe and Asia. Mary Robinson, as I remarked,
was addressing the Irish diaspora, and exploring how the experience of those
Irish emigrants could, in some way, be folded back into Irish experience, so
that it could have meaning within contemporary Ireland.

In the work of his first books, Clifton often tries to relate his experiences
in Asia or Africa to Ireland, and his own status as a kind of exile. However, in
his later work from the 1990s and 2000s, he has become more willing to let
the Irish context slip. Many of his poems are portraits of writers, artists and
politicians who have become unmoored from their homes and drift through
the world constantly negotiating their identity against the background of a
foreign language, foreign mores and foreign cityscapes. In one poem he takes
the voice of God, who finds himself in reputedly the most atheistic country in
the world, France. He thoroughly enjoys the experience, as he is not bothered
with supplications, prayers, etc.:

> I would sit here, I would wait –
>   A dinner, a *café crème,*
> A chaser of grog. Whatever else, there was time –
> Let Judgement take care of itself. To celebrate –
> That was the one imperative. Randomness, flux,
> Drew themselves about me as I ate,
> Protected by the nearnesses of women, their sex
> Blown sheer through summer dresses, loving my food,
> My freedom, as they say a man should.[37]

This is reminiscent of 'the sunny, secular and self-confident pleasures of
Horace's oak tree' which Hufstader described in Grennan's poetry. One implication of this might be that freedom, randomness and flux are not attainable
in Ireland, and that one must mitch from the country in order to experience
them. But Clifton's work is not merely reaction against Ireland, but engagement
with foreign experience for its own sake. Where Delanty cannot make sense of

American experience without reference to the Ireland he left behind, Clifton proves more capacious and can comprehend much more of the world.

In the way that they deal with the experience of being a privileged Westerner in Third World countries, many of his earlier poems resemble those of Fergus Allen (b. 1921), whose first book, *The Brown Parrots of Providencia*, was published in 1993. In 'Aside' a dog passes him by, looks at him and writes him off; similarly, 'the strutting man / With the nightstick and dark, sun-flashing glasses, / He sees me as one to be disregarded'. These data gather in violence, with helicopters and looters swirling around the speaker, and he concludes: 'Curled up in my form, / I hold my breath as uncountable hooves / Drum across a summer-hardened savannah.'[38] The Westerner of this poem is no heroic neo-Imperialist, but frail and vulnerable, possibly also culpable. Allen's poetry in *The Brown Parrots of Providencia* and *Who Goes There?* (1996), like Grennan's and for the most part like Clifton's, is uninterested in the historical fate and crises of Ireland in the twentieth century.

Another time-honoured destination for Irish émigrés is England. Sam Gardiner (b. 1936), Peter McDonald (b. 1962), Bernard O'Donoghue (b. 1945), Matthew Sweeney (b. 1952) and Maurice Riordan (b. 1953) were born in Ireland and all now live in England. The similarities end there. McDonald has been influenced by the poetry of Michael Longley as well as that of Louis MacNeice (he has written excellent criticism on both poets). A poem such as 'The Victory Weekend' exceeds both those influences and also deals in a complex way with McDonald's own birthplace, Belfast. The poet and his wife are in London for the fiftieth anniversary of VE day. In retrospect this turns out to be a celebration of the 'nation' rather than the 'empire' (the latter idea is absent from the poem), and McDonald casts an unconvinced eye on the celebrations ('cheap victory; boozy fellowship; a free / people forgetting everything again').[39] The poem remains preoccupied with the legacy of the war; it refuses to assess that legacy, but instead pans over the sea to the Belfast that McDonald grew up in with its 'bombs not yet exploded'.[40] The poem ends by watching how the dead of that struggle march past, 'in a simple, strict parade, / until the fireworks split up in the dark'.[41] When questioned in 1997 about his views on the Irish diaspora, he remarked:

> I don't consider myself to be living abroad, though I might do so if I found myself holed up in Berlin, Tokyo, or Dublin. Then again, I might love it in those places, and decide that they could be added to the expanding catchment area (where, in my experience, poems happen) that I like to think of as a kind of personal Greater Belfast.[42]

In 'The Victory Weekend' we see how his Greater Belfast stretches to include the European conflict, but without any reference to Robinson's idea of the Irish diaspora, with its nostalgic idea of a homeland with candles burning in the windows. McDonald is at home in England, as much as Grennan and Muldoon are at home in America. It is also worth remarking that because McDonald comes from a Unionist background, he is at home in a different, perhaps more complex way, in England.

One of his finest poems is 'Three Rivers', dedicated to his daughter, in which three generations are traced out beside three rivers, the Isis (which is what Oxonians call the Thames), the Lagan (which flows through McDonald's hometown) and the Jordan. In the first part, McDonald is driving his baby daughter home and he looks at the Isis, thinking that it is the same river he himself saw when he first came to Oxford to study, and was homesick and disoriented. At that time, the words of Thomas Traherne, another Oxford poet, were echoing in his mind: '*How like, / How like, How like an angel I came down*' and McDonald remarks how he was straining his 'eyes in case they broke with tears'. He turns then to the river running beside the moving car, and also beside his life, in which his family is 'held safe and moving fast / on a road over acres of floodwater, / sending us home through rain and daylight fall'.[43] Despite the way that McDonald registers his resident alien status, the poem is primarily about homecoming – that of his daughter, and also of McDonald himself; after all, he is no longer homesick in his adopted country. It is a moment of pure transformation although they remain in the same place.

The theme of World War II also appears in the poetry of Tom Paulin. Paulin was born in Leeds in 1949, brought up in Northern Ireland and has spent most of his working life in England (now at Oxford University). From the publication of his first book, *A State of Justice* (1977), he has been preoccupied with political questions of Ireland and Europe, and *The Invasion Handbook* (2002), which tries to understand the run-up to World War II, is the first instalment of a larger work. Despite its obvious historical and poetic ambitions, the book is a flimsy affair that peddles biographical titbits about political leaders as profound insight. For instance, Clemenceau, through Paulin's ventriloquism, tells us the following: 'no one knows I made war / with 40 grammes of sugar in my blood'. Clemenceau also reveals that he's 'known men who saw Napoleon / with their own eyes / America is far away / protected by the Ocean . . .'[44] Perhaps this is intended to be breathtakingly banal, as Paulin displays the simplistic ideas of great statesmen; however, Paulin's collage *in toto* does not provide anything more complex.

Less ambitious but more convincing is Bernard O'Donoghue, whose poems delicately interleave accounts of professional life in England (he is a mediævalist at Oxford University) with memories of childhood and holidays in Ireland. The tone is equable and objective, humorously and calmly recounting connections and breakdowns between the two countries. Then there is Ian Duhig (b. 1954), born of Irish parents in England, and who wittily writes as much about his Irish heritage as his English home. Is the lien becoming too tenuous? In what way might it be discharged? Should our idea of Irish poetry stretch to include the likes of Duhig or exclude them? As we will see in the final chapter, in the last decade or so, the tendency is away from the diaspora model employed by Boland and Delanty, and towards McDonald's idea. Yeats established an Irish poetic tradition that depended minimally on the Irish language, and could assert his poetry's Irishness purely by use of Irish themes; this, in its turn, was sustained by nationalist ideology. As that ideology has withdrawn, there appears to be no means – or indeed desire – to restrict our idea of Irish poetry. The concept will be stretched so thin that it will lose all explanatory power. Perhaps we should listen again to what Patrick Kavanagh said in 1950: 'As far as I am concerned, Auden and Dylan Thomas, Moravia, Sartre, Pound are all Irish poets. They have all said the thing which delighted me, a man born in Ireland, so they must have a great deal of Irish in them.'[45]

Chapter 12

The disappearance of Ireland

Paul Durcan, Dennis O'Driscoll, Kevin Higgins, Ciaran Carson, Peter Sirr, Sinéad Morrissey, David Wheatley, Vona Groarke, Conor O'Callaghan, Caitríona O'Reilly

Under Seán Lemass, the government in the period 1959–66 developed industry in Ireland on an unprecedented scale, and the consequences of this policy are still felt to this day. Michael Hartnett remarked that in the 1970s this led to a dismissal with many things connected with traditional Ireland – small farmers, small shops and the Irish language. These were perceived as signs of an unmodern atavism that the country wished to abandon, especially after it joined the European Economic Community in 1973.[1] There was an attendant loosening of the strictures of Catholic morality, spearheaded especially by Gay Byrne's *The Late Late Show* and a soap opera entitled the *Riordans*.[2] In the mid 1990s, these developments were galvanised by large in-flows of foreign investment; multinational companies were attracted by the country's well-educated young population and by fiscal policies which maximised their tax-breaks and minimised their long-term responsibilities. In 1994, the investment bankers Morgan Stanley called the phenomenon the 'Celtic Tiger'.[3]

In his novel, *The Very Man* (2003), Chris Binchy has his protagonist leave Ireland in the early 1990s and return when the boom is at its height. This is what he sees:

> It was as if the changes had happened over night. That was exactly how it was. All the cranes and new buildings and pubs, builders in hard hats everywhere. Streets with no names. Everybody on Grafton Street and in the pubs wearing the clothes but never quite getting it right, great smells coming out of cafés but when you went in it took twenty minutes for them to get to you and when they did they could never understand you. People in shops were sloppy and rude. It was like all this money had just landed out of nowhere and nobody really knew what to do, or they knew what they should be doing, they just didn't know how and they could only make a half-assed attempt at sophistication. There was an edge in the way people dealt with each other. Everywhere you walked on the street you could hear it – fuck him, fuck it, fuck off, fucking prick, cunt, bitch. Everywhere and everybody.[4]

Derek Mahon put this even more pithily: 'The isle is full of intolerable noises.'[5] Binchy catches a lot of the aggression, speed, colour and vulgarity that has come into Irish life during the period. This sudden release of energy has had several effects, among them the weakening of both the Catholic Church, as the country's moral arbiter, and of nationalist ideology. At least since the beginning of the Troubles in the late 1960s it had been clear that the Republic's nationalism would not prompt it into action – it was happy with a few flags, fine speeches and the occasional wreath-laying ceremony.

In an editorial of *Poetry Ireland Review* in 1986, Terence Brown remarked that very few of the submissions he received address 'political or social issues directly'. He continued: 'Reading the bulk of the submissions it is sometimes possible to forget that we are living through a period of profound social and political crisis.'[6] This lack of satire could hardly have been for lack of targets. Over a decade later, there were several government tribunals that investigated the connections between big business and government, revealing the unethical if not illegal practices of Fianna Fáil politicians, especially the late Charles J. Haughey. At the same time, there were a large number of high-profile court cases against pederasts in the ranks of the Catholic clergy. This was crowned by the publication of the Ferns Report in 2005, which revealed a child-abuse network tolerated by bishops and archbishops.

In the 1980s, poets such as Paul Durcan (b. 1944) and Brendan Kennelly (b. 1936) were consistently critical of social policy (deploring attitudes towards poverty above all) and of the atmosphere of sexual repression, as orchestrated by the Catholic Church. Durcan's main instrument was Surrealism as he targeted Ireland's bourgeois philistinism, its plutocracy and, on a basic level, its people's inability to express their deepest emotions. A further aspect of his work is his emotional directness when dealing with family relations. For instance, half of *The Berlin Wall Café* (1985) is about the break-up of a marriage, and half of *Daddy, Daddy* (1990) is about his troubled relationship with his father. Durcan was aware of the connection between Ireland's systemic hypocrisy and its emotional inarticulateness, and his work found wide audiences at the very time that practices such as group therapy, psychoanalysis and support groups were taking root in the country. A previous generation would simply have considered that kind of talk insane, and indeed in many poems he refers to his time in mental asylums as a young man.

While not generally satirical, much of the poetry of Dennis O'Driscoll (b. 1954) can be characterised as social criticism. In his poems of the 1980s he is concerned with the humdrum nature of office life (O'Driscoll has worked as a civil servant from the age of sixteen), elegies for loved ones and satires of poets and the poetry scene. There is also a strong tendency in his poetry to perceive all the world as *vanitas vanitatum*: the first poem in his *New and Selected Poems* (2004) imagines all the people who are going to die on this particular day and how futile their aspirations are. The tone is unclear: on a superficial level, it expresses tenderness, but when the mode is repeated throughout his œuvre (for instance in 'Out of Control', where he says 'Worry on, mothers: you have / good reason to lose sleep'[7]) one feels he ever so slightly relishes the damage. When the Celtic Tiger phenomenon began in the 1990s, O'Driscoll was able to marshal some of these strands to meet the moment. Well attuned to the language of business, he had no difficulty in catching the new commercial speech rhythms that were now flowing through the island. The register of the elegies for his parents was also employed to depict an older generation left behind by the new dispensation. And as Chris Binchy suggests, there was no shortage of aggressive vanity in the 1990s, which served to fuel O'Driscoll.

Kevin Higgins (b. 1967) has demonstrated a good satirical savagery when facing the new Ireland. His first collection, *The Boy with No Face* (2005), contains many poems in conventional lyrical modes (in which he is weaker) and others with a social critique as lithe and imaginative as that of the con-merchants who run the show. He has perhaps acquired much of his sharpness by taking part in poetry slams. 'The Voice of Reason' depicts a man who 'will do any gymnastics necessary to hide / the cut-throat razor he has behind his back'. Higgins reports the spiel: 'He wants to keep you talking / about the gold he's seen in those Romanian teeth, / while they sneak Liam Lawlor out the back door.'[8] (Lawlor was a Fianna Fáil politician convicted and jailed several times for not co-operating with government tribunals.) Explaining his satirical bent elsewhere, he says that he sees 'words not as decorations / but weapons, knives with which to cut / others down to size'.[9] A satire which eschews moderation and openly admits its own savagery can only succeed.

As the authors of *Reinventing Ireland* point out, Irish attitudes to modernity have also changed from the 1970s. The distant past of ancient Ireland is now acceptable for use in the heritage industry, while the recent past (of Catholic and nationalist repression) is used to warn what might happen if the country does not fully embrace the globalised free market.[10] Consonant with this, as I remarked in chapter 9, there is a change in attitude towards the Irish language, as it has become independent of nationalist ideology and is viewed now more as an expression of individuality. The authors also remark the erosion of the sense of place in Ireland during the 1990s: increasingly it is difficult to say whether you are standing on a high street in Dublin, London, Budapest or

Stockholm.[11] But this is a somewhat superficial view of the issue, fuelled by a left-wing prejudice against capitalism (though it must be admitted that the Republic's investment in health and childcare is below European standards). The view from the high street might be disorienting, but high streets have back streets adjacent to them, and the relationship between the two should show us the specific ways that global capital impacts on individual countries. Globalisation is different everywhere.

The distant past is of course very present in the conflict in Northern Ireland; unfortunately that has not been globalised out of existence. It is of note, however, that while the younger generation of Northern Irish poets – among them Leontia Flynn (b. 1974) and Alan Gillis (b. 1973) – might occasionally refer to the Troubles, they do not reach for a nationalist framework in order to understand the events unfolding around them; Gillis for one is more likely to reach for the logarithms of electronic games to make sense of his world. It might also be argued that the past persists in the strong interest in the Gaelic Athletic Association (GAA), the Irish language and the hundreds of thousands of visitors to the Fleadh Cheoil na hÉireann every year. Yet as I remarked in chapter 9 in relation to the Irish language, the Irish language has moved out of the orbit of nationalism, at least in the south of the country. In Dublin for instance, Irish-language schools, which also foster Gaelic games, are in general filled with children whose parents know that a bilingual education is better than a monolingual one; this is a resistance to the global monoculture of the English language, rather than to whatever is left of the British Empire. It is a crucial distinction.

The ebbing of nationalist ideology from Irish culture has had several important effects on poetry also. The break comes, roughly, after Heaney, Boland and Kinsella – all three poets who in their different ways engage deeply with the issue of nationalism. With the generation that emerged in the last two decades of the twentieth century, such an engagement is almost completely absent (with the exception of McGuckian, as I remarked earlier). It is not that these poets avoid all experience particular to Ireland, rather, on no level do they attempt to link that experience with nationalist ideology (neither to aggrandise nor attack it). For the preceding two centuries that nationalist framework, whether rejected or embraced, generally served to define what was understood by the term 'Irish poetry'. A good example of this is the contrasting uses to which Thomas Kinsella and Peter Sirr (b. 1960) put Dublin history: for the first, it is slotted into the colonial narrative; for the second, it is part of the meditations of the poet-citizen on his city. Just as some visitors to the city complain that Dublin lost its 'character' in the boom period of the 1990s, so it may be asked if the poetry also has not lost a vital element as it abandons the fruit-ful postcolonial dichotomy of writing in the oppressor's tongue, i.e., to what extent is this new poetry still 'Irish'? In the introduction to her anthology, *The New Irish Poets* (2004), Selina Guinness remarks that '[I]t must be pointed out then that the "new" in the title applies as much to the term "Irish" as it does to the poets here represented. Ireland now is a country where the "imagined community" is often bewildered by the rapid pace of modernity which has left individual members out on "the bypass"' (the last phrase is from Conor O'Callaghan).[12]

One significant pattern of response is immersion in the local. There is Sirr's *Bring Everything* (2000) and David Wheatley's (b. 1970) phantasmagoric excursion through Dublin's history in the title poem of *Misery Hill* (2000). Conor O'Callaghan's (b. 1968) imaginative archæological roaming around the littorals of Dundalk and Carlingford offers a locality beyond Dublin. While Ciaran Carson's (b. 1948) poetry is more often discussed in the context of Northern Irish poetry, a book like *Belfast Confetti* (1989), with its mixture of urban legend and academic history, belongs more properly in this context. Also significant is the way that Irish poets have reacted to the impact of feminism. Thanks to a poet-critic such as Eavan Boland, a new generation of Irish female poets have the opportunity to explore further the implications of changing gender roles both in cultural representations and on a practical level as working writers. Two indices of the change: an Irish male poet, of whatever generation, will think twice now about depicting the land as female; and a female poet will not necessarily be viewed as a fey poetess if she writes about domesticity. The first might still go ahead with the depiction and the second might turn out to be a fey poetess in the end, but the general point still holds.

Just as poets such as Heaney, Mahon and Longley took their ideas of poetry and criticism from the New Criticism which reigned in the universities they attended, so now does this generation absorb Deleuze, Žižek and Butler in one form or another. Perhaps the most important development in Irish literary criticism in the 1990s has been the emergence of readers whose theoretical sophistication does not blind them to local conditions; on the contrary, the many discourses of critical theory often bring those very conditions into even sharper focus. These critics both review new collections and are frequently colleagues of poets in English departments (the practices of literary criticism and creative writing are not as institutionally distant as in the USA), which explains a good deal of the osmosis. (Many poets have considerable experience of both sides – for instance, David Wheatley, Leontia Flynn, Caitríona O'Reilly, Sinéad Morrissey, Cathal McCabe and John Redmond all possess doctorates in literature.) Thus if a poet now uses an epigraph from Deleuze for a poem, he or she is not necessarily trying to introduce a new term or idea, but is connecting with an ongoing debate.

Indeed the isle is full of noises, but not all of them are as intolerable as Derek Mahon would have us believe.

The first poem in Ciaran Carson's collection, *First Language* (1993), is entitled, 'La Je-Ne-Sais-Quoi' and it is not written in English. It is not written in French either. It is written in Irish, which is the author's first language. Carson is famed for his long lines which stretch all the way to the right-hand margin and loop back to the left indent, often ending with a rhyme that is phonically lost in the sprawl. There are many honourable ways to lose your rhymes – that is, to render them imperceptible to first-time readers – and Carson has added another to these. The first thing one notices about the Irish poem is that its lines are extremely short, mostly made up of three to five words. If the non-Irish speaker thinks that Carson is a different type of poet in his own language, he would be right. It is a poem that plays on puns and general ambiguity of reference, as it describes the act of love-making, which is also a description of the mechanism of language, and more particularly the way a man and wife communicate:

> I bhfaiteadh na mbéal
> I bhfriotal na súl
> Fáscadh agus teannadh
> Go dtí nach raibh ann
> Ach scáth an scátháin eadrainn,
> Tocht i do chluais istigh.[13]

The fifth line conveys the physical closeness of the bodies and the sixth the way that proximity is part of, or associated with, the language of emotion entering the ear of the lover. There is a classical restraint to the address, for all the sensuality of the subject. The poem employs the traditional verbal elements of love poetry – mouths, eyes, sudden kisses – and there is hardly anything to indicate that the encounter takes place in the modern world. On turning the page, we enter history, of a sort. The poem is entitled, 'Second Language'.

> English not being yet a language, I wrapped my lubber-lips around my thumb;
> Brain-deaf as an embryo, I was snuggled in my comfort-blanket dumb.
>
> Growling figures campaniled above me, and twanged their carillons of bronze
> Sienna consonants embedded with the vowels *alexandrite, emerald* and *topaz*.

> The topos of their discourse seemed to do with me and convoluted
> genealogy;
> Wordy whorls and braids and skeins and spiral helices, unskeletoned from
> laminate geology . . .[14]

In the first line, Carson winningly implies the primacy of the Irish language, at least for Carson himself, although he knows that English and Irish occupy opposite positions in the country. Language goes back and forth almost incomprehensibly above the child, who has silenced himself with his thumb. That silence contrasts pointedly with the flamboyant verboseness of these lines: the difference marks how far Carson has come. The switch to English releases a large amount of *things* into the poem, as well as different modes of speech (namely, the academic-speak of 'topos of their discourse'). In the last line here it is as though Carson is so dazzled by their variety that he is unable to link them in more complex syntactical forms, and resorts to repeated copula ('whorls and braids and skeins and spiral helices').

The superabundance of Carson's long lines is often fuelled by a wild, digressive story-telling impulse. On a first reading (and perhaps even on a second) it is difficult to see what is going on in the poem 'Dresden' from *The Irish for No* (1987). The narrator embarks on so many digressions (about a frying pan; about Flynn's arrest and subsequent learning of Irish; about Master McGinty) and makes so many amusing observations (for instance, about the village where 'men were known to eat their dinner from a drawer. / Which they'd slide shut the minute you'd walk in'[15]), that by the time he returns to the story of Horse Boyle the reader has forgotten what the point was.

In many of his poems Carson employs this technique, which has different stories colliding chaotically with each other, making frantic connections, throwing up occasional thumbnail vignettes of people or places and ultimately disorienting the reader before unexpectedly drawing everything together at the end of the poem. 'Dresden' reveals itself with the account of Horse Boyle's flight over the city of that name on the gratuitous RAF bombing mission at the end of World War II. Neil Corcoran comments that '[f]or all its noises of lighter timbre, the noise that this poem called "Dresden" really echoes with is the noise of exploding bombs . . .'[16] Through the depiction of the destruction of the Dresden figurines ('Shepherdesses, figurines of Hope and Peace and Victory, delicate bone fragments'[17]), the suffering of the victims of violence is evoked with pathos. The humour and cynicism of the narrator fade at this point to reveal compassion and the ludicrous confusions of military violence (an Irish man bombing the Germans for the English).

Many of the poems of *Belfast Confetti* employ the same techniques as 'Dresden': narrators reeling off yarns within yarns within yarns, the ever present shadow of paramilitary violence, the black humour and the characteristic long line sauntering over the page. But in *Belfast Confetti* Carson employs all these devices in order to write what is essentially a book celebrating his native city, with all its violence, humour, humanity and troubled history. The first poem in the book, 'Turn Again', sets the key signature. This is how it opens:

> There is a map of the city which shows the bridge that was never built.
> A map which shows the bridge that collapsed; the streets that never existed
>
> · · ·
>
> Today's plan is already yesterday's – the streets that were there are gone.
> And the shape of the jails cannot be shown for security reasons.[18]

Belfast is like a palimpsest, a document that is written upon again and again, constantly changing its meaning and appearance. Each poem of the book is like another 'turn', another way of storying the city. In this respect, the agency of language is like that of bombs that erase whole sections of streets or large buildings; or like that of assassins who erase people. Belfast is a place whose every mile is known and monitored by the conflicting forces of the city. As Carson says in one of the prose sections of the book: 'We are all being watched through peep-holes, one-way mirrors, security cameras, talked about on walkie-talkies, car 'phones, Pye Pocketfones.'[19]

Carson delights in mixing these levels together so that the various aspects of writing become metaphors for violence. For instance in the poem, 'Punctuation', the full stop that put an end to sentences turns into the bullets that put an end to a life. The poem opens with a panorama of night-time Belfast:

> This frosty night is jittering with lines and angles, invisible trajectories:
> Crackly, chalky diagrams in geometry, rubbed out the instant they're
>   sketched,
> But lingering in the head.[20]

Those diagrams could be plans for paramilitary action or plans to spoil those actions. Equally they could be the proposals and revisions of the poet's imagination. He imagines the bullets coming from unknown directions and asks: 'This bullet, is your name on it? / For the moment, everything is *X*, a blank not yet filled in.'[21] This is macabre. The head of the speaker is a blank to be filled in by a bullet, as the paramilitary plan comes to fruition. Possibilities hang in the air: which of the several invisible trajectories will turn out to be the real one? Which of the stories will come true? The speaker walks on thinking: 'I can / See my hand, a mile away in the future, just about to turn the latch-key in the lock, / When another shadow steps out from behind the hedge, going, dot, dot, dot,

dot, dot . . .'[22] This spray of full-stops is also a spray of bullets, one of which will also bring a stop to the life of the speaker.

The Alexandrine Plan (1998) is a collection of extremely loose versions of sonnets by Stéphane Mallarmé, Arthur Rimbaud and Charles Baudelaire, and in the same year he published *The Twelfth of Never*, made up of more sonnets, this time tricksy and postmodernist, which mixed ballad elements with a flakey, spaced-out delivery. Carson has also published several books of prose – they might be categorised 'creative non-fiction' – and one of these, *The Star Factory* (1997), is preoccupied with Belfast as an imperial city. The collection *Breaking News* (2003) brings Carson to the troubled depths of Pax Britannica to consider the various wars and uprisings that the British Empire had to deal with in the nineteenth century. It is a kind of retro-globalism, as Carson sees the Victorian aspect of Belfast echoed in the imperial reach of Britain, and vice versa. Thus in 'Exile' he talks of walking the night streets of

> Sevastopol
> Crimea
>
> Inkerman
> Odessa
>
> Balkan
> Lucknow
>
> Belfast
> is many
>
> places then
> as now[23]

The first striking thing about these lines is their brevity, and this is typical of many poems in the book. Through a simple list of cities which ends with Belfast, Carson opens out his native city to the world. He also acknowledges that globalism is no new phenomenon, and he goes on to state that the poet's job is to save the entire truth of one city 'from oblivion'.[24] It is an act of recuperation, and what is engaging is that Carson does not wish to restrict the meaning of the city to a merely Irish significance, but rather to show how that Irishness contains multitudes of other identities.

Dublin is the city celebrated by Peter Sirr in his collection *Bring Everything*. It represents the perfection of a mode that Sirr has been working on in previous books, encompassing a rich imaginative profusion and amazing sensual force. Though it includes love poems, its central character is the city of Dublin itself as it has never been seen before in Irish poetry. He relishes the huge variety of commodity that is now available, he goes into Habitat shops, he looks at the headlines, he listens to the city's noises, he relishes the odours and perfumes of the city breathing, leans closer to consider them: 'admiring the stalls, running our fingers along bright fabrics, sniffing cheeses, wandering wherever the crowd took us'.[25] Put simply, the collection takes pleasure in every aspect of the place, without turning away from the greed and deception which help compose the whole scene. The title itself indicates the expansive generosity of this contemplation. It is like the poetry of Frank O'Hara as he wandered around New York on his lunch breaks. With the important exceptions of Thomas Kinsella, Derek Mahon and Michael Hartnett, Irish poetry has overlooked the city as subject, preferring landscape. Sirr then is like one of the first pioneers discovering a new continent and conveying it to our imaginative ownership.

For Sirr the city, by gathering commodities from far-flung countries, corrals the hinterlands of those things as well, and so the self has access to the various geographies of the world: 'There's a moment the air will thicken and the light shift, as if / another country has poured itself in' and you might find yourself in China or Turkestan.[26] Sirr's book is exuberant and capacious, truly suggesting a space into which everything can be brought. The usual jeremiads about globalism dwell on the debilitating effects of the free flow of capital; the wide-ranging locales of Sirr's poems catch something of that movement as well as the refreshing sense that Ireland in the last ten years has been invaded by so many foreign things, foodstuffs and people. Rather than wringing his hands about this, he delights in the freedoms such change brings: the freedom to inhabit other selves temporarily, to taste other countries, to buy their furniture in the Habitat store.

Those same Jeremiahs also believe that one of the first casualties of this loosening up is an older idea of place. Certainly, in Sirr's book Dublin occasionally lifts off and floats through the stratosphere, but the consequence of this is that the city is rediscovered, seen anew. The history of Dublin comes to the fore in later poems such as 'After a Day in the History of the City', 'Cathedral', 'Essex Street'. What is evident here is that his global gaze is rooted in place in a different way from, say, Kinsella's in Thomas Street and its environs. For the older poet the imperatives of nationalism inform his reconstructions of urban history, whereas Sirr lacks such a framework. For the latter, the bloodshed of the past becomes dreamily commutative with that which happened in other cities of the world. So in a sense, indeed, the nationalist idea of place is erased, but a different idea replaces it and who is to say that one has more purchase than the other?

The outstanding and most surprising pages of *Nonetheless* (2004) are to be found in the section entitled 'Edge Songs', which are 'workings, adaptations, versions, "skeleton" translations of poems in Old Irish, Middle Irish and Latin, as they might be remembered or misremembered by an imagined Irish poet, and sometimes original poems written in response to or in the shadow of poems from that tradition', as Sirr puts it in a note.[27] For over two centuries, this kind of material has been used to fuel variations on nationalist ideology: so, reading these poems in *Nonetheless* is somewhat like watching butterflies take flight from museum cases. It is startling that Sirr's intense engagement with the dirt and glitter of recent developments in Ireland has given him access to some of its most ancient origins. Moreover, the great liberties he takes with the Irish and Latin sources come out of a deeper faithfulness to the mode of translation often practised in the Middle Ages in which *inventio* was a integral element in the process of bringing material over from one language to another. This is the ground which many previous Irish poets appropriated for themselves and their times; Sirr's entranced revision of this past is the new brink.

Sinéad Morrissey's second collection, *Between Here and There*, has many poems set in Japan and New Zealand, in which places she lived for some years. The last lines of the book read: 'I want to see it, / finger it, believe it, be amazed.'[28] She is particularly adept at recording the feelings of an observer who has stepped beyond the bounds of European culture to witness scenes like the following:

> What do you think when you see a mâché vagina
> being rammed with a penis as broad as a battering ram
> so that children disguised as elements shriek with joy?
>
> You think: *we are disembodied, while the moon herself has a body.*
> *She is over by the beer stands disguised as a man. One stagger and she'll trigger*
> *the collapse of the dancers. The moon came to watch us and we all fell down.*[29]

The first tercet is deliberately provocative in its word choices (namely, the repetition in 'rammed' and 'battering ram'): this is the kind of thing that one strand of feminism has taught us to deplore. Morrissey's response is interesting because she is shocked, not into outrage, but meditation, on her own body and those of the people about her, as well as how those bodies connect with natural cycles (the poem's title is 'Summer Festival'). Also striking is the use of italics which flags a dramatic change of tone (a favourite device). Her next collection, *The State of the Prisons* (2005), has a sequence about an extended trip to China. It is vividly observed, but does not rise above a journalistic account. Indeed, the collection as a whole emphasises narrative over lyrical effects, and the title poem is a long sequence based on the life of an eighteenth-century prison reformer. Such excursions to Japan and China cannot be categorised as emigration poetry like that of Delanty and Boland discussed in the previous chapter, which in spite of itself 'harp[s] on / about those Micks who fashioned' America.[30] This rather fits Peter McDonald's idea of poetic homeland which stretches to include the world, and it might be called rooted cosmopolitanism.

The locales of David Wheatley's first two collections are for the most part Irish, with occasional excursions to Europe. They are set around Bray, Co. Wicklow, where he was brought up, and Dublin City. Esenin, Mandelstam, Chamfort, Mac Gill-Eain, Verlaine, among others, all make appearances in his first collection, *Thirst* (1997), and this breadth of reference tweaked more than one Irish reviewer. What they failed to recognise was that this linguistic range (for Wheatley translates from these languages) was an index of a movement away from the usual demarcations of Irish poetry. If Seamus Heaney uses Dante to get another take on the old binaries of Ireland and England, Wheatley uses these other voices to get closer to Irish experience that is for the most part unconcerned with its relation to England as colonial oppressor.

Dublin's present and vivid past is the setting for Wheatley's second book *Misery Hill*, and its overriding theme is cultural amnesia. As an academic, Wheatley is interested in the nineteenth-century Irish poet, James Clarence Mangan, and that research is used in a sonnet cycle addressed to him. The sequence often strikes a note of bitter irony about the destruction of the city, and it develops by evoking a lost world of Dublin characters, foremost among which is Mangan himself. The city's history is transposed to one chaotic present in Wheatley's vision – with the legendary street-singer Zozimus rubbing shoulders with a bullish present of 'double-glazing, hedges, / hose pipes, patios and second cars'.[31] But the triumph in this synchronous mode is the title poem 'Misery Hill'. It is a capacious work taking in illegal immigrants, soaring property prices in Dublin, cartoon characters all jostling through a bizarre underworld. On a technical level, its *terza rima* contains long stretches of ingenious rhyming. Counterpointing the romping burlesque and slapstick metamorphoses of the poem is an elegiac undertow for all that has been lost – people, buildings, the whole city itself.

Most of the poems of *Mocker* (2006) are set in Hull, where Wheatley moved in 2000. Increasingly apparent is a wry humour, finely observant of the details of urban life and its hinterlands, as in the prose poems of 'Bankside-Wincolmlee by Instamatic', written in homage to another Hull poet, Peter Didsbury: 'Do they all lift, all these bridges, even this far up the river? Picture it unstitched the whole of its length, like a gutted haddock. Behind B&Q three teenage boys are fixing their lines and casting into the puddle of sludge between the river's cowpat banks. Who shall have a fishy?'[32] The childlike question at the end sweetly counterpoints the preceding urban grunge. The book also explores the limits of the traditional lyric, for instance in 'Fintan and the Hawk of Achill' and 'Sonnet', but Wheatley does not burn his bridges: he insists on including disjunctive registers along with older modes. Some of the latter provide the outstanding moments of the book, as in 'An Errancy', which mixes a ballad register with a contemporary voice:

On Luggala I heard the news,
oh boy, that it was time to choose

the straight or crooked path back home
and choosing neither chose to roam

across the gap beyond all reason,
out of love and out of season,

and coming to a clear stream fell
and bathed my face and drank my fill.[33]

The interjection in the second line is reminiscent of Muldoon and perhaps the Beatles, but the proceeding lines strike a very different note, as the poem avoids the tricksiness of the older poet and remains much closer to the ballad idiom. Wheatley avoids the choice that he is presented with – avoids the simplistic terms in which it is put – in favour of a rich errancy. Inconsequence, drift, detritus, odds and ends, hesitancy, doodles, scrimshaw, randomness, axolotls, misgiving: these are the phenomena to which Wheatley is most sharply attuned and from which he writes his finest poems.

As I remarked at the end of chapter 10, in 1999 Vona Groarke (b. 1964) expressed the wish that special issues of poetry magazines dealing with Irish women's poetry 'will eventually be redundant'.[34] The hardest pioneering work of feminists, both in the political and cultural spheres, had been carried out, and there was now an opportunity for a balanced appraisal of its implications for poetic tradition: poets could now decide which elements were still viable, which were more problematic. For instance, poets will still clearly need to write love poems, but theoretical considerations have made this terrain a minefield: it is too easy to regress to previous gender positions under the pressure of form and intonation. Those readers who find 'theoretical considerations' out of place in love poetry might be reminded that Philip Sidney shows that love is about nothing else. The word 'theory' itself comes from the Greek word θεωρία, which means looking at, viewing, contemplation; and lovers do a lot of that.

In 'Song', from her latest collection, *Juniper Street* (2006), Groarke recalls a blackbird singing years before she meets the dedicatee of her poem, her husband, the poet Conor O'Callaghan. The implication at the end of the poem is that it is O'Callaghan who has stirred 'that blackbird / into song'.[35] The poem is a response to his poem entitled 'Cover Version', from his collection, *Fiction* (2005), in which he makes the following complaint: 'Sugar. Isn't it odd that we've never had a song? / You know, where your pre-history mimes in sync / with mine for three otherwise unremarkable minutes.'[36] He then goes on to imagine what the song would possibly be like if it did exist, and that leads him on a trip through the strange emotional and historical detritus of the couple's past. This conversation has been going on between the two poets from their very first books. For instance, O'Callaghan's first book was entitled *The History of Rain* (1993) and the last line of the last poem in Groarke's first book, *Shale* (1994), reads: 'Your hand, when you lean to touch me, smells of rain.'[37] Eavan Boland has written persuasively about women as objects represented in poems talking back to their creators. Groarke and O'Callaghan offer a new model of conversation, a type of *renga* that is their marriage.

O'Callaghan is almost programmatically anti-transcendental, continually pushing away any high-flown rhetoric of revelation, only to let it emerge in the negative spaces of the poem (for example, that 'cloudless blue that yields a minute's rainfall'[38]). One of the best examples of this is the final poem of his second collection, *Seatown* (1999), 'Slip'. Over five pages long, the poem's force is difficult to convey in brief quotation. It economically sketches out the gradual obsolescence of the slip in the harbour, and an episode when the speaker looks at it – himself almost as erased as the viewed object by the sea – before turning back to 'an aimless life'.[39] As illustrative anecdote, this is fairly conventional: what is striking is the way the speaker's personality drifts in and out of focus throughout the poem. The poem end by syntactically refusing the use of an 'I', and the austerity and restraint of the lines are counterpointed by the lavish, humorous descriptions that are to be found elsewhere in the same book, as in the group of poems that describe Dundalk, where he lived for many years. Here one appreciates the balanced detailing, the accurate and yet indulgent eye, the luxuriant and unexpected juxtapositions. His more recent work has explored that 'common ground' even further, as he charts the transition to middle age: 'We wear this weather the tennis shirts / we once thought a scream. We compromise / when it comes to cuisine and the arts.'[40] This turns down the wattage to a dangerously low level, and the challenge for O'Callaghan is obviously to find the staves and notes in the ambient background noise of middle-class lives without falsifying them. It would be too easy to soup up some consolation, and it is only by remaining clear-eyed and unromantic that he can maintain his poetry's integrity.

The tone of Groarke's first book, *Shale*, moved between the incantatory and the discursive. In her second book, *Other People's Houses* (1999), she took the idea of the house and looked at it from every possible angle, with an imagination that combined wit and sweet lyricism. 'House Style' follows family resemblances through the generations; 'Domestic Arrangements' considers in turn the rooms of a Big House. The title poem, 'Other People's Houses', is about the places she lived with her husband before they purchased their own place. It is also a stunning love poem, and it should be said that this is a mode in which Groarke excels. The sharper edge of this is the mordant eroticism of 'Folderol'. The speaker sees the amorous graffiti on the walls and remarks that it

> reminds me of you, and the twenty-four
> words for 'nonsense' I wrote on your thighs and back
> (the night you came home from her house with some cock-
> and-bull story of missed connections and loose ends)
> with passion-fruit lipstick and mascara pens.[41]

One is wittily reminded of the etymology of the word 'enjambment' in the third line here. The speaker wakes to find herself smudged all over 'while you, of course, had vanished without a trace'.[42] This is a kind of *aisling* with the man as elusive lover and the woman, quite literally, as scribe. Groarke subverts the academic piety that empowers women: as the poem progresses, it seems that the female at last 'writes back', only to be foiled in the conclusion. This kind of witty sexual politics informs the whole collection.

Her third was entitled *Flight* (2002). The 'flight' of the title resonates on several levels: first, it is the flight from one's parents and one's hometown into adulthood; second, it the occasional flight from one's own responsibilities as a parent and the blankness of middle age; and third, it is the unalloyed joy in the flight of the imagination at the height of its powers. Many of the poems have domestic settings and relate mundane scenes, but these are cross-hatched with an impulse towards abstraction. So one poem will be about watching her son drawing with markers, and another will have an altogether more hazy provenance and trajectory. The title poem of the collection, 'Flight', is about imaginative extravagance and also about the way this can be harnessed in a poem; it is a flight beyond the ken of domesticity that still looks over its shoulder back down to 'home'. It suggests that the final horizon for all the domestic poems is not sentimental, but something much more wide-ranging and difficult to pin down ('And who's to say just what occurs // when something loses the run / of itself and slips airborne'[43]).

Juniper Street continues this extravagance and is her finest collection to date. Etymologically, extravagance is a wandering beyond limits, and the way in which Groarke can take mundane situations and range beyond them is breath-taking. 'The Local Accent' begins with a river going through a town, and through detailed descriptions explores the way the landscape is connected to the way people speak. In some way the landscape must be speaking through them, even as they think they are expressing themselves. Such double-talk becomes Groarke's method as she puns on words like 'pronounce' and 'inflection'.

Groarke was born in Co. Longford in the Irish midlands and *Juniper Street*, though it takes its title from the name of a street in Philadelphia (the city where she lived in 2004) returns to the locales of her birthplace, especially in the long poem 'Athlones'. Her eye ranges over the town, dwelling on its qualities of middleness. That is a conventional enough approach. What makes the poem so impressive is, first, the kind of thing that Groarke notices and, second, the way she slides from one observation to the next. She is particularly brilliant on picking up the play of light through the town, and this becomes a way of describing human co-existence as a marvellous conversation of light and shadow. The people impinge on one another in ways that they are only half aware of, and these, connected with the ways they are fully aware of, make up the life of the town.

Groarke now works at Wake Forest University in North Carolina (where her husband also works), and she has not been slow to adapt to the new terrain. She has published a diary of her time in Philadelphia,[44] and the title poem of *Juniper Street* is a statement of love, and also a way of imaginatively settling in America. She employs the conventional image of the lover's hand, but one is reminded of the last lines of *Shale* ('Your hand, when you lean to touch me ...') and that the hand in the later poem is also that of a writer. This is a rooted cosmopolitanism, as we witness Groarke's 'Greater Midlands' in *Juniper Street* effortlessly involving the whole of America.

Caitríona O'Reilly (b. 1973) has published two collections, *The Nowhere Birds* (2001) and *The Sea Cabinet* (2006). A favourite metaphor is sculpture and this is reflected in the cool, beautiful surfaces of O'Reilly's work, even when dealing with difficult material, for instance with anorexia in 'Skin'. The detached tone enables a luxurious description of the body: the speaker is fascinated, proud and a little aghast at her predicament. As Maria Johnston remarks, O'Reilly has learned this kind of delivery from Plath, but unlike the many other poets who have been influenced by the American, O'Reilly is not overwhelmed.[45] Even when writing in freer modes, she gives an impression of incredible compactness and discipline; and she plays this off against a precise gaudiness of diction.

The title poem of her second collection is set in the Town Docks Museum in Hull and is for the most part concerned with whales and the practice of whaling. The echo chamber for the poem is the oceans themselves, the large, chilling inhuman spaces that we know so little about. The fascination is the same as Melville's, a passage from whose *Moby-Dick* she uses as the collection's epigraph. For Melville the sea seemed to offer a vast critique of humanity and all its doings: what are kings and countries compared to the ancient forces moving through the brine? Part II of the poem is about the exhibition of a 'mermaid' with a 'crudely-stitched seam between skin and scale'.[46] Such a creature of fascination and fetish draws many stares from visitors. O'Reilly's imagination keeps returning to the gaze between the sexes, with its mixture of desire, disgust, tenderness, deception and pleasure. She knows what happens between the cynosure and the devotee, and describes that action as it plays itself out on the bodies of the participants.

> When I draw
> his blade across my
>
> arm it resembles
> water dripping over
>
> a stone lip
> in the stone garden,
>
> runny wax
> from a candle . . .[47]

There is a striking tension at the first enjambment here as one wonders *what* the knife is cutting – a body part or merely a possession? While the worst is confirmed in the next line, it is immediately mitigated by the garden imagery; but the description also serves to focus more clearly the hideous nature of the scene. That the speaker is matter-of-fact also helps this effect.

The third section of 'The Sea Cabinet' is about an Eskimo couple who were exhibited in York some time in the nineteenth century. Taken out of their element, they do not fare well: 'she dies on board ship of measles only weeks / from home. Memiadluk went back alone.'[48] For the couple, leaving their element proves a fatal experience. However, poets of this generation have prospered in foreign places, and have significantly extended the imaginative domain of Irish poetry.

In his poem 'The Disappearing Island', Seamus Heaney takes the voice of St Brendan's crew, who hauled up on an island and made a fire there, only to discover that they were actually on top of a whale, and the island disappeared beneath them. Heaney provides a shocking image as terra firma dissolves beneath their feet. As the epigraph to this book, I quoted another reported disappearance of an island, this time Ireland. Poets such as Heaney and Hartnett, even though they have invested much of their imaginative life in matters of 'Ireland', clearly also relish the prospect of getting rid of it. These more recent poets do not move in concert with a larger nationalist objective, as the poets of a century before did. Rather, they bear witness to the multitudes the island contains, and have extended its borders to include a fair piece of the known world.

Notes

Introduction

1. Epigraph to Eamon Grennan's *Facing the Music: Irish Poetry in the Twentieth Century* (Omaha: Creighton University Press, 1999).
2. Harry Thomas, ed., *Talking with Poets* (New York: Handsel Books, 2002), p. 48.
3. Although *Translations* has been translated *in toto* into Irish, there has only been one unofficial bilingual production by Aisteorí Ildaite at UCD in 1995, directed by Síle Ní Bhroin and Karen O'Shea.
4. W. B. Yeats, *Collected Poems*, ed. Richard J. Finneran (London: Palgrave, 1999), pp. 161–2.
5. Vona Groarke, Interview with Fionnuala Dillane and John McAuliffe, *Review of Postgraduate English Studies* 5 (1997), pp. 59–60.
6. Niall Ferguson, *Empire: How Britain Made the Modern World* (London: Penguin, 2003), p. xxiv.

1 The appearance of Ireland

1. Tomás Ó Duinnshléibhe, *Taidhgín* (Inverin: Cló Iar-Chonnachta, 1995), p. 98. In English: 'A nation can lose and win its freedom, and lose and win it again and yet again, but if the language is lost, we will never regain it. A nation cannot lose its language without losing its soul, and when its soul is lost, it is finished as a nation.'
2. Robert Welch, 'Constitution, Language and Tradition in Nineteenth-Century Irish Poetry', *Tradition and Influence in Anglo-Irish Poetry*, eds. Terence Brown and Nicholas Grene (London: Macmillan, 1989), p. 13.
3. Matthew Campbell, 'Poetry in English, 1830–1890: From Catholic Emancipation to the Fall of Parnell', *Cambridge History of Irish Literature*, vol. I, eds. Margaret Kelleher and Philip O'Leary (Cambridge: Cambridge University Press, 2006), p. 500.
4. Welch, 'Constitution, Language and Tradition', throughout.
5. Thomas Moore, *Moore's Irish Melodies, Lalla Rookh, National Airs, Legendary Ballads, Songs, Etc., with a Memoir by J. F. Waller, L.L.D., Superb Illustrations on Steel and Wood.* London: William MacKenzie. There is no date, but it is most likely late nineteenth century.

211

6. George Saintsbury, 'Lesser Poets, 1790–1837', *Cambridge History of English Literature*, eds. A. W. Ward and A. R. Waller, vol. XII (Cambridge: Cambridge University Press, 1921), pp. 102–3.

7. As he remarked in one prefatory note to the Melodies: 'I cannot help thinking that it is possible to love our country very zealously, and to feel deeply interested in her honour and happiness, without believing that Irish was the language spoken in Paradise.' Thomas Moore, *Poetical Works of Thomas Moore* (London: Frederick Warne, 1891), p. 192.

8. *Ibid.*, p. 191.

9. *Ibid.*, pp. 196–7.

10. *Ibid.*, p. 213.

11. Terence Brown, *Ireland's Literature: Selected Essays* (Mullingar: Lilliput Press, 1988), p. 19.

12. Moore, *Poetical Works* (1891), pp. 193–4.

13. Stephen Gwynn, *Thomas Moore* (London: Macmillan, 1905), p. 70.

14. Moore, *Poetical Works* (1891), p. 218.

15. *Literature Online.* 2 November 2005. http: \\ lion.chadwyck.co.uk.

16. What follows is taken from the preface to the French English-language edition of Moore's works in 1829:

   For Lalla Rookh Mr Moore received 3,000 guineas of Messrs Longman and Co. For the Life of Sheridan he was paid 2,000 guineas by the same house – Mr Moore enjoys an annuity of 500 *l.* from Power, the music-seller, for the Irish Melodies and other lyrical pieces; and he is engaged to write for the Times newspaper, at a salary of 500 *l.* a year. It is well known that the Memoirs of Lord Byron, written by himself, had been deposited in the keeping of Mr Moore, and designed as a legacy for his benefit. It is also known that the latter, with the consent and at the desire of his lordship, had long ago sold the manuscript to Mr Murray, the bookseller, for the sum of two thousand guineas.

   J. W. Lake, 'A Biographical and Critical Sketch of Thomas Moore, Esq.', *The Poetical Works of Thomas Moore* (Paris: A. and W. Galignani, 1829), p. xvii.

17. Gregory A. Schirmer, *Out of What Began: A History of Irish Poetry in English* (Cornell: Cornell University Press, 1998).

18. Moore, *Poetical Works* (1891), p. 443.

19. Brown, *Ireland's Literature*, p. 18.

20. Gwynn, *Thomas Moore*, p. 83.

21. Brown, *Ireland's Literature*, p. 26.

22. Gwynn, *Thomas Moore*, p. 90.

23. J. J. Callanan, *The Recluse of Inchidony and Other Poems* (London: Hurst, Chance and Co., 1829). I give the full publication details as the date is occasionally given wrongly as 1830.

24. J. J. Callanan, *The Irish Poems of J. J. Callanan*, ed. Gregory A. Schirmer (Gerrards Cross: Colin Smythe, 2005).

25. Callanan, *The Recluse*, p. 27.

26. Schirmer, Introduction, *The Irish Poems of J. J. Callanan*, p. 20.

27. Callanan, *The Irish Poems*, pp. 49–50, 52.

28. *Ibid.*, p. 105.

29. Robert Welch, *A History of Verse Translation from the Irish 1789–1897* (Gerrards Cross: Colin Smythe, 1988), pp. 69–70.

30. Callanan, *The Irish Poems*, p. 94.

31. Welch, *A History*, p. 67.

32. L. G. Kelly, *The True Interpreter: A History of Translation Theory in the West* (Oxford: Basil Blackwell, 1979), p. 49.

33. Welch remarks that 'Her versions tend to envelop the general content of the Irish in clouds of rhetoric which sail far above the literal detail, creating elaborate but hybrid shapes as they float past.' *A History*, p. 42. Also, see Schirmer, *Out of What Began*, p. 84.

34. Seamus Deane, 'Thomas Moore', *The Field Day Anthology of Irish Writing*, ed. Seamus Deane *et al.*, vol. I (Derry: Field Day Publications, 1991), pp. 1055–6.

35. John Mitchel, Introduction, *Poems of James Clarence Mangan*, ed. D. J. O'Donoghue (Dublin: M. H. Gill, 1910), p. xxviii.

36. David Lloyd, *Nationalism and Minor Literature: James Clarence Mangan and the Emergence of Irish Cultural Nationalism* (Berkeley: University of California Press, 1987).

37. Anthony Cronin, Foreword, *Selected Poems of James Clarence Mangan*, ed. Michael Smith (Dublin: Gallery Press, 1973), pp. 11–13.

38. David Wheatley, *Misery Hill* (Loughcrew: Gallery Press, 2000), pp. 12–25.

39. Brian Moore, *The Mangan Inheritance* (London: Jonathan Cape, 1979).

40. Susan Howe, *The Nonconformist's Memorial* (New York: New Directions, 1993), pp. 106–8.

41. James McCabe, 'James Clarence Mangan's Lost Memoir: The Desert and the Solitude', *Metre* 10 (Autumn 2001), pp. 115–25.

42. Sean Ryder, Introduction, *James Clarence Mangan: Selected Writings* (Dublin: UCD Press, 2004), p. 1.

43. Thomas Kinsella and Seán Ó Tuama, eds., *An Duanaire: Poems of the Dispossessed 1600–1900* (Mountrath: Dolmen Press, 1981), pp. 308–11.

44. Mangan, *Selected Writings*, pp. 222, 224.

45. *Ibid.*, pp. 64–5.

46. Lloyd, *Nationalism and Minor Literature*, pp. 118–19.

47. Mangan, *Selected Writings*, pp. 212–13.

48. *Ibid.*, p. 214. The numbers in parentheses refer the reader to Mangan's mock-academic notes.

2 Tennyson's Ireland

1. Cormac Ó Gráda, *The Great Irish Famine* (Dublin: Gill and Macmillan, 1989), p. 75.

2. Joep Leerssen, *Remembrance and Imagination: Patterns in the Historical and Literary Representation of Ireland in the Nineteenth Century* (Cork: Cork University Press, 1996), pp. 157–8.

3. Austin Clarke, 'Gaelic Ireland Rediscovered: The Early Period', *Irish Poets in English: The Thomas Davis Lectures on Anglo-Irish Poetry*, ed. Seán Lucy (Dublin: Mercier Press, 1973), p. 31.

4. Kathleen Tillotson has remarked on the newness of his material, and that 'in 1842, Arthurian story was still strange to the ordinary reader, and even felt to be unacceptable as a subject for poetry'. 'Tennyson's Serial Poem', *Mid-Victorian Studies* (London: University of London-Athlone Press, 1965), pp. 82. See also Michael Thorn, *Tennyson* (London: Abacus, 1993), p. 211.

5. James Henry, *Poematia* (Dresden: C. C. Meinhold and Sons, 1866), p. 111.

6. J. P. Mahaffy, 'Obituary: Dr. James Henry', *The Academy* 12 August 1876, rpt. in *Selected Poems of James Henry*, ed. Christopher Ricks (New York: Handsel Books, 2002), p. 13.

7. James Henry, *Selected Poems of James Henry*, p. 54.

8. *Ibid.*, p. 55.

9. *Ibid.*, p. 113.

10. *Ibid.*, p. 115.

11. *Ibid.*, p. 104.

12. Peter Denman, *Samuel Ferguson: The Literary Achievement* (Gerrards Cross: Colin Smythe, 1990), p. 8.

13. Gréagóir Ó Dúill, *Samuel Ferguson: Beatha agus Saothar* (Dublin: An Clóchomhar Tta, 1993), p. 185. In English:

    Ferguson was frequently uncertain of his own view of the characters and events in the ancient legends he dealt with. He was an Anglo-Irish gentleman scholar, an Ulsterman who was a New Light Presbyterian covenanter, he was a nationalist and almost ready to admit at certain times that the tie with England should be broken – he was three persons in one poet.

14. *Ibid.*, p. 143.

15. *Field Day Anthology of Irish Writing*, ed. Seamus Deane, vol. II (Derry: Field Day Publications, 1991), p. 50.

16. *Ibid.*

17. It is of note that Alfred Perceval Graves, in his selection of Ferguson's work, took the liberty of lopping off this final stanza from the poem, as he did in one other case, remarking 'I have, in the exercise of my editorial discretion, got rid of these two moralising tags in the condensed version of *The Tain Quest* and the otherwise uncut text of *The Welshmen of Tirawley*, to be found within these pages.' *The Poems of Samuel Ferguson*, ed. Alfred Perceval Graves (Dublin: Talbot Press, 1916), pp. xxxii–xxxiii. *Literature Online*, 3 November 2005, http: \\ lion.chadwyck.co.uk.

18. *Literature Online*, 3 November 2005, http: \\ lion.chadwyck.co.uk.

19. *Ibid.*

20. Denman, *Samuel Ferguson*, p. 123.

21. Samuel Ferguson, *Congal: A Poem, in Five Books* (Dublin: Edward Ponsonby, 1872), p. 145.

22. Denman, *Samuel Ferguson*, p. 5.

23. W. B. Yeats, 'The Poetry of Samuel Ferguson', *Dublin University Review* (November 1886), rpt. in *Uncollected Prose by W. B. Yeats*, vol. I, ed. John P. Frayne (London: Macmillan, 1970), p. 103.

24. In another version of the same essay, Yeats compliments Ferguson on the 'barbarous truth' of his work. It is important to note that this is hardly a compliment that would have pleased the earlier poet. *Ibid.*, p. 87.

25. Ó Dúill, *Samuel Ferguson*, p. 35.

26. William Allingham, *A Diary*, eds. H. Allingham and D. Radford (London: Macmillan, 1907), pp. 297–8.

27. William Allingham, *Poems*, ed. H. Allingham (London: Macmillan, 1912), p. 39.

28. *Ibid.*, p. 40.

29. William Allingham, ed., *The Ballad Book: A Selection of the Choicest British Ballads* (London: Macmillan, 1865), p. x.

30. Allingham, *Poems*, p. 29.

31. *Ibid.*, p. 31.

32. *Ibid.*, p. 54.

33. *Ibid.*, p. 55.

34. *Literature Online*, 3 November 2005, http: \\ lion.chadwyck.co.uk.

35. *Ibid.*

36. Gregory Schirmer, for instance, suggests that Allingham did not have the 'insider's authority' of a later figure like Kavanagh when he wrote about Irish peasant life. *Out of What Began: A History of Irish Poetry in English* (Cornell: Cornell University Press, 1998) p. 129.

3 Revival

1. Ezra Pound, *The Cantos* (London: Faber and Faber, 1987), p. 532.

2. F. R. Higgins, quoted in *The Faber Book of Contemporary Irish Poetry*, ed. Paul Muldoon (London: Faber and Faber, 1986), p. 18.

3. John Hutchinson, *The Dynamics of Cultural Nationalism: The Gaelic Revival and the Creation of the Irish Nation State* (London: Allen and Unwin, 1987), p. 39.

4. Douglas Hyde, *Abhráin Grádh Chúige Connacht/Love Songs of Connacht* (1893; Dublin: Irish Academic Press, 1987), pp. 66–7. Here I reproduce Hyde's original font, as the introduction of Gaelic fonts to printed texts during the Revival was an important design innovation which emphasised other cultural differences between English and Irish.

5. *Ibid.*, p. 65. Also compare this version with Samuel Ferguson's, 'Pastheen Finn: Irish Rustic Song', 16 Febuary 2007, http: \\ lion.chadwyck.co.uk. Ferguson smoothes out the contradictions and difficulties of the poem in order, one imagines, to make it more palatable to a Victorian audience.

6. Hyde, *Abhráin Grádh Chúige Connacht*, p. 147.

7. *Ibid.*, pp. 70–1.

8. Robert Welch, *A History of Verse Translation from the Irish 1789–1897* (Gerrards Cross: Colin Smythe, 1988), pp. 151–2.

9. Katharine Tynan, *Shamrocks* (London: Kegan Paul, Trench, 1887), p. 4.

10. Ethna Carbery, *The Four Winds of Eirinn*, ed. Seamas McManus (1902; Dublin: M. H. Gill and Son, 1934), p. 44.

11. Emily Lawless, *With the Wild Geese* (London: Isbister, 1902), p. 5.

12. W. B. Yeats, *Collected Poems*, ed. Richard J. Finneran (London: Palgrave, 1991), p. 233.

13. *Ibid.*

14. *Literature Online*, 9 November 2005, http: \\ lion.chadwyck.co.uk.

15. *Ibid.*

16. *Ibid.*

17. George Sigerson, *Bards of the Gael and Gall: Examples of the Poetic Literature of Erin* (1897; Dublin: Talbot Press, 1925), p. 107.

18. Declan Kiberd, *Inventing Ireland: The Literature of the Modern State* (London: Jonathan Cape, 1995), p. 136.

19. Edward Dunsany, Introduction, *Songs of the Fields* by Francis Ledwidge (London: Herbert Jenkins Ltd, 1918), pp. 7–8.

20. P. J. Mathews, *Revival: The Abbey Theatre, Sinn Féin, the Gaelic League and the Co-Operative Movement* (Cork: Cork University Press – Field Day Publications, 2003), p. 44.

21. Padraic Colum, *Wild Earth and Other Poems* (1909; New York: Henry Holt, 1916), p. 3.

22. Eilís Ní Dhuibhne, ed., *Voices on the Wind: Women Poets of the Celtic Twilight* (Dublin: New Island Books, 1995), p. 67.

23. *Ibid.*

24. Ledwidge, *Songs of the Fields*, p. 28.

25. J. M. Synge, *Collected Works*, vol. I, ed. Robin Skelton (Gerrard's Cross: Colin Smythe, 1982), p. 42.

26. Kiberd, *Inventing Ireland*, p. 627.

27. Synge, *Collected Works*, vol. I, p. 60.

28. *Ibid.*, p. 64.

4 W. B. Yeats

1. Edna Longley, *Poetry in the Wars* (Newcastle: Bloodaxe, 1986), p. 15.

2. *Ibid.*, p. 16.

3. R. F. Foster, *W. B. Yeats: A Life*, vol. I, *The Apprentice Mage* (Oxford: Oxford University Press, 1997), p. 598.

4. W. B. Yeats, *Collected Works*, vol. X, *Later Articles and Reviews*, ed. Colton Johnson (New York: Scribner's, 2000), p. 16.

5. *Ibid.*, p. 29.

6. *Collected Works of W. B. Yeats: Later Essays*, vol. V, ed. William H. O'Donnell (New York: Scribner's, 1994), p. 207.

7. *Ibid.*, pp. 210–11.

8. Seamus Deane argues that the occult served as a kind of substitution for the Irish language: like Irish, the occult, 'was an old language in which much that had belonged to the world before the onset of print culture had been preserved'. *Strange Country: Modernity and Nationhood in Irish Writing since 1790* (Oxford: Clarendon Press, 1997), pp. 110–11.

9. Thomas Carlyle, *Sartor Resartus: The Life and Opinions of Herr Teufelsdröckh* (London: George Routledge and Sons, 1926), p. 174.

10. Foster, *W. B. Yeats*, p. 89.

11. Yeats, *Collected Works*, vol. II, *The Plays*, eds. David R. Clark and Rosalind E. Clark (London: Palgrave, 2001), p. 79.

12. See, for instance, Yug Mohit Chaudhry, *Yeats, the Irish Literary Revival and the Politics of Print* (Cork: Cork University Press, 2001), pp. 132–84.

13. *Collected Poems of W. B. Yeats*, revised edn, ed. Richard J. Finneran (Houndmills: Palgrave, 1991), p. 19.

14. See for instance the first chapter of Ernie O'Malley's *On Another Man's Wound* (Dublin: Anvil Book, 1997) for an account of how mythology prepared him to fight as a revolutionary.

15. Terence Brown, *The Life of W. B. Yeats: A Critical Biography* (Dublin: Gill and Macmillan, 1999), p. 82.

16. Yeats, *Collected Poems*, p. 50.

17. *Ibid.*

18. Email to the author, October 2006.

19. Yeats, *Collected Poems*, p. 127.

20. Yeats, *Collected Works*, vol. X, p. 191.

21. Yeats, *Collected Works*, vol. V, p. 213.

22. F. R. Higgins, quotd in *The Faber Book of Contemporary Irish Poetry*, ed. Paul Muldoon (London: Faber and Faber, 1986), p. 18.

23. Yeats, *Collected Poems*, p. 131.

24. *Ibid.*, p. 134.

25. *Ibid.*, p. 149.

26. *Ibid.*

27. *Ibid.*, p. 193.

28. *Ibid.*, p. 194.

29. *Ibid.*

30. *Ibid.*, pp. 195–6.

31. *Ibid.*, p. 198.

32. *Ibid.*, p. 199.

33. *Ibid.*

34. *Ibid.*, p. 198.

35. *Ibid.*, p. 200.

36. *Ibid.*, p. 204.
37. *Ibid.*, p. 206.
38. *Ibid.*, p. 207.
39. *Ibid.*, p. 216.
40. *Ibid.*
41. *Ibid.*, p. 217.
42. *Ibid.*, p. 337.
43. *Ibid.*, p. 340.
44. *Ibid.*, p. 197.
45. Peter Allt and Russell K. Alspach, eds., *Variorum Edition of the Poems of W. B. Yeats* (London: Macmillan, 1957), pp. 119–20; and Yeats, *Collected Poems*, p. 40.
46. Yeats, *Collected Works*, vol. V, pp. 241–2.
47. *Ibid.*, p. 240.

5 Wild earth

1. W. B. Yeats, *The Collected Poems of W. B. Yeats*, ed. Richard J. Finneran (London: Palgrave, 1991), p. 327.
2. Padraic Colum, *Wild Earth and Other Poems* (1909; New York: Henry Holt, 1916), pp. 59–60.
3. Padraic Colum, Preface to *Anna Livia Plurabelle*, by James Joyce (New York: Crosbie Gaige, 1928), pp. vii, xiv.
4. Terence Brown, 'Ireland, Modernism and the 1930s', *Modernism and Ireland: The Poetry of the 1930s*, eds. Patricia Coughlan and Alex Davis (Cork: Cork University Press, 1995), p. 36. On the same page, he reminds us that Joyce wished for James Stephens, a Revival writer in the same mould as Colum, to take over from him if he should die before completing *Finnegans Wake*.
5. Peter Denman, 'Austin Clarke: Tradition, Memory and Our Lot', *Tradition and Influence in Anglo-Irish Poetry*, eds. Terence Brown and Nicholas Grene (London: Macmillan, 1989), p. 66.
6. Austin Clarke, *Collected Poems* (Dublin: Dolmen Press, 1974), p. 153.
7. Austin Clarke, *A Penny in the Clouds: More Memories of Ireland and England* (London: Routledge and Kegan Paul, 1968), p. 84.
8. Clarke, *Collected Poems*, p. 154.
9. Seán Ó Ríordáin, *Brosna* (1964; Dublin: Sáirséal agus Dill, 1979), p. 14.
10. Clarke, *Collected Poems*, p. 178.
11. Alan Gillis, *Irish Poetry of the 1930s* (Oxford: Oxford University Press, 2005), p. 93.
12. Gregory Schirmer, *The Poetry of Austin Clarke* (Mountrath: Dolmen Press, 1983), p. 102.
13. Clarke, *Collected Poems*, p. 327.
14. *Ibid.*, p. 518.
15. *Ibid.*, pp. 519–20.
16. *Ibid.*, p. 520.

17. Antoinette Quinn, *Patrick Kavanagh: A Biography*, revd edn (Dublin: Gill and Macmillan, 2003), p. 70.
18. Patrick Kavanagh, *Collected Poems*, ed. Antoinette Quinn (London: Penguin, 2004), p. 15.
19. Antoinette Quinn, *Patrick Kavanagh: Born-Again Romantic* (Dublin: Gill and Macmillan, 1993), p. 152.
20. Author's note to *Collected Poems* (1964), quoted in *Collected Poems*, ed. Quinn, p. 292.
21. Quinn, *Patrick Kavanagh: Born-Again Romantic*, p. 296.
22. Kavanagh, *Collected Poems*, p. 90.
23. *Ibid.*, p. 184.
24. *Ibid.*
25. Quinn, *Patrick Kavanagh: Born-Again Romantic*, p. 396.
26. Kavanagh, *Collected Poems*, p. 227.
27. Austin Clarke, *Poetry in Modern Ireland* (Dublin: Cultural Relations Committee, 1961), pp. 59–60.
28. Peter McDonald, *Louis MacNeice: A Poet in His Contexts* (Oxford: Oxford University Press, 1991), p. 1.
29. Louis MacNeice, *Selected Prose*, ed. Alan Heuser (Oxford: Oxford University Press, 1990), p. 88.
30. Jon Stallworthy, *Louis MacNeice* (New York: W. W. Norton, 1995), p. 219.
31. Louis MacNeice, *Collected Poems*, ed. Peter McDonald (London: Faber and Faber, 2007), p. 17.
32. *Ibid.*
33. McDonald, *Louis MacNeice*, p. 83.
34. Derek Mahon, *Journalism*, ed. Terence Brown (Loughcrew: Gallery Press, 1996), pp. 22–3.
35. MacNeice, *Collected Poems*, p. 99.
36. *Ibid.*, pp. 138, 139, 140.
37. Edna Longley, *Louis MacNeice: A Study* (London: Faber and Faber, 1988), p. 135.
38. MacNeice, *Collected Poems*, p. 533.
39. *Ibid.*, p. 584.
40. Devin A. Garrity, ed., *New Irish Poets: Representative Selections from the Work of 37 Contemporaries* (New York: Devin-Adair, 1948), p. 45.

6 The ends of Modernism: Kinsella and Irish experiment

1. J. C. C. Mays, Introduction, *Collected Poems of Denis Devlin*, ed. J. C. C. Mays (Dublin: Dedalus, 1989), p. 25.
2. The meaning of the title is ambiguous and is perhaps taken from Seneca, Letter CXVII (and not, as Brian Coffey, supposed, Horace): 'Quod bonum est prodest', 'the good is useful'.
3. Devlin, *Collected Poems*, p. 84.

4. *Ibid.*, p. 132.
5. *Ibid.*, p. 134.
6. *Ibid.*, p. 135.
7. Brian Coffey, *The Death of Hektor* (London: Menard Press, 1982), p. 15.
8. Seamus Deane, *Celtic Revivals* (London: Faber and Faber, 1985), p. 135.
9. F. S. L. Lyons, *Ireland Since the Famine* (London: Fontana, 1973), p. 683.
10. Andrew Fitzsimons, 'The Sea of Disappointment: Thomas Kinsella's Pursuit of the Real', unpublished doctoral dissertation (Dublin: Trinity College, 2005), chapters 1 and 2.
11. Ezra Pound, *Gaudier-Brzeska: A Memoir* (New York: New Directions, 1970), p. 92.
12. *Ibid.*, p. 117.
13. *Ibid.*, p. 111.
14. Thomas Kinsella, Interview with Ian Flanagan, *Metre* 2 (Spring 1997), p. 109.
15. Kinsella, *Collected Poems 1956–2001* (Manchester: Carcanet, 2001), p. 177.
16. *Ibid.*, p. 144.
17. *Ibid.*, p. 146.
18. *Ibid.*, p. 159.
19. Donatella Abbate Badin, *Thomas Kinsella* (New York: Twayne, 1996), p. 108.
20. Kinsella, *Collected Poems*, p. 159.
21. *Ibid.*, p. 160.
22. *Ibid.*, p. 161.
23. *Ibid.*, p. 164.
24. *Ibid.*
25. *Ibid.*, p. 165.
26. *Ibid.*, p. 172.
27. *Ibid.*, p. 173.
28. John Montague, *Collected Poems* (Loughcrew: Gallery, 1995), p. 213.
29. *Ibid.*
30. Steven Matthews, *Irish Poetry: Politics, History, Negotiation. The Evolving Debate, 1969 to the Present* (London: Macmillan, 1997), p. 131.
31. Montague, *Collected Poems*, p. 80.
32. *Ibid.*, p. 83.
33. *Ibid.*, p. 120.
34. *Ibid.*
35. Randolph Healy, *Green 532: Selected Poems 1983–2000* (Applecross: Salt, 2002), p. 43.
36. *Ibid.*, p. 40.
37. Maurice Scully, *Livelihood* (Bray: Wild Honey Press, 2004).
38. Interview with Kit Fryatt, *Metre* 17 (Spring 2005), p. 139.
39. *Ibid.*, p. 141.
40. Scully, *Livelihood*, p. 159.
41. 'Fite fuaite ina chéile' is a common phrase in Irish.
42. Scully, *Livelihood*, p. 163.
43. Interview, p. 142.

7 Ireland's Empire

1. Richard Murphy, *Collected Poems* (Loughcrew: Gallery Press, 2000), p. 233.
2. *Ibid.*, p. 21.
3. Bernard O'Donoghue, 'The Lost Link: Richard Murphy's Early Poetry', *Metre* 10 (Autumn 2001), pp. 138–9.
4. See Terence Brown, *Ireland's Literature: Selected Essays* (Dublin: Lilliput, 1988), p. 202.
5. *Ibid.*, p. 194.
6. Murphy, *Collected Poems*, p. 67.
7. *Ibid.*, p. 81.
8. *Ibid.*, p. 67.
9. *Ibid.*, p. 101.
10. *Ibid.*, p. 116.
11. *Ibid.*, p. 211.
12. *Ibid.*, p. 206.
13. *Ibid.*, p. 230.
14. Derek Mahon, *Collected Poems* (Loughcrew: Gallery Press, 1999), p. 85.
15. *Ibid.*, p. 86.
16. Peter Denman, 'Know the One? Insolent Ontologies and Mahon's Revisions', *Irish University Review* 24.1 (Spring–Summer 1994), p. 34.
17. Mahon, *Collected Poems*, p. 127.
18. Fran Brearton, *The Great War and Irish Poetry: W. B. Yeats to Michael Longley* (Oxford: Oxford University Press, 2000), p. 186.
19. Derek Mahon, *Journalism*, ed. Terence Brown (Loughcrew: Gallery, 1996), p. 94.
20. Mahon, *Collected Poems*, p. 141.
21. *Ibid.*, p. 120.
22. Brearton, *The Great War*, p. 174.
23. *Ibid.*, pp. 174–5.
24. Derek Mahon, *The Hudson Letter* (Loughcrew: Gallery Press, 1995), p. 39.
25. *Ibid.*, p. 56.
26. Derek Mahon, *The Yellow Book* (Loughcrew: Gallery Press, 1997), p. 57.
27. Terence Brown, 'Mahon and Longley: Place and Placelessness', *The Cambridge Companion to Contemporary Irish Poetry*, ed. Matthew Campbell (Cambridge: Cambridge University Press, 2003), p. 140.
28. Michael Longley, Interview with Eileen Battersby, *Irish Times* (9 March 2000), p. 13.
29. Quoted in Brearton, *The Great War*, p. 255.
30. *Ibid.*, p. 284.
31. Michael Longley, Interview with Fran Brearton, *Irish Studies Review* 18 (Spring 1997), p. 37.
32. Richard Kirkland, *Literature and Culture in Northern Ireland Since 1965: Moments of Danger* (Harlow: Longman, 1996), throughout. And Michael Allen, 'Rhythm and Development in Michael Longley's Earlier Poetry', *Contemporary Irish Poetry*, ed. Elmer Andrews (Basingstoke: Macmillan, 1992).

33. Michael Longley, *Collected Poems* (London: Cape, 2006), p. 58. Mahon would publicly and privately disagree with Longley about these lines. See Fran Brearton, *Reading Michael Longley* (Tarset: Bloodaxe, 2006), p. 90.

34. Longley, *Collected Poems*, p. 62.

35. *Ibid.*, p. 62.

36. Brearton, *The Great War*, p. 258.

37. Longley, *Collected Poems*, p. 186.

38. Michael Longley, *Gorse Fires* (London: Secker and Warburg, 1991), p. 52.

39. Michael Longley, Interview with Sarah Broom, *Metre* 4 (Spring–Summer 1998), p. 18.

40. Longley, *Collected Poems*, p. 225.

41. *Ibid.*, p. 307.

42. *Ibid.*, p. 192.

43. *Ibid.*, p. 1.

8 Seamus Heaney

1. Seamus Heaney, *Electric Light* (London: Faber and Faber, 2001), p. 77.

2. Frank Sewell suggests that Heaney learnt this technique from Seán Ó Ríordáin. *Modern Irish Poetry: A New Alhambra* (Oxford: Oxford University Press, 2000), p. 59.

3. Seamus Heaney, *North* (London: Faber and Faber, 1975), p. 16.

4. Seamus Deane, 'Unhappy and at Home: Interview with Seamus Heaney', *Crane Bag Book of Irish Studies*, eds. Mark Patrick Hederman and Richard Kearney (Dublin: Blackwater Press, 1982), p. 66.

5. Michael Parker has shown how closely the poem is connected with political events in Northern Ireland in 1972 and 1973. *Seamus Heaney: The Making of a Poet* (London: Macmillan, 1993), pp. 124–5.

6. Seamus Heaney, *North*, pp. 49–50.

7. Michael Parker feels that it is prophetic of the Protestant strike of 1974, but goes on to comment: 'Although the monstrous, "ignorant", "parasitical" child sired by England is generally taken to be a reference to Protestant paramilitaries, as some commentators have pointed out, the IRA can equally be viewed as the offspring of the rape.' *Seamus Heaney*, p. 144.

8. James Simmons, 'The Trouble with Seamus', *Seamus Heaney: A Collection of Critical Essays*, ed. Elmer Andrews (London: Macmillan, 1992), p. 57; and Edna Longley: 'In any case, the poem hardly persuades as a man's emotion towards his wife or child ("parasitical / And ignorant little fists").' *Poetry in the Wars* (Newcastle: Bloodaxe, 1986), p. 157. Ciaran Carson, 'Escaped from the Massacre?', *Honest Ulsterman* 50 (Winter 1975), p. 185.

9. Patricia Coughlan, '"Bog Queens": The Representation of Women in the Poetry of John Montague and Seamus Heaney', *Gender in Irish Writing*, eds. Toni O'Brien Johnson and David Cairns (Milton Keynes and Philadelphia: Open University Press, 1991), p. 89.

10. Seamus Deane, *Celtic Revivals: Essays in Modern Irish Literature, 1880–1980* (London: Faber and Faber, 1985), p. 175.

11. *Ibid.*, p. 178.

12. Longley, *Poetry in the Wars*, p. 157.

13. *Ibid.*, p. 169.

14. Seamus Heaney, *Death of a Naturalist* (1966; London: Faber and Faber, 1991), p. 44.

15. Heaney, *Field Work* (London: Faber and Faber, 1979), p. 31.

16. Seamus Heaney, *Station Island* (London: Faber and Faber, 1984), p. 92.

17. Seamus Heaney, *The Spirit Level* (London: Faber and Faber, 1996), p. 25.

18. Seamus Heaney, *Seeing Things* (London: Faber and Faber, 1991), p. 76.

19. *Ibid.*, p. 16.

20. *Ibid.*, p. 18.

21. *Ibid.*, p. 55.

22. Seamus Heaney, *District and Circle* (London: Faber and Faber, 2006), p. 19.

23. Seamus Heaney, *Preoccupations: Selected Prose 1969–1978* (London: Faber and Faber, 1980), p. 116.

24. Seamus Heaney, *Finders Keepers: Selected Prose 1971–1991* (London: Faber and Faber, 2002), p. 59.

25. Seamus Heaney, *Beowulf: A New Translation* (London: Faber and Faber, 1999), p. xxiii.

26. Harry Thomas, ed., *Talking with Poets* (New York: Handsel Books, 2002), p. 48.

27. Deane, Interview: 'Unhappy and at Home', p. 67.

9 Irsko po Polsku: poetry and translation

1. Tomás Ó Duinnshléibhe, *Taidhgín* (Inverin: Cló Iar-Chonnachta, 1995), p. 98. In English: 'A nation cannot lose its language without losing its soul, and when its soul is lost, it is finished as a nation.'

2. Tony Crowley, *Wars of Words: The Politics of Language in Ireland 1537–2004* (Oxford: Oxford University Press, 2005).

3. Perry Share and Hilary Tovey, *A Sociology of Ireland*, 2nd edn (Dublin: Gill and Macmillan, 2003), p. 334.

4. Michael Cronin, *Translating Ireland: Translations, Languages, Cultures* (Cork: Cork University Press, 1996), p. 39.

5. Padraic Colum, *Wild Earth and Other Poems* (1909; New York: Henry Holt, 1916), p. 60.

6. Eavan Boland, *The Lost Land* (Manchester: Carcanet, 1998), p. 13.

7. David Wheatley, 'Ceist na Teangan/The Language Issue', *Metre* 11 (Winter 2001–2), Michael Harnett Special Issue, p. 177.

8. Michael Longley, *Collected Poems* (London: Cape, 2006), p. 128.

9. Seán Ó Ríordáin, *Eireaball Spideoige* (1952; Dublin: Sáirséal Ó Marcaigh, 1986), p. 44.

10. See Seán Ó Coileáin, *Seán Ó Ríordáin: Beatha agus Saothar* (Dublin: An Clóchomhar Teoranta, 1982), p. 241.

11. Thomas Kinsella, *The Dual Tradition: An Essay on Poetry and Politics in Ireland* (Manchester: Carcanet, 1995), p. 5.

12. *Ibid.*, p. 4.

13. Seán Ó Ríordáin, *Brosna* (1964; Dublin: Sáirséal agus Dill, 1979), p. 17.

14. Máirtín Ó Direáin, *Tacar Dánta/Selected Poems*, trans. Tomás Mac Síomóin and Douglas Sealy (Newbridge: Goldsmith Press, 1984), p. 12.

15. *Ibid.*, p. 13.

16. *Ibid.*, p. 12.

17. *Ibid.*, p. 13.

18. Nuala Ní Dhomhnaill, *Feis* (Maynooth: An Sagart, 1991), p. 128.

19. Nuala Ní Dhomhnaill, *Pharoah's Daughter*, trans. Paul Muldoon (Loughcrew: Gallery Press, 1990), p. 155.

20. Nuala Ní Dhomhnaill, *The Astrakhan Cloak*, trans. Paul Muldoon (Loughcrew: Gallery Press, 1992), pp. 66–7.

21. Gearóid Mac Lochlainn, *Sruth Teangacha, Stream of Tongues* (Inverin: Cló Iar-Chonnachta, 2002), p. 62.

22. Michael Hartnett, 'Why Write in Irish?', *Irish Times* (26 August 1975); rpt in *Metre* 11 (Winter 2001–2), p. 134.

23. *Ibid.* '*Deoch uisce*' is 'a drink of water'.

24. Michael Hartnett, *Collected Poems*, ed. Peter Fallon (Loughcrew: Gallery, 2001), p. 147. This book omits Hartnett's poems in Irish and Louis de Paor has fairly commented that it is 'a deeply flawed publication and an unreliable guide to the trajectory of the poet's development . . . The decision not to include any of Ó hAirtnéide's work in Irish represents a staggering revision of the poet's career'. 'Micheál Ó hAirtnéide's Collected Poems in Irish', *Remembering Michael Harnett*, eds. John McDonagh and Stephen Newman (Dublin: Four Courts Press, 2006), p. 66.

25. Nuala Ní Dhomhnaill, 'Foighne Crainn: The Patience of a Tree', *Metre* 11 (Winter 2001–2), p. 151.

26. 'Tá na Gaeil amhrasach romham / 'ceapann na Gaill gur / as mo mheabhair atáim.' Michael Hartnett, *Do Nuala: Foidhne Chrainn* (Dublin: Coiscéim, 1984), p. 22. For a discussion of the reception of the book see de Paor, 'Micheál Ó hAirtnéide's Collected Poems', pp. 68–9.

27. Hartnett, *Collected Poems*, p. 149.

28. *Ibid.*, p. 151.

29. *Ibid.*, pp. 164–5.

30. Ní Dhomhnaill, 'Foighne Crainn', p. 148.

31. Hartnett, *Collected Poems*, p. 122.

32. Michael Hartnett, *A Book of Strays*, ed. Peter Fallon (Loughcrew: Gallery, 2002), p. 43.

33. Hartnett, *Collected Poems*, p. 169.

34. To name but a few: Michael Hartnett, Seamus Heaney, Pearse Hutchinson, Trevor Joyce, Thomas Kinsella, Medbh McGuckian, Paul Muldoon, Eiléan Ní Chuilleanáin

and Bernard O'Donoghue from Irish; Mary O'Donnell and Eavan Boland from German; Harry Clifton, Derek Mahon, John Montague and David Wheatley from French; Peter Fallon, Michael Hartnett, Michael Longley and Louis MacNeice from Latin; Ciaran Carson, Eamon Grennan and Hutchinson from Italian; Longley and MacNeice again from ancient Greek; Cathal McCabe from Polish; Hutchinson again from Catalan and Dutch; Desmond O'Grady from modern Greek; Heaney and O'Donoghue again from Old English; and Ní Chuilleanáin again from Romanian.

35. Although Longley remarked in interview that his 'Latin and Greek are worse than rusty', he also said that '[t]he classics have left me with some images and themes, and with a sense of syntactical possibilities – playing a long sentence off against the metrical units'. Interview with Dermot Healy. *Southern Review* 31.3 (Summer 1995), p. 559.
36. Michael Longley, *Collected Poems*, p. 205.
37. Fran Brearton, *Reading Michael Longley* (Tarset: Bloodaxe, 2006), p. 194.
38. Longley, *Collected Poems*, p. 307.
39. John Kerrigan, 'Ulster Ovids', *The Chosen Ground: Essays on the Contemporary Poetry of Northern Ireland*, ed. Neil Corcoran (Bridgend: Seren, 1992), p. 258.
40. Derek Mahon, *Collected Poems* (Loughcrew: Gallery, 2000), p. 131.
41. Peter Fallon, *The Georgics of Virgil* (Loughcrew: Gallery, 2004) p. 22.
42. Paul Valéry, *Poésies* (Paris: Gallimard, 1958), p. 101. Derek Mahon, *Harbour Lights* (Loughcrew: Gallery, 2005), p. 72.
43. Valéry, *Poésies* p. 105. Mahon, *Harbour Lights*, p. 75.
44. Wallace Stevens, *Opus Posthumous: Poems, Plays, Prose*, ed. Milton J. Bates (New York: Vintage, 1990), p. 202.
45. Aidan Rooney published his first collection under the name Aidan Rooney-Céspedes. *Day Release* (Loughcrew: Gallery, 2000), p. 42.
46. Samuel Beckett, *Poems 1930–1989* (London: Calder Publications, 2002), p. 74.
47. Translation mine.
48. Unpublished translation.
49. J[ames]. C[ampbell]., 'N. B.', *Times Literary Supplement* (7 July 2006), p. 16.
50. Samuel Beckett, *Poems 1930–1989*, p. 77.
51. Derek Mahon, 'Watt Is the Word: The "Brief Scattered Lights" of Beckett's Poems', *Times Literary Supplement* (3 November 2006), p. 13.

10 Feminism and Irish poetry

1. Ailbhe Smith, 'Paying our Disrespects to the Bloody State We're in: Women, Violence, Culture and the State' (1994), rpt. in *The Field Day Anthology of Irish Writing*, vol. V, ed. Angela Bourke *et al.* (Cork: Cork University Press, 2002), p. 407.
2. Patricia Coughlan, '"The Whole Strange Growth": Heaney, Orpheus and Women', *Irish Review* 35 (2007), pp. 25–45.
3. Medbh McGuckian and Nuala Ní Dhomhnaill, 'Comhrá', by Laura O'Connor. *Southern Review* 31.3 (Summer 1995), pp. 596–7.

4. *Ibid.*, pp. 606–7.
5. Eavan Boland, 'Aspects of Pearse'. *Dublin Magazine* 5.1 (Spring 1966), pp. 46–55.
6. Eavan Boland, *Collected Poems* (Manchester: Carcanet, 1995), p. 200.
7. *Ibid.*, p. 102.
8. *Ibid.*, p. 202.
9. Paula Meehan, *Dharmakaya* (Manchester: Carcanet, 2000), p. 28.
10. Catherine Walsh, *City West* (Exeter: Shearsman, 2005), p. 68.
11. *Ibid.*, p. 9.
12. Moynagh Sullivan, 'The In-Formal Poetics of Medbh McGuckian', *Nordic Irish Studies* 3.1 (2004), pp. 75–92.
13. Clair Wills, *Improprieties: Politics and Sexuality in Northern Irish Poetry* (Oxford: Oxford University Press, 1993), pp. 168–9.
14. Michael Allen, 'The Poetry of Medbh McGuckian'. *Contemporary Irish Poetry: A Collection of Critical Essays*, ed. Elmer Andrews (London: Macmillan, 1992), p. 304.
15. Medbh McGuckian, *Venus and the Rain*, revd edn. (Loughcrew: Gallery, 1994), p. 11
16. Medbh McGuckian, Interview with Vona Groarke. *Verse* 16.2 (1999), p. 38.
17. McGuckian, *Venus*, p. 25.
18. *Ibid.*
19. Edna Longley, *The Living Stream: Literature and Revisionism in Ireland* (Newcastle upon Tyne: Bloodaxe, 1994), p. 54.
20. Medbh McGuckian, *Had I a Thousand Lives* (Loughcrew: Gallery, 2003), p. 38.
21. *Ibid.*, p. 34.
22. *Ibid.*
23. *Ibid.*, p. 35.
24. Moynagh Sullivan, 'Dreamin' My Dreams of You: Medbh McGuckian and the Theatre of Dreams', *Metre* 17 (Spring 2005), p. 109.
25. Medbh McGuckian, *The Book of the Angel* (Loughcrew: Gallery, 2004), p. 32.
26. *Ibid.*, p. 35.
27. *Ibid.*, p. 32.
28. *Ibid.*, p. 19.
29. Guinn Batten and Dillon Johnston, 'Contemporary Poetry in English: 1940–2000'. *Cambridge History of Irish Literature*, eds. Margaret Kelleher and Philip O'Leary, vol. II (Cambridge: Cambridge University Press, 2006), p. 405.
30. Eiléan Ní Chuilleanáin, *The Girl Who Married a Reindeer* (Loughcrew: Gallery, 2001), p. 46.
31. *Ibid.*, p. 25.
32. Eiléan Ní Chuilleanáin, *The Second Voyage* (Dublin: Gallery, 1986), p. 65.
33. Vona Groarke, Editorial, *Verse* 16.2 (1999), p. 8.

11 Out of Ireland: Muldoon and other émigrés

1. Aleš Debeljak, *Svěrací kazajka anonymity: slovinská poezie a bílé místo na literární mapě USA* (Prague: Volvox Globator, 1999), p. 48.

2. Quoted in R. F. Foster, *W. B. Yeats: A Life*, vol. I (Oxford: Oxford University Press, 1998), p. 327.

3. Dennis O'Driscoll, 'Golden Newies', *Metre* 7/8 (Spring–Summer 2000), p. 259.

4. Tim Kendall, *Paul Muldoon* (Bridgend: Seren, 1996), p. 101.

5. Paul Muldoon, *Selected Poems 1968–1983* (London: Faber and Faber, 1986), p. 8.

6. *Ibid.*

7. John Haffenden, Interview with Paul Muldoon, *Viewpoints* (London: Faber and Faber, 1981), p. 133.

8. Kendall, *Paul Muldoon*, p. 114.

9. Paul Muldoon, *Quoof* (London: Faber and Faber, 1983), p. 8.

10. *Ibid.*, p. 9.

11. *Ibid.*

12. Paul Muldoon, *Meeting the British* (London: Faber and Faber, 1987), p. 59.

13. Kendall, *Paul Muldoon*, p. 170.

14. Paul Muldoon, *Madoc – A Mystery* (London: Faber and Faber, 1990), p. 224.

15. *Ibid.*

16. Edna Longley, *The Living Stream: Literature and Revisionism in Ireland* (Newcastle: Bloodaxe, 1994), p. 51. Kendall, *Paul Muldoon*, p. 167, Clair Wills, *Reading Paul Muldoon* (Newcastle: Bloodaxe, 1998), p. 140.

17. Michael Allen, 'Rhyme and Reconciliation in Muldoon', *Paul Muldoon: Critical Essays*, eds. Tim Kendall and Peter McDonald (Liverpool: Liverpool University Press, 2004), p. 64.

18. Michael Hofmann, 'Muldoon – A Mystery', *London Review of Books* (20 December 1990), p. 19.

19. Paul Muldoon, *The Annals of Chile* (London: Faber and Faber, 1994), p. 15.

20. See Kendall, *Paul Muldoon*, pp. 227–9, for a good account of this.

21. Joseph Conte, *Unending Design: The Forms of Postmodern Poetry* (Ithaca: Cornell University Press, 1991), p. 3.

22. Wills, *Reading Paul Muldoon*, p. 172.

23. *Ibid.*, p. 157.

24. Emily Dickinson, *Complete Poems*, ed. Thomas H. Johnson (London: Faber and Faber, 1975), p. 635.

25. Greg Delanty, *The Hellbox* (Oxford: Oxford University Press, 1998), p. 33.

26. *Ibid.*, p. 34.

27. Eavan Boland, *Code* (Manchester: Carcanet, 2001), p. 36.

28. David Wheatley, 'Changing the Story: Eavan Boland and Literary History', *Irish Review* 31 (Spring–Summer 2004), pp. 103–20; Carol Rumens, Review of *The Lost Land*, by Eavan Boland, *Verse* 16.2 (Summer 1999), special issue on Women Irish Poets, ed. Vona Groarke, p. 126; Peggy O'Brien, Review of *Code*, by Eavan Boland, *Metre* 11 (Winter 2001–2), p. 111.

29. Peter Fallon, *News of the World: Selected and New Poems* (Loughcrew: Gallery, 1998), p. 137.

30. Jonathan Hufstader, 'Horace's Oak Tree', Review of *Relations: New and Selected Poems*, by Eamon Grennan, *Metre* 6 (Summer 1999), p. 66.
31. *Ibid.*, p. 69.
32. Eamon Grennan, *Relations: New and Selected Poems* (St Paul: Graywolf, 1998), p. 144.
33. *Ibid.*, pp. 144–5.
34. Eamon Grennan, 'What I Heard There', *Metre* 7/8 (Spring–Summer 2000), p. 263.
35. Eamon Grennan, Interview with Justin Quinn, *Metre* 9 (Spring–Summer 2001), p. 16.
36. Harry Clifton, Interview with David Wheatley, *Metre* 1 (Autumn 1996), pp. 40–1.
37. Harry Clifton, *God in France: A Paris Sequence 1994–1998* (Dublin: Metre Editions, 2003), p. 31.
38. Fergus Allen, *The Brown Parrots of Providencia* (London: Faber and Faber, 1993), p. 22.
39. Peter McDonald, *Pastorals* (Manchester: Carcanet, 2004), p. 23.
40. *Ibid.*, p. 26.
41. *Ibid.*
42. Peter McDonald, Response to 'Irish Poetry and the Diaspora', *Metre* 3 (Autumn 1997), p. 17.
43. Peter McDonald, *The House of Clay* (Manchester: Carcanet, 2006), p. 32.
44. Tom Paulin, *The Invasion Handbook* (London: Faber and Faber, 2002), pp. 6–7.
45. Patrick Kavanagh, 'Diary', *Envoy: A Review of Literature and Art* 2.7 (June 1950), p. 85.

12 The disappearance of Ireland

1. Michael Hartnett, 'Why Write in Irish?', *Irish Times* (26 August 1975); rpt. in *Metre* 11 (Winter 2001–2), p. 134.
2. Luke Gibbons, *Transformations in Irish Culture* (Cork: Cork University Press, 1996).
3. Peadar Kirby, Luke Gibbons and Michael Cronin, eds., *Reinventing Ireland: Culture, Society and the Global Economy* (London: Pluto Press, 2002), pp. 17–18.
4. Chris Binchy, *The Very Man* (London: Macmillan, 2003), p. 25.
5. Derek Mahon, *Collected Poems* (Loughcrew: Gallery, 1999), p. 285.
6. Terence Brown, Editorial, *Poetry Ireland Review* 16 (Summer 1986), p. 5.
7. Dennis O'Driscoll, *New and Selected Poems* (London: Anvil, 2004), p. 187.
8. Kevin Higgins, *The Boy with No Face* (Cliffs of Moher: Salmon Poetry, 2005), p. 34.
9. *Ibid.*, p. 15.
10. Kirby *et al.*, *Reinventing Ireland*, p. 7.
11. *Ibid.*, p. 12.
12. Selina Guinness, *The New Irish Poets* (Tarset: Bloodaxe, 2004), p. 15.
13. Ciaran Carson, *First Language* (Loughcrew: Gallery, 1993), p. 9. A literal translation of this might run: 'In a flutter of mouths / in the words of eyes / pressing and straining / until there was nothing there / but a shadow of a shadow between us / caught

inside your ear.' But 'tocht' also means a gasp or catch in the breath, only here it takes places in the ear.

14. *Ibid.*, p. 10.
15. Ciaran Carson, *Selected Poems* (Winston-Salem: Wake Forest University Press, 2001), p. 14.
16. Neil Corcoran, 'One Step Forward, Two Steps Back', *The Chosen Ground: Essays on the Contemporary Poetry of Northern Ireland*, ed. Neil Corcoran (Bridgend: Seren, 1992), p. 221.
17. Carson, *Selected Poems*, p. 15.
18. Ciaran Carson, *Belfast Confetti* (Loughcrew: Gallery, 1989), p. 11.
19. *Ibid.*, p. 78.
20. *Ibid.*, p. 64.
21. *Ibid.*
22. *Ibid.*
23. Ciaran Carson, *Breaking News* (Loughcrew: Gallery, 2003), p. 51.
24. *Ibid.*, p. 52.
25. Peter Sirr, *Bring Everything* (Loughcrew: Gallery, 2000), p. 37.
26. *Ibid.*, p. 14.
27. Peter Sirr, *Nonetheless* (Loughcrew: Gallery, 2004), p. 78.
28. Sinéad Morrissey, *Between Here and There* (Manchester: Carcanet, 2002), p. 58.
29. *Ibid.*, p. 50.
30. Greg Delanty, *The Hellbox* (Oxford: Oxford University Press, 1998), p. 33.
31. David Wheatley, *Misery Hill* (Loughcrew: Gallery, 2000), p. 21.
32. David Wheatley, *Mocker* (Loughcrew: Gallery, 2006), p. 15.
33. *Ibid.*, p. 51.
34. Vona Groarke, Editorial, *Verse* 16.2 (1999), p. 8.
35. Vona Groarke, *Juniper Street* (Loughcrew: Gallery, 2006), p. 25.
36. Conor O'Callaghan, *Fiction* (Loughcrew: Gallery, 2005), p. 61.
37. Vona Groarke, *Shale* (Loughcrew: Gallery, 1994), p. 58.
38. O'Callaghan, *Fiction*, p. 61.
39. Conor O'Callaghan, *Seatown* (Loughcrew: Gallery, 1999), p. 60.
40. O'Callaghan, *Fiction*, p. 32.
41. Vona Groarke, *Other People's Houses* (Loughcrew: Gallery, 1999), p. 19.
42. *Ibid.*
43. Vona Groarke, *Flight* (Loughcrew: Gallery, 2002), p. 16.
44. Vona Groarke, 'Foreignism: A Philadelphia Diary', *Dublin Review* 18 (Spring 2005), pp. 40–72.
45. Maria Johnston, *Contemporary Poetry Review* www.cprw.com.
46. Caitríona O'Reilly, *The Sea Cabinet* (High Green: Bloodaxe, 2006), p. 40.
47. *Ibid.*, p. 25.
48. *Ibid.*, p. 42.

Guide to further reading

The following guide provides suggestions for further reading and is not meant as an exhaustive bibliography. The most important section is the first, which lists books that have fundamentally changed perceptions of Irish poetry, and in a good few cases, of Irish literature in general. The subsequent sections pertain to individual writers and periods, and are referenced to the appropriate chapters.

General

Andrews, Elmer, ed. *Contemporary Irish Poetry: A Collection of Critical Essays.* London: Macmillan, 1992.

Brearton, Fran. *The Great War and Irish Poetry: W. B. Yeats to Michael Longley.* Oxford: Oxford University Press, 2000.

Brown, Terence. *Ireland's Literature: Selected Essays.* Mullingar: Lilliput Press, 1988.

Brown, Terence and Nicholas Grene, eds. *Tradition and Influence in Anglo-Irish Poetry.* London: Macmillan, 1989.

Campbell, Matthew, ed. *Cambridge Companion to Contemporary Irish Poetry.* Cambridge: Cambridge University Press, 2003.

Corcoran, Neil, ed. *The Chosen Ground: Essays on the Contemporary Poetry of Northern Ireland.* Bridgend: Seren, 1992.

Poets of Modern Ireland. Cardiff: University of Wales Press, 1999.

Cronin, Michael. *Translating Ireland: Translations, Languages, Cultures.* Cork: Cork University Press, 1996.

Crotty, Patrick, ed. *Modern Irish Poetry.* Belfast: Blackstaff, 1995.

Deane, Seamus. *Celtic Revivals.* London: Faber and Faber, 1985.

Deane, Seamus, *et al.*, eds. *The Field Day Anthology of Irish Writing.* 5 vols. Derry: Field Day Publications, 1991, 2002.

Heaney, Seamus. *Finders Keepers: Selected Prose 1971–1991.* London: Faber and Faber, 2002.

Johnston, Dillon. *The Poetic Economies of England and Ireland 1912–2000.* London: Palgrave-Macmillan, 2001.

Kelleher, Margaret and Philip O'Leary, eds. *Cambridge History of Irish Literature.* 2 vols. Cambridge: Cambridge University Press, 2006.

Kinsella, Thomas. *The Dual Tradition: An Essay on Poetry and Politics in Ireland.*
    Manchester: Carcanet, 1995.
Longley, Edna. *Poetry in the Wars.* Newcastle: Bloodaxe, 1986.
    The Living Stream: Literature and Revisionism in Ireland. Newcastle:
        Bloodaxe, 1994.
    Poetry and Posterity. Newcastle: Bloodaxe, 2000.
Mahon, Derek. *Journalism.* Ed. Terence Brown. Loughcrew: Gallery, 1996.
O'Driscoll, Dennis. *Troubled Thoughts, Majestic Dreams: Selected Prose Writings.*
    Loughcrew: Gallery, 2001.
Ó Tuama, Seán, ed. *An Duanaire: Poems of the Dispossessed 1600–1900.* With
    translations by Thomas Kinsella. Mountrath: Dolmen Press, 1981.
Southern Review 31.3 (Summer 1995). Special Issue on Irish Poetry.
Vance, Norman. *Irish Literature Since 1800.* London: Longman, 2002.
Welch, Robert. *A History of Verse Translation from the Irish 1789–1897.* Gerrards
    Cross: Colin Smythe, 1988.

Chapter 1: The appearance of Ireland

Thomas Moore, J. J. Callanan, James Clarence Mangan

Gwynn, Stephen. *Thomas Moore.* London: Macmillan, 1905.
Leerssen, Joep. *Remembrance and Imagination: Patterns in the Historical and
    Literary Representation of Ireland in the Nineteenth Century.* Cork: Cork
    University Press, 1996.
Lloyd, David. *Nationalism and Minor Literature: James Clarence Mangan and the
    Emergence of Irish Cultural Nationalism.* Berkeley: University of
    California Press, 1987.
Welch, Robert. *Irish Poetry from Moore to Yeats.* Gerrards Cross: Colin Smythe,
    1980.

Chapter 2: Tennyson's Ireland

James Henry, Samuel Ferguson, William Allingham

Denman, Peter. *Samuel Ferguson: The Literary Achievement.* Gerrards Cross:
    Colin Smythe, 1990.
Graham, Colin. *Ideologies of Epic: Nation, Empire and Victorian Epic Poetry.*
    Edinburgh: Edinburgh University Press, 2001.
Ó Dúill, Gréagóir. *Samuel Ferguson: Beatha agus Saothar.* Dublin: An
    Clóchomhar Tta, 1993.
Patten, Eve. *Samuel Ferguson and the Culture of Nineteenth-Century Ireland.*
    Dublin: Four Courts Press, 2004.

Ricks, Christopher, Introductory materials. *Selected Poems of James Henry*, ed. Christopher Ricks. New York: Handsel Books, 2002.

Chapter 3: Revival

Douglas Hyde, Katharine Tynan, Ethna Carbery, Emily Lawless, Eva Gore-Booth, Padraic Colum, Susan L. Mitchell, Francis Ledwidge, J. M. Synge, Oscar Wilde

Given the lack of secondary material directly related to poetry in this period, readers are directed to Patrick Crotty's essay in volume II of Kelleher and O'Leary, eds., *Cambridge History of Irish Literature* (2006).

Chapter 4: W. B. Yeats

Brown, Terence. *The Life of W. B. Yeats: A Critical Biography*. Dublin: Gill and Macmillan, 1999.
Cullingford, Elizabeth. *Gender and History in Yeats's Love Poetry*. Syracuse: Syracuse University Press, 1993.
Ellmann, Richard. *The Identity of Yeats*. London: Macmillan, 1954.
    Yeats: The Man and the Masks. New York: W. W. Norton, 1978.
Foster, R. F. *W. B. Yeats: A Life*. 2 vols. Oxford: Oxford University, Press, 1997, 2003.
Howes, Marjorie. *Yeats's Nations: Gender, Class and Irishness*. Cambridge: Cambridge University Press, 1999.
Howes, Marjorie and John Kelly, eds. *The Cambridge Companion to W. B. Yeats*. Cambridge: Cambridge University Press, 2006.
Kermode, Frank. *Romantic Image*. London: Routledge, 1957.
Longenbach, James. *Stone Cottage: Pound, Yeats and Modernism*. New York: Oxford University Press, 1988.

Chapter 5: Wild earth

Padraic Colum, Austin Clarke, Patrick Kavanagh, Louis MacNeice

Brown, Terence. *Louis MacNeice: Sceptical Vision*. Dublin: Gill and Macmillan, 1975.
Gillis, Alan. *Irish Poetry of the 1930s*. Oxford: Oxford University Press, 2005.
Longley, Edna. *Louis MacNeice: A Study*. London: Faber and Faber, 1988.
McDonald, Peter. *Louis MacNeice: A Poet in His Contexts*. Oxford: Oxford University Press, 1991.

Quinn, Antoinette. *Patrick Kavanagh: Born-Again Romantic*. Dublin: Gill and
     Macmillan, 1993.
     Patrick Kavanagh: A Biography. Revd edn. Dublin: Gill and Macmillan, 2003.
Schirmer, Gregory A. *The Poetry of Austin Clarke*. Mountrath: Dolmen Press,
     1983.
Stallworthy, Jon. *Louis MacNeice*. New York: W. W. Norton, 1995.

Chapter 6: The ends of Modernism: Kinsella and Irish experiment

*Denis Devlin, Brian Coffey, Thomas Kinsella, John Montague,
Trevor Joyce, Randolph Healy, Maurice Scully*

Badin, Donatella Abbate. *Thomas Kinsella*. New York: Twayne, 1996.
Coughlan, Patricia and Alex Davis. *Modernism and Ireland: The Poetry of the
     1930s*. Cork: Cork University Press, 1995.
Davis, Alex. *A Broken Line: Denis Devlin and Irish Poetic Modernism*. Dublin:
     UCD Press, 2000.
Gillis, Alan. *Irish Poetry of the 1930s*. Oxford: Oxford University Press, 2005.
Mays, J. C. C. Introduction. *Collected Poems of Denis Devlin*, ed. J. C. C. Mays.
     Dublin: Dedalus, 1989.
Tubridy, Derval. *The Peppercanister Poems*. Dublin: UCD Press, 2000.

Chapter 7: Ireland's Empire

Richard Murphy, Derek Mahon, Michael Longley

Brearton, Fran. *Reading Michael Longley*. Tarset: Bloodaxe, 2006.
Irish University Review 7.1 (Spring 1977). Richard Murphy Special Issue.
Irish University Review 24.1 (Spring–Summer 1994). Derek Mahon Special Issue.
Kennedy-Andrews, Elmer, ed. *The Poetry of Derek Mahon*. Gerrards Cross: Colin
     Smythe, 2002.
Kirkland, Richard. *Literature and Culture in Northern Ireland Since 1965:
     Moments of Danger*. Harlow: Longman, 1996.

Chapter 8: Seamus Heaney

Allen, Michael, ed. *Seamus Heaney: A Collection of Critical Essays*. New York: St
     Martin's Press, 1997.
Corcoran, Neil. *The Poetry of Seamus Heaney*. London: Faber and Faber, 1998.
Coughlan, Patricia. '"Bog Queens": The Representation of Women in the Poetry
     of John Montague and Seamus Heaney'. *Gender in Irish Writing*, eds.
     Toni O'Brien Johnson and David Cairns. Milton Keynes and
     Philadelphia: Open University Press, 1991.

Chapter 9: Irsko po Polsku: poetry and translation

*Seán Ó Ríordáin, Máirtín Ó Direáin, Nuala Ní Dhomhnaill,
Gearóid Mac Lochlainn, Michael Hartnett, Michael Longley,
Derek Mahon, Peter Fallon, Aidan Rooney, Samuel Beckett*

Mahon, Derek. 'Watt Is the Word: The "Brief Scattered Lights" of Beckett's
    Poems'. *Times Literary Supplement* 3 November 2006.
McDonagh, John and Stephen Newman, eds. *Remembering Michael Harnett.*
    Dublin: Four Courts Press, 2006.
Metre 11 (Winter 2001–2), Michael Harnett Special Issue.
Ní Dhomhnaill, Nuala. *Selected Essays.* Ed. Oona Frawley. Dublin: New Island
    Books, 2005.
Ó Coileáin, Seán. *Seán Ó Ríordáin: Beatha agus Saothar.* Dublin: An Clóchomhar
    Teoranta, 1982.
Ó Tuama, Seán. *Repossessions: Selected Essays on the Irish Literary Heritage.* Cork:
    Cork University Press, 1995.
Sewell, Frank. *Modern Irish Poetry: A New Alhambra.* Oxford: Oxford University
    Press, 2000.

Chapter 10: Feminism and Irish Poetry

*Eavan Boland, Paula Meehan, Catherine Walsh, Medbh McGuckian,
Eiléan Ní Chuilleanáin*

Ryan, Ray, ed. *Writing in the Irish Republic: Literature, Culture, Politics 1949–1999.*
    London: Palgrave, 2000.
Sullivan, Moynagh. 'Dreamin' My Dreams of You: Medbh McGuckian and the
    Theatre of Dreams'. *Metre* 17 (Spring 2005).
Wheatley, David. 'Changing the Story: Eavan Boland and Literary History'. *Irish
    Review* 31 (Spring–Summer 2004).
Wills, Clair. *Improprieties: Politics and Sexuality in Northern Irish Poetry.* Oxford:
    Oxford University Press, 1993.

Chapter 11: Out of Ireland: Muldoon and other émigrés

*Paul Muldoon, Greg Delanty, Eavan Boland, Peter Fallon,
Eamon Grennan, Harry Clifton, Peter McDonald, Tom Paulin,
Bernard O'Donoghue, Ian Duhig*

Kendall, Tim. *Paul Muldoon.* Bridgend: Seren, 1996.
Kendall, Tim and Peter McDonald, eds. *Paul Muldoon: Critical Essays.* Liverpool:
    Liverpool University Press, 2004.
Wills, Clair. *Reading Paul Muldoon.* Newcastle: Bloodaxe, 1998.

Chapter 12: The disappearance of Ireland

Paul Durcan, Dennis O'Driscoll, Kevin Higgins, Ciaran Carson, Peter Sirr, Sinéad Morrissey, David Wheatley, Vona Groarke, Conor O'Callaghan, Caitríona O'Reilly,

Guinness, Selina, ed. *The New Irish Poets.* Tarset: Bloodaxe, 2004.

Index